AGRICULTURE ISSUES AND POLICIES

AGRICULTURE DISASTER AND CROP INSURANCE: BACKGROUND AND ISSUES

AGRICULTURE ISSUES AND POLICIES

Additional books in this series can be found on Nova's website under the Series tab.

Additional E-books in this series can be found on Nova's website under the E-book tab.

AGRICULTURE ISSUES AND POLICIES

AGRICULTURE DISASTER AND CROP INSURANCE: BACKGROUND AND ISSUES

ANGELA M. GIL
EDITOR

Nova Science Publishers, Inc.
New York

For permission to use material from this book please contact us:
Telephone 631-231-7269; Fax 631-231-8175
Web Site: http://www.novapublishers.com

LIBRARY OF CONGRESS CATALOGING-IN-PUBLICATION DATA

Agriculture disaster and crop insurance : background and issues / editor: Angela M. Gil.
p. cm.
Includes index.
ISBN 978-1-61761-559-7 (hardcover)
1. Crop insurance--United States. 2. Disaster relief--United States. I. Gil, Angela M.
HG9968.A36 2011
368.1'2100973--dc22

2010034001

Published by Nova Science Publishers, Inc. † New York

CONTENTS

PREFACE

The U.S. Department of Agriculture (USDA) offers several permanently authorized programs to help farmers recover financially from a natural disaster, including federal crop insurance, the Noninsured Crop Disaster Assistance Program (NAP), and emergency disaster loans. The federal crop insurance program is designed to protect crop producers from unavoidable risks associated with adverse weather, and weather-related plant diseases and insect infestations. Under the emergency disaster loan program, when a county has been declared a disaster area by either the President or the Secretary of Agriculture, agricultural producers in that county may become eligible for low-interest loans. This book provides an overview and history of the current USDA disaster assistance programs

Chapter 1- The U.S. Department of Agriculture (USDA) offers several permanently authorized programs to help farmers recover financially from a natural disaster, including federal crop insurance, the Noninsured Crop Disaster Assistance Program (NAP), and emergency disaster loans. The federal crop insurance program is designed to protect crop producers from unavoidable risks associated with adverse weather, and weather-related plant diseases and insect infestations. Producers who grow a crop that is currently ineligible for crop insurance may be eligible for a direct payment under NAP. Under the emergency disaster (EM) loan program, when a county has been declared a disaster area by either the President or the Secretary of Agriculture, agricultural producers in that county may become eligible for low-interest loans.

Chapter 2- In an effort to end the ad-hoc nature of emergency crop disaster assistance to farmers, Congress authorized a new Supplemental Revenue Assistance Payments Program (SURE) in the Food, Conservation, and Energy Act of 2008. The program provides payments to producers for crop revenue losses due to natural disaster or adverse weather incurred on or before September 30, 2011. It essentially compensates eligible producers for a portion of losses that are not eligible for an indemnity payment under a crop insurance policy. The program departs from both traditional disaster assistance and crop yield insurance by calculating and reimbursing losses using total crop revenue for the entire farm (i.e., summing revenue from all crops for an individual farmer).

Chapter 3- The federal government has relied primarily on two policy tools in recent years to help mitigate the financial losses experienced by crop farmers as a result of natural disasters—a federal crop insurance program and congressionally mandated *ad-hoc* crop disaster payments. Congress has made several modifications to the crop insurance program since the 1980s, in an effort to forestall the demand for supplemental disaster payments.

Although the scope of the crop insurance program has widened significantly over the past 25 years, the anticipated goal of crop insurance replacing disaster payments has not been achieved.

Chapter 4- The 111th Congress is considering the effectiveness and operations of the federal crop insurance program. The House Committee on Agriculture has been seeking input from farmers and others on the program in advance of the next farm bill debate. Meanwhile, concern about the federal budget deficit is coinciding with the rising cost of the federal crop insurance program. This report provides a primer on the federal crop insurance program and discusses related issues.

The federal crop insurance program began in 1938 when Congress authorized the Federal Crop Insurance Corporation. The current program, which is administered by the U.S. Department of Agriculture's Risk Management Agency (RMA), provides producers with risk management tools to address crop yield and/or revenue losses on their farms. In purchasing a policy, a producer growing an insurable crop selects a level of coverage and pays a portion of the premium—or none of it in the case of catastrophic coverage—which increases as the level of coverage rises. The federal government pays the rest of the premium (averaging nearly 60% of the total).

Chapter 5- Under the federal crop insurance program, farmers can purchase crop insurance policies to manage financial risks associated with declines in crop yields and/or revenue. The program covers more than 100 crops and is administered by the U.S. Department of Agriculture's (USDA's) Risk Management Agency (RMA), which acts as both regulator and reinsurer. To encourage farmer participation and reduce the need for ad hoc disaster assistance, the federal government subsidizes the purchase of crop insurance policies, which are sold and serviced through 15 approved private insurance companies. Insurance company losses are reinsured by USDA, and their administrative and operating (A&O) costs are reimbursed by the government.

Chapter 6- The U.S. Department of Agriculture's (USDA) Farm Service Agency (FSA) provides programs to help farmers recover financially from natural disasters. Congress has historically supplemented these programs with ad hoc programs that pay farmers who experienced crop losses. The 2008 farm bill established a program through 2011 to pay farmers who lose crops. To receive these payments, farmers must purchase coverage under federal crop insurance or the Noninsured Crop Disaster Assistance Program, and receive claims payments for losses.

GAO was asked to evaluate (1) how FSA administered the crop disaster programs for losses from 2001 through 2007 and the results of payments under these programs and (2) what lessons FSA can learn from the previous crop disaster programs to manage its new crop disaster program. GAO reviewed statutes, regulations, and guidance; analyzed USDA data; and interviewed USDA officials.

In: Agriculture Disaster and Crop Insurance: Background… ISBN: 978-1-61761-559-7
Editor: Angela M. Gil

Chapter 1

AGRICULTURAL DISASTER ASSISTANCE

Dennis A. Shields and Ralph M. Chite

SUMMARY

The U.S. Department of Agriculture (USDA) offers several permanently authorized programs to help farmers recover financially from a natural disaster, including federal crop insurance, the Noninsured Crop Disaster Assistance Program (NAP), and emergency disaster loans. The federal crop insurance program is designed to protect crop producers from unavoidable risks associated with adverse weather, and weather-related plant diseases and insect infestations. Producers who grow a crop that is currently ineligible for crop insurance may be eligible for a direct payment under NAP. Under the emergency disaster (EM) loan program, when a county has been declared a disaster area by either the President or the Secretary of Agriculture, agricultural producers in that county may become eligible for low-interest loans.

In order to provide a regular supplement to crop insurance and NAP payments, the Food, Conservation, and Energy Act of 2008 (P.L. 110-246, the 2008 farm bill) included authorization and funding for five new disaster programs to cover losses through FY2011. The largest of the new programs is the Supplemental Revenue Assistance Payments Program (SURE), which is designed to compensate eligible producers for a portion of crop losses that are not eligible for an indemnity payment under the crop insurance program.

The 2008 farm bill also authorized three new livestock assistance programs and a tree assistance program. The Livestock Indemnity Program (LIP) compensates ranchers at a rate of 75% of market value for livestock mortality caused by a disaster. The Livestock Forage Disaster Program (LFP) assists ranchers who graze livestock on drought-affected pastureland or grazing land. The Emergency Assistance for Livestock, Honey Bees, and Farm-Raised Fish Program (ELAP) compensates producers for disaster losses not covered under other disaster programs. Finally, the Tree Assistance Program (TAP) provides payments to eligible orchardists and nursery tree growers to cover 70% of the cost of replanting trees or nursery stock following a natural disaster. For individual producers, combined payments under

SURE, LIP, LFP, and ELAP may not exceed $100,000. For TAP, a separate limit of $100,000 per year per producer applies.

The new programs are designed to address the ad hoc nature of disaster assistance provided to producers during the last two decades. Since 1988, Congress has regularly made emergency financial assistance available to farmers and ranchers, primarily in the form of crop disaster payments and livestock assistance.

Following losses to 2009 crops due to excessive rain across much of the country, legislation was introduced in late 2009 in both chambers (S. 2810 and H.R. 4177) to make emergency payments to producers for losses in calendar year 2009. The Senate Finance Committee subsequently attached emergency agricultural assistance to the House-passed version of the Tax Extenders Act of 2009 (H.R. 4213). The Senate amended and passed the bill on March 10, 2010. The legislation would provide a supplemental "direct payment" to producers in designated disaster counties who receive direct payments for crops under the 2008 farm bill (e.g., wheat, corn, upland cotton, rice, peanuts, and soybeans). The threshold for loss due to a natural disaster is 5%, much lower than historical norms, and the payment would be 90% of a farm's direct payment in 2009. (The loss threshold compares with previous disaster programs that typically paid for losses in excess of 35% at 65% of established prices.) Provisions are also included for payments to specialty crop producers ($300 million), producers and first handlers of cottonseed ($42 million), and aquaculture producers ($25 million) for high feed costs in 2009. The Congressional Budget Office estimates the total cost at $1.48 billion.

Over the years, USDA has had at its disposal three major programs designed to help crop Oproducers recover from the financial effects of natural disasters—federal crop insurance, the Noninsured Crop Disaster Assistance Program (NAP), and emergency disaster loans. All three of these programs have permanent authorization and receive regular annual funding. In addition to benefits provided under these standing programs, Congress has regularly made emergency financial assistance available to farmers and ranchers in the form of disaster payments.

During the congressional debate on the omnibus 2008 farm bill, some policymakers wanted to make permanent some level of disaster payments to supplement the crop insurance program and attempt to end the ad hoc (but regular) nature of emergency disaster assistance. Consequently, Title XV of the Food, Conservation, and Energy Act of 2008 (P.L. 110-246, the 2008 farm bill) authorizes a new $3.8 billion trust fund to cover the cost of making agricultural disaster assistance available on an ongoing basis over four years (FY2008-FY2011) through five new programs.

This report has two sections. The first provides an overview of the current USDA disaster assistance programs: federal crop insurance, NAP payments, emergency disaster loans, the new Supplemental Revenue Assistance Payments Program (SURE), and four other smaller disaster programs authorized in the 2008 farm bill. The second section reviews the recent history of emergency supplemental farm disaster assistance.

MAJOR USDA DISASTER ASSISTANCE PROGRAMS

Federal Crop Insurance

The federal crop insurance program is administered by USDA's Risk Management Agency. The program is designed to protect crop producers from unavoidable risks associated with adverse weather, and weather-related plant diseases and insect infestations. A producer who chooses to purchase an insurance policy must do so by an administratively determined deadline date, which varies by crop and usually coincides with the planting season. Crop insurance is available for most major crops. Insurance products that protect against loss in revenue (yield times price) are also available.

The federal crop insurance program was instituted in the 1930s and was subject to major legislative reforms in 1980, and again in 1994 and 2000. The Agriculture Risk Protection Act of 2000 (P.L. 106-224) pumped $8.2 billion in new federal spending over a five-year period into the program primarily through more generous premium subsidies to help make the program more affordable to farmers and enhance farmer participation levels, in an effort to preclude the need for ad-hoc emergency disaster payments. Between 2000 and 2009, the federal subsidy to the crop insurance program averaged $3.7 billion per year, up from an annual average of $1.1 billion in the 1990s and about $500 million in the 1980s. Nearly three-fourths of federal spending during 2000-2009 was used to subsidize producer premiums, and the balance primarily covered the government share of program losses and reimbursed participating private insurance companies for their administrative and operating expenses. In 2007 and 2008, program costs rose sharply, mainly because premium subsidies and company reimbursements are based on total premiums, and total premiums increased in tandem with farm commodity prices.[1]

Under the current crop insurance program, a producer who grows an insurable crop selects a level of crop yield and price coverage and pays a premium that increases as the levels of yield and price coverage rises. However, all eligible producers can receive catastrophic (CAT) coverage without paying a premium. The premium for this portion of coverage is completely subsidized by the federal government. Under CAT coverage, participating producers can receive a payment equal to 55% of the estimated market price of the commodity, on crop losses in excess of 50% of normal yield, or 50/55 coverage.

Although eligible producers do not have to pay a premium for CAT coverage, they are required to pay upon enrollment a $300 administrative fee per covered crop for each county where they grow the crop.[2] The fee can be waived by USDA for financial hardship cases. Any producer who opts for CAT coverage has the opportunity to purchase additional insurance coverage from a private crop insurance company. For an additional premium paid by the producer, and partially subsidized by the government, a producer can increase the 50/55 catastrophic coverage to any equivalent level of coverage between 50/100 and 85/100, (i.e., 85% of yield and 100% of the estimated market price), in increments of 5%.

For many insurable commodities, an eligible producer can purchase revenue insurance. Under such a policy, a farmer potentially can receive an indemnity payment when actual farm revenue falls below the target level of revenue, regardless of whether the shortfall in revenue was caused by poor production or low farm commodity prices. Insured producers also can be eligible for reduced coverage if they are late or prevented from planting because of flooding.

(For more information on the federal crop insurance program, see CRS Report RL34207, *Crop Insurance and Disaster Assistance in the 2008 Farm Bill*; and CRS Report R40532, *Federal Crop Insurance: Background and Issues*.)

Noninsured Crop Disaster Assistance Program (NAP)

Producers who grow a crop that is currently ineligible for crop insurance may be eligible for a direct payment under USDA's Noninsured Crop Disaster Assistance Program (NAP). NAP has permanent authority under the Federal Crop Insurance Reform Act of 1994 (P.L. 103-354, as amended), and is administered by USDA's Farm Service Agency. The program's principal clientele are farmers who grow a crop that is ineligible for federal crop insurance. NAP is not subject to annual appropriations. Instead, it receives such sums as are necessary through USDA's Commodity Credit Corporation, which has a line of credit with the U.S. Treasury to fund an array of farm programs.

Eligible crops under NAP include any commercial crops grown for food or fiber that are ineligible for crop insurance, and include mushrooms, floriculture, ornamental nursery, Christmas tree crops, turfgrass sod, aquaculture, and ginseng. Trees grown for wood paper or pulp products are not eligible. To be eligible for a NAP payment, a producer first must apply for coverage under the program by the application closing date, which varies by crop, but is generally about thirty days prior to the final planting date for an annual crop. Like catastrophic crop insurance, NAP applicants must also pay an administrative fee. The NAP fee is $250 per crop payable at the time of application (rising from $150 per crop, as required by the 2008 farm bill).

In order to receive a NAP payment, a producer must experience at least a 50% crop loss caused by a natural disaster, or be prevented from planting more than 35% of intended crop acreage. For any losses in excess of the minimum loss threshold, a producer can receive 55% of the average market price for the covered commodity. Hence, NAP is similar to catastrophic crop insurance coverage in that it pays 55% of the market price for losses in excess of 50% of normal historic production. A producer of a noninsured crop is subject to a payment limit of $100,000 per person and is ineligible for a payment if the producer's qualifying gross revenues exceed $2 million. NAP payments were $110 million in FY2005, $66 million in FY2006, $127 million in FY2007, $74 million in FY2008, and an estimated $82 million in FY2009.[3]

Emergency Disaster Loans

When a county has been declared a disaster area by either the President or the Secretary of Agriculture, agricultural producers in that county may become eligible for low-interest emergency disaster (EM) loans available through USDA's Farm Service Agency. Producers in counties that are contiguous to a county with a disaster designation also become eligible for an EM loan. EM loan funds may be used to help eligible farmers, ranchers, and aquaculture producers recover from *production* losses (when the producer suffers a significant loss of an annual crop) or from *physical* losses (such as repairing or replacing damaged or destroyed structures or equipment, or for the replanting of permanent crops such as orchards). A qualified applicant can then borrow up to 100% of actual production or physical losses (not to exceed $500,000) at a below-market interest rate.

Once a county is declared eligible, an individual producer within the county (or a contiguous county) must also meet the following requirements for an EM loan. A producer must (1) be a family farmer and a citizen or permanent resident of the U.S.; (2) experience a crop loss of more than 30% or a physical loss of livestock, livestock products, real estate or property; and (3) be unable to obtain credit from a commercial lender, but still show the potential to repay the loan. Applications must be received within eight months of the county's disaster designation date. Loans for non real estate purposes generally must be repaid within one to seven years; loans for physical losses to real estate have terms up to 20 years. Depending on the repayment ability of the producer and other circumstances, these terms can be extended to 20 years for non real estate losses and up to 40 years for real estate losses.

The EM loan program is permanently authorized by Title III of the Consolidated Farm and Rural Development Act (P.L. 87-128), as amended, and is subject to annual appropriations. Traditionally, an appropriation was made for EM loans within the regular agriculture appropriations bill. However, most of the funding for the program in recent years has been provided through emergency supplemental appropriations. Emergency provisions in the Consolidated Appropriations Act of 2000 (P.L. 106-113) provided funding to make $547 million in EM loans over a multi-year period. Total EM loans made were $90 million in FY2001, $58 million in FY2002, just under $100 million in FY2003, $30 million in FY2004, $23 million in FY2005, $51 million in FY2006, $75 million in FY2007, $45 million in FY2008, $30 million in FY2009, and $4 million thus far in FY2010 (through January 8, 2010).[4]

Supplemental Revenue Assistance Payments Program (SURE)

The largest of the new farm disaster assistance programs authorized through the 2008 farm bill is the Supplemental Revenue Assistance Payments Program (SURE) for crop producers for losses occurring from crop year 2008 through September 30, 2011.[5] The program is designed to compensate eligible producers for a portion of crop losses that are not eligible for an indemnity payment under the crop insurance program (i.e., the portion of losses that is part of the deductible on the policy.) An eligible producer can receive a payment equal to 60% of the difference between a target level of revenue and the actual total farm revenue for the entire farm. The target level of revenue will be based on the level of crop insurance coverage selected by the farmer, thus increasing if a farmer opts for higher levels of coverage. To be eligible for a payment, a producer must be in or contiguous to a county that has been declared a disaster area by the Secretary of Agriculture, or have an overall 50% farm loss. Payments are limited so that the disaster program guarantee level cannot exceed 90% of what income likely would have been in the absence of a natural disaster. The producer also must have at least the minimum level of crop insurance (CAT) coverage for insurable crops and participate in the NAP program for non-insurable crops.[6]

Given the complexity of the program, USDA took 18 months to issue regulations for the SURE program, with farmer signup for 2008 crop losses beginning January 4, 2010. Prior to publication of the regulations, some farm groups and legislators had expressed concern for timely publication so farmers could learn about program details and sign up.

A concern many have with the program is that payments for crop losses cannot be determined until after the marketing year ends, since a portion of the disaster payment formula is based on the average market year prices (published after the year ends), as defined in statute. For example, the marketing year for the 2008 corn crop ended August 31, 2009, and USDA published the market year average price on September 29, 2009. After that date, revenue calculations could be determined for farms producing corn. Thus, crop disaster payments in any year could be delayed more than a year after the actual loss.

Other 2008 Farm Bill Disaster Programs

In addition to SURE, described above, the 2008 farm bill also authorizes and funds four smaller disaster programs through FY2011: (1) Livestock Indemnity Program (LIP), which compensates ranchers at a rate of 75% of market value for livestock mortality caused by a disaster;[7] (2) Livestock Forage Disaster Program (LFP), to assist ranchers who graze livestock on drought-affected pastureland or grazing land;[8] (3) Emergency Assistance for Livestock, Honey Bees, and Farm-Raised Fish Program (ELAP), which provides up to $50 million to compensate these producers for disaster losses not covered under other disaster programs;[9] and (4) Tree Assistance Program (TAP), under which eligible orchardists and nursery growers can receive a payment to cover 70% of the cost of replanting trees or nursery stock following a natural disaster.

For individual producers, combined payments under SURE, LIP, LFP, and ELAP may not exceed $100,000. For TAP, a separate limit of $100,000 per year per producer applies.

Emergency Supplemental Farm Disaster Assistance

In virtually every crop year between 1988 and 2007, Congress provided ad hoc disaster assistance to farmers and ranchers with significant weather-related production losses. Ad-hoc assistance has been made available primarily through emergency supplemental appropriations to a wide array of USDA programs.[10]

While disaster programs authorized in the 2008 farm bill are meant to replace the need for ad hoc payments, it is an open question whether Congress will continue to pass additional emergency payments for producers. This is particularly true for crop losses, because of the potential time lag between actual losses and government payments.[11] The sections below describe the most recent emergency funding, beginning with 2005 losses and ending with congressional action in March 2010 for 2009-crop losses.

2005-2007 Supplemental Assistance

Title IX of the FY2007 Iraq war supplemental appropriations act (P.L. 110-28) provided emergency agricultural disaster assistance, primarily for crop and livestock losses in any one of years 2005, 2006, or 2007 (for crops planted before February 28, 2007). Subsequently, Congress extended the assistance for crop and livestock losses in all of 2007 in the FY2008

Consolidated Appropriations Act (P.L. 110-161, Division A, Section 743). Both laws limited payments to one of the three years, as selected by the producer. The cost of 2005-2007 assistance was $2.45 billion, including $2.03 billion for crop loss assistance and $383 million for livestock feed and mortality losses.[12]

The following is a description of the major agricultural disaster provisions.[13] The producer signup period for 2005-2007 crop years ended on February 27, 2009.

Crop Loss Assistance

P.L. 110-28, as amended by P.L. 110-161, provided such sums as necessary to fund a crop disaster payment program for 2005, 2006, or 2007 production losses. Payments under the crop loss provisions were $2.03 billion. In order to contain program costs, a producer could not receive a payment for more than one crop year. Eligible producers could receive a payment on losses in excess of 35% of normal crop yields. The payment rate was 42% of the established market price for the commodity. The act also prohibited any crop disaster payments to a producer who either waived crop insurance or did not participate in the Noninsured Crop Disaster Assistance Program in the year of the loss. Also, the sum of disaster payments, crop insurance indemnities, and crop marketings could not exceed 95% of what the value of the crop would have been in the absence of losses. P.L. 110-28 also required USDA to make payments to farmers who experienced quality losses to their 2005-2007 crops, as well as for quantity losses.

Livestock Assistance

P.L. 110-28, as amended by P.L. 110-161, contained necessary sums to fund a Livestock Compensation Program (LCP) to reimburse livestock growers for feed losses caused by a natural disaster. Payments under the LCP provision were $341 million. Payments were made to producers of beef, dairy, poultry, hogs, sheep, goats, and catfish, in any county that was declared a disaster area by the President or Secretary of Agriculture between January 1, 2005, and December 31, 2007, with payments limited to one year of losses. To contain costs, the act limited the payment rate to 61% of the payment rate used in previous years. For the same time period, P.L. 110-28, as amended, contained necessary funds (payments totaled $42 million) for a Livestock Indemnity Program to reimburse producers for replacing livestock killed by a natural disaster, at a payment rate of at least 26% of the market value of the livestock prior to death. The statute also included payments to dairy producers for production losses in disaster-designated counties (payments totaled $12 million).

Conservation

P.L. 110-28 contained $16 million in additional funding for the Emergency Conservation Program (ECP) to assist farmers in the cleanup and restoration of farmland damaged by a natural disaster. Separately, P.L. 110-28 in effect provided additional funds for the Emergency Forestry Conservation Reserve Program, a program that helps restore forest lands in the South that were damaged by the 2005 hurricanes. The act removed statutory language that prohibited any spending beyond calendar year 2006, which CBO estimated at $115 million for FY2007.

2008 Supplemental Assistance

Primarily in response to the 2008 Midwest floods, the FY2008 Supplemental Appropriations Act (P.L. 110-252) contained a total of nearly $480 million in emergency funding to eligible farmers to defray the cost of clean-up and rehabilitation of farmland and watersheds following a disaster. Of the total amount available, $89.4 million was for the Emergency Conservation Program (ECP), which assists farmers in the cleanup and restoration of farmland damaged by a natural disaster, and $390.5 million was for the Emergency Watershed Protection Program (EWPP), which is designed to relieve imminent hazards created by natural disasters and to alleviate future flood risk. Second supplemental amounts of $115 million for ECP and $100 million for the EWPP were provided under the Consolidated Security, Disaster Assistance, and Continuing Appropriations Act of 2009 (P.L. 110-329).[14] No emergency supplemental disaster assistance was authorized for 2008 crop and livestock losses, since new programs were authorized and funded through the 2008 farm bill, as described above.

American Recovery and Reinvestment Act of 2009

The enacted American Recovery and Reinvestment Act of 2009 (ARRA, P.L. 111-5) contains provisions worth $744 million, as estimated by CBO, to directly assist farmers, including $674 million for crop disaster programs (primarily SURE). The SURE program changes affect 2008 crop payments by altering the payment formula and program dates.

The enacted ARRA also authorizes a new $50 million grant program for aquaculture producers to compensate them for their share of high feed prices in 2008. Under the Aquaculture Grant Program, USDA's Farm Service Agency provides grants to state governments for distribution to farmers. USDA implemented the program through a notice of funds availability published in the *Federal Register* on June 2, 2009.[15] State departments of agriculture began announcing program availability on June 18, 2009.[16]

The final component of ARRA related to farm disaster assistance is $20 million in budget authority (loan subsidy) for the Farm Service Agency to support $173 million in direct farm operating loans. FSA lends to farmers and ranchers who are not able to obtain credit from commercial lenders.

For more information on ARRA, see CRS Report R40160, *Agriculture, Nutrition, and Rural Provisions in the American Recovery and Reinvestment Act (ARRA) of 2009*, coordinated by Jim Monke.

Potential Disaster Assistance for 2009-Crop Losses

Following losses to 2009 crops due to excessive rain across much of the country, legislation was introduced in late 2009 in both chambers (S. 2810 and H.R. 4177) to make emergency payments to producers for losses in calendar year 2009. The bills were referred to committees in both chambers. Subsequently, the Senate Finance Committee attached emergency agricultural assistance to the House-passed version of the Tax Extenders Act of

2009 (H.R. 4213), which does not contain provisions for agricultural disaster payments.[17] The Senate passed the amended bill on March 10, 2010.

The legislation would provide a supplemental "direct payment" to producers in counties designated as primary natural disaster areas (i.e., excluding contiguous counties) who receive direct payments for 2009 crops under Section 1103 of the 2008 farm bill (wheat, corn, grain sorghum, barley, oats, upland cotton, long grain rice, medium grain rice, soybeans, and other oilseeds) and under Section 1303 (peanuts). The yield threshold for a crop loss due to a natural disaster is 5%, much lower than historical norms, and the payment would be 90% of a farm's total direct payments for all crops in 2009. At 5%, the proposed loss threshold is much lower than in previous disaster programs that paid for losses in excess of 35% at 65% of established prices. Eligible producers need not have purchased crop insurance.

Provisions in the Senate bill are also included for payments to specialty crop producers ($300 million), producers and first handlers of cottonseed ($42 million), and aquaculture producers ($25 million) for high feed costs in 2009. USDA is also directed to make a $21 million payment to an agricultural transportation cooperative in Hawaii for assistance to maintain and develop employment. Additional provisions authorize $75 million in no-interest emergency loans to poultry producers who have suffered financial losses associated with the termination or nonrenewal of a contract with a poultry company that has filed under Chapter 11 of the U.S. Bankruptcy Code. Finally, provisions that trigger payments for 2009 losses under the existing Livestock Forage Disaster Program are loosened. The Congressional Budget Office estimates the total cost at $1.48 billion.

To avoid paying a producer twice for the same loss, the legislation stipulates that any payments would be included in the calculation of farm revenue for a producer's payment under the SURE program (see "Supplemental Revenue Assistance Payments Program (SURE)").

Some Members of Congress are concerned that payments under the legislation could be too generous because of the low loss threshold. Normal variation in crop yields can be more than 5%. As a result, payments could go to producers and landowners (receiving direct payments) who had not experienced weather-related disasters.

End Notes

[1] In December 2009, USDA proposed changes to how company reimbursements are calculated. For more information, see CRS Report R40966, *Renegotiation of the Standard Reinsurance Agreement (SRA) for Federal Crop Insurance*, by Dennis A. Shields.

[2] The 2008 farm bill (P.L. 110-246) increased the fee to $300 per crop per county from the existing $100 fee.

[3] U.S. Department of Agriculture, http://www.ers.usda.gov/publications/ agoutlook/aotables/ 2009/ 11Nov/aotab35.xls.

[4] For more information on emergency disaster loan funding and program details, see http://www.fsa.usda.gov/FSA/ webapp?area=home&subject=fmlp&topic=fun.

[5] For more information on the SURE program, see CRS Report R40452, *A Whole-Farm Crop Disaster Program: Supplemental Revenue Assistance Payments (SURE)*, by Dennis A. Shields. USDA program information is available at http://www.fsa.usda.gov/FSA/webapp?area=home&subject=diap&topic=sure. Also, see Farm Service Agency, USDA, "Supplemental Revenue Assistance Payments Program," 74 *Federal Register* 68480-68498, December 28, 2009.

[6] The 2008 farm bill made an exception to the crop insurance/NAP requirement for the 2008 crop year by allowing producers who did not purchase crop insurance or NAP coverage in advance to be eligible for the program, as long as they pay the equivalent administrative fee for coverage within 90 days of enactment. Subsequently,

language contained in P.L. 110-398 and P.L. 111-5 (the economic stimulus bill) modified program details for the 2008 and 2009 crops.

[7] See USDA fact sheet at http://www.fsa.usda.gov/Internet/FSA_File/lip09.pdf. Also see Farm Service Agency and Commodity Credit Corporation, USDA, "Livestock Indemnity Program and General Provisions for Supplemental Agricultural Disaster Assistance Programs," 74 *Federal Register* 31567-31578, July 2, 2009.

[8] See USDA fact sheet at http://www.fsa.usda.gov/FSA/webapp?area=home&subject=diap&topic=lfp. Also see Farm Service Agency, USDA, "Livestock Forage Disaster Program and Emergency Assistance for Livestock, Honeybees, and Farm-Raised Fish; Supplemental Agricultural Disaster Assistance," 74 *Federal Register* 46665-46683, September 11, 2009.

[9] See Farm Service Agency, USDA, "Livestock Forage Disaster Program and Emergency Assistance for Livestock, Honeybees, and Farm-Raised Fish; Supplemental Agricultural Disaster Assistance," 74 *Federal Register* 46665-46683, September 11, 2009.

[10] For a history of the congressional response to agricultural disasters, see CRS Report RL31095, *Emergency Funding for Agriculture: A Brief History of Supplemental Appropriations, FY1989-FY2009*, by Ralph M. Chite.

[11] In contrast to crop disaster payments under the 2008 farm bill, the method for determining loss under the livestock programs is more streamlined, and livestock payments arrive more quickly. Livestock death losses for individual producers immediately trigger Livestock Indemnity Program payments, while the weekly publication "U.S. Drought Monitor" is used to determine payments for grazing losses under the Livestock Forage Disaster Program. As of early January 2010, USDA had made more than $175 million in disaster payments under both programs.

[12] Payment figures in this section are from U.S. Department of Agriculture, Economic Research Service, *Agricultural Outlook: Statistical Indicators*, Table 35—CCC Net Outlays by Commodity and Function, http://www.ers.usda.gov/ publications/agoutlook/aotables/2009/11Nov/aotab35.xls.

[13] For more information on these disaster programs, see various USDA fact sheets accessed at http://www.fsa.usda.gov/ FSA/webapp?area=home&subject=diap&topic=landing.

[14] U.S. Department of Agriculture, Farm Service Agency, *FY2010 USDA Budget Explanatory Notes for Committee on Appropriations*, Farm Service Agency, June 3, 2009, p. 68, http://www.obpa.usda.gov/18fsa2010notes.pdf.

[15] For the notice and additional information on the program, see http://www. fsa. usda.gov/ FSA/webapp?area=home& subject=landing&topic=aqua.

[16] Florida Department of Agriculture and Consumer Services, "Bronson Announces 2008 Aquaculture Grant Program," press release, June 18, 2009, http://www.doacs.state.fl.us/press/2009/06182009.html.

[17] Senate Finance Committee, "Baucus, Reid Introduce Package to Restore Aid for Out-of-Work Americans, Improve Tax Certainty for Families, Businesses to Bolster Job Creation," press release, March 1, 2010, http://finance.senate.gov/press/Bpress/2010press/prb030110b.pdf. The proposed legislation is at http://finance.senate.gov/sitepages/leg/LEG%202010/030110_Workers_State_Business_Relief_Act.pdf.

In: Agriculture Disaster and Crop Insurance: Background... ISBN: 978-1-61761-559-7
Editor: Angela M. Gil

Chapter 2

A WHOLE-FARM CROP DISASTER PROGRAM: SUPPLEMENTAL REVENUE ASSISTANCE PAYMENTS (SURE)

Dennis A. Shields

SUMMARY

In an effort to end the ad-hoc nature of emergency crop disaster assistance to farmers, Congress authorized a new Supplemental Revenue Assistance Payments Program (SURE) in the Food, Conservation, and Energy Act of 2008. The program provides payments to producers for crop revenue losses due to natural disaster or adverse weather incurred on or before September 30, 2011. It essentially compensates eligible producers for a portion of losses that are not eligible for an indemnity payment under a crop insurance policy. The program departs from both traditional disaster assistance and crop yield insurance by calculating and reimbursing losses using total crop revenue for the entire farm (i.e., summing revenue from all crops for an individual farmer).

Under SURE, a farmer's revenue from *all* crops in *all* counties is compared with a guaranteed level that is computed mostly from expected or average yields and prices. As a result, the program considers the disaster's impact on a farmer's entire enterprise and not on just the crop(s) that were adversely affected. If the actual farm revenue (including farm program payments and insurance indemnities) is less than the farm's guaranteed level, the producer receives a payment, calculated as 60% of the difference between the two amounts. In contrast, if actual whole farm revenue does not fall below the guarantee, whereby losses for one crop are offset by revenue gains for another, no disaster payment is made. Payments are limited so that the guaranteed level cannot exceed 90% of expected farm income in the absence of a natural disaster.

On December 28, 2009, USDA issued regulations for SURE. Previously, farm groups had been calling for their publication so that farmers could learn program details, sign up, and consider related business issues such as appropriate insurance coverage levels. Farmer signup for 2008 crop losses began January 4, 2010, and USDA began making payments shortly thereafter.

USDA officials say that SURE is the most complex program USDA's Farm Service Agency (FSA) has undertaken. It has faced a number of implementation challenges in terms of program administration, such as collecting and tabulating a significant amount of data for individual farmers, as well as crop price data that are not readily available. Another issue has been accounting for various insurance products when determining the farmer's guarantee level.

Part of the motivation behind SURE was to provide a pre-designed program that farmers could incorporate in their risk management planning. Also, payments would be presumably more timely because legislation would already be in place when disaster strikes. However, disaster payments under SURE arrive well after the crop loss because some of the data needed to compute payment rates become available more than one year after harvest. Computing actual farm revenue requires season-average prices, which USDA publishes after the market year ends. Also, government commodity payments, which are also needed for the revenue calculation, can occur 1 1/2 years after the crop is harvested. Thus, SURE program payments may not be as timely as some farmers and policymakers would like. In fact, legislation was introduced in late 2009 in both chambers (S. 2810 and H.R. 4177) that would make emergency payments for losses in calendar 2009.

In the next farm bill debate, Congress will likely be interested in program effectiveness. Major questions are likely to be (1) whether the SURE program in fact eliminates the need for ad-hoc crop disaster legislation for crop farmers, and (2) how well this whole-farm approach helps manage farm-level risk. Some farmers have already complained that the whole-farm approach typically does not result in disaster payments for diversified operations. In contrast, where farmers have qualified for payments, the initial reaction has been generally favorable.

The Food, Conservation, and Energy Act of 2008 (P.L. 110-246, 2008 farm bill) created a set of disaster programs called "Supplemental Agricultural Disaster Assistance." The programs supplement crop insurance coverage and provide disaster assistance for livestock (including aquaculture and honey bees), forage, and tree and nursery crops.

The largest component of Supplemental Agricultural Disaster Assistance is a new crop disaster program called the Supplemental Revenue Assistance Payments Program (SURE). The program pays producers for crop revenue losses due to natural disaster or adverse weather. It essentially compensates eligible producers for a portion of losses that are not eligible for an indemnity payment under a crop insurance policy. The program departs, however, from both traditional disaster assistance and crop yield insurance by calculating and reimbursing losses using total crop revenue for the entire farm (i.e., summing revenue from all crops for an individual farmer). Because of the size and complexity of SURE, this report focuses on the program's mechanics, how it relates to other farm disaster programs, and some funding and implementation issues.

On December 28, 2009, USDA issued regulations for SURE.[1] Previously, farm groups had been calling for their publication so that farmers could learn program details, sign up, and consider related business issues such as appropriate insurance coverage levels. USDA officials say that this is the most complex program USDA's Farm Service Agency has undertaken, and the Department has faced a number of issues as it implements the program.

Federal Programs for Crop Disaster

Historically, three ongoing federal programs help farmers deal with risk associated with crop losses.[2] Each has permanent authorization and receives regular annual funding. *Crop insurance* indemnifies participating producers for yield or revenue losses for their farms. USDA's *noninsured crop disaster assistance program (NAP)* provides crop-loss coverage for crops not covered by insurance policies. *Emergency disaster loans* are available to producers when a county has been declared a disaster area either by the President or the Secretary of Agriculture.

In recent decades, when these programs did not provide sufficient financial assistance to producers, Congress has provided "ad-hoc" emergency crop disaster assistance. In virtually every crop year between 1988 and 2007, Congress provided disaster assistance to farmers and ranchers with significant weather-related production losses. During this period, federal ad-hoc crop disaster programs provided approximately $1 billion per fiscal year to farmers who experienced a major crop loss caused by a natural disaster. Ad-hoc assistance has been made available primarily through emergency supplemental appropriations to a wide array of USDA programs.[3]

In an effort to end the ad-hoc nature of emergency assistance, with legislation enacted *after* the disaster occurred, Congress authorized the SURE program in the 2008 farm bill to cover crop revenue losses incurred on or before September 30, 2011. Part of the motivation was to provide a pre-designed program that farmers could incorporate in their risk management planning. Also, payments would be presumably more timely because legislation would already be in place when disaster strikes.

How SURE Works

A major distinction of SURE is that payments are based on whole-farm crop revenue, not crop- specific losses. In previous disaster programs, producer payments were based on individual crop losses. If a farmer experienced a yield loss, the farmer would be eligible for a payment specific to that crop loss, assuming other criteria were met. Revenue losses are, in general, determined by the calendar year of harvest.

Under the new program, a farmer's revenue from *all* crops in *all* counties is compared with a guaranteed level of revenue that is computed mostly from expected or average yields and prices. As a result, the program considers the disaster's impact on a farmer's entire enterprise and not on just the crop(s) that were adversely affected. If the actual farm revenue (including farm program payments and insurance indemnities) is less than the farm's guaranteed level, the producer receives a payment. In contrast, if actual whole farm revenue does not fall below the guaranteed level, whereby losses for one crop are offset by revenue gains for another, no disaster payment is made. Payments are limited so that the guaranteed level cannot exceed 90% of expected farm income in the absence of a natural disaster.

Eligibility Requirements

The law specifies that farmers must purchase insurance on all crops in their farming operation, including field crops, hay, double-crop plantings, and fruits and vegetables. Requiring insurance coverage ensures that SURE is supplemental, not primary, insurance, which limits expenditures. This requirement covers production in all counties and states where a farmer has a share in the production. If crop insurance is not available, producers must purchase Noninsured Crop Disaster Assistance Program (NAP) coverage. The value of any crop not eligible to be insured under either program will not be considered under SURE.

Producers are not required to purchase insurance or NAP coverage if the crop is not economically significant or if the NAP administrative fee (currently $250 per crop) exceeds 10% of the value of the coverage. Economic significance is defined by the crop having at least a 5% share of the producer's total expected revenue from all crops grown.

Finally, eligible farmers must have a financial interest and be at risk in the production of crops located in a secretarial-disaster-declared county (or a contiguous county), or have an overall production loss greater than 50%. At least one crop of economic significance must suffer at least a 10% production loss due to disaster, adverse weather, or disaster-related conditions.

Payment Calculation

SURE payments will be made when an individual producer's *program guarantee* total is greater than the *farm revenue*. The payment is 60% of the difference between the two. Both revenue and guarantee are calculated by summing the values for all crops across all locations for an individual producer. The SURE calculation described below is summarized in "Box 1. Supplemental Revenue Assistance Payment Mechanism." A hypothetical scenario for an individual farmer is shown in "Box 2. SURE Payment—Hypothetical Example for Wheat/Watermelon Farm."[4]

SURE Guarantee

The guaranteed revenue level in the SURE program is essentially the sum of a farm's crop insurance guarantees increased by 15%, and NAP guarantees increased by 20%. These factors are designed to partly fill the gap left by insurance or NAP coverage.[5] Values for both insured and NAP crops are summed to arrive at a farmer's total revenue guarantee.

For insurable crops, the guarantee is the product of the 1.15 factor, the (adjusted) actual production history (APH) yield,[6] the insurance coverage level, planted or prevented planted acreage, and price election. The yield for determining federal counter-cyclical payments (Direct and Counter-Cyclical Payment Program) is used if it is higher than the adjusted APH yield. Including the insurance coverage level is designed to encourage farmers to purchase higher levels of coverage. For non-insurable crops, a similar calculation is made. The guarantee is the product of a 1.20 factor, the NAP price, planted and prevented planted acreage, and 50% of the adjusted NAP yield (or the counter-cyclical payment yield, if higher).

Box 1. Supplemental Revenue Assistance Payment Mechanism

Title XV of the 2008 farm bill (P.L. 110-246) authorizes a new crop disaster program for FY2008-FY20 11. Eligible farmers must be in or contiguous to a disaster-declared county, or have a production loss greater than 50%. They must have purchased crop insurance or have coverage under the Noninsured Crop Disaster Assistance Program (NAP), where applicable. Amounts for insurable and non-insurable crops are added together for whole-farm totals (for both the guarantee and farm revenue calculations).

I. Payment Formula

Eligible crop producers can receive a supplemental payment equal to:

60% of (Program Guarantee minus Total Farm Revenue)

Formula is based on the revenue of the entire farm. The Guarantee cannot exceed 90% of Expected Revenue.

II. How to Calculate the Program Guarantee:

A. Insurable Crops

Program Guarantee = 115% of (Payment Rate X Payment Acres X Payment Yield)

Payment Rate = Crop Insurance Price Election

Payment Acres = Planted and Prevented Planting Acreage

Payment Yield = Selected Crop Insurance Coverage Level X Adjusted Crop Insurance Yield or Counter-Cyclical Payment (CCP) Yield, whichever is higher

B. Non-insurable Crops

Program Guarantee = 120% of (Payment Rate X Payment Acres X Payment Yield)

Payment Rate = 100% of the Noninsured Assistance Program (NAP) Price

Payment Acres = Planted and Prevented Planting Acreage

Payment Yield = 50% X Adjusted NAP yield or Counter-Cyclical Payment (CCP) yield, whichever is higher

III. How to Calculate Total Farm Revenue:

Total Farm Revenue = Estimated Actual Value for each crop produced on the farm =

Value of Actual Crop Production + 15% of Direct Payments + CCP or Average Crop Revenue (ACRE) Payments + Loan Deficiency Payments (LDP) or Marketing Loan Gains (MLG) + Net Crop Insurance Payments (Indemnities – Premiums) + NAP Payments + Other Disaster Payments + Crop Salvage Value

Where the Value of Actual Crop Production = Actual Harvested Production X National Average Market Price

For NAP eligible crops, the National Average Market Price cannot be greater than 100% of NAP Price.

IV. How to Calculate Expected Revenue:

Program Guarantee cannot exceed 90% of Expected Revenue

Expected Revenue = (Adjusted APH or CCP Yield X Planted and Prevented Planted Acreage X Price Guarantee) + (Adjusted NAP Yield X NAP Price)

Source: Adapted from CRS Report RL34207, *Crop Insurance and Disaster Assistance in the 2008 Farm Bill*, by Ralph M. Chite and Dennis A. Shields.

Box 2. SURE Payment—Hypothetical Example for Wheat/Watermelon Farm

Farmer Martin has just two crops on his farm: 500 acres of wheat and 100 acres of watermelon. To remain eligible for SURE, he purchases (1) crop insurance for wheat and (2) Noninsured Crop Disaster Assistance Program (NAP) coverage for watermelon because crop insurance is not available. The watermelon crop is economically significant because it accounts for at least 5% of expected value of all crops grown by the producer. Assume poor weather adversely affects both crops, and one of the fields is located in a county that has been designated as a disaster county. Using the formula outlined in Box 1, Farmer Martin's SURE payment would be $15,203.

I. Payment Formula

60% of (Program Guarantee minus Total Farm Revenue)
SURE Payment = 60% X ($156,488 - $131,149) = $15,203

II. How to Calculate the Program Guarantee:

A.Insurable Crops (wheat in this example)
Program Guarantee = 115% of (Payment Rate X Payment Acres X Payment Yield)
Program Guarantee = 115% X $7.35/bu. X 500 acres X 30 bu./ac. = $126,788
Payment Rate = $7.35 per bushel
Payment Acres = 500 acres
Payment Yield = 75% X 40 bu./ac. = 30 bu./ac.

B. Non-insurable Crops (watermelon in this example)
Program Guarantee = 120% of (Payment Rate X Payment Acres X Payment Yield)
Program Guarantee = 120% X $8.25/cwt. X 100 acres X 30 cwt./acre = $29,700
Payment Rate = $8.25 per cwt.
Payment Acres = 100 acres
Payment Yield = 30 hundredweight (cwt.)/ac. (50% of average yield); (i.e., 3,000 lbs./ac.)

Total Program Guarantee = $126,788 + $29,700 = $156,488

III. How to Calculate Total Farm Revenue:

Total Farm Revenue = Estimated Actual Value for each crop produced on the farm = Value of Actual Crop Production + 15% of Direct Payments + Other government payments + Net Crop Insurance Payments (Indemnities – Premiums) + NAP Payments + Other Disaster Payments + Crop Salvage Value

Revenue = wheat (13,000 bu. X $7/bu.) + watermelon (4,200 cwt. X $5.75/cwt.) = $115,150;

Direct Payments = 15% X $8,663 = $1,299; Net Crop Insurance Payments (Indemnities – Premiums) = $14,700

Total Farm Revenue = $115,150 + $1,299 + $14,700 = $131,149

IV. How to Calculate Expected Revenue:

Program Guarantee cannot exceed 90% of Expected Revenue (Acre X Yield X Price) = **90% X $196,500 = $176,850**

Expected Revenue = [500 ac. X 40 bu./ac. X $7.35/bu.] + [100 ac. X 60 cwt./ac. X $8.25 per cwt.] = $196,500

Source: Adapted from U.S. Department of Agriculture, Oklahoma Farm Service Agency, *Supplemental Revenue Assistance Payments (SURE)*, Farm Bill 2008 Information Sheet, Oklahoma City, OK, November 2008, http://www.fsa.usda.gov/Internet/FSAFile/surefactsheetok.pdf.

The program guarantee cannot exceed 90% of total expected revenue. The expected revenue is calculated the same as the guarantee, except the 1.15 factor, 1.20 factor, and insurance coverage level are not included in the calculations. The effect of this limit is that the SURE guarantee cannot be greater than a 90% insurance guarantee across all crops.

Total Farm Revenue

The formula for total farm revenue is the actual value for all crops, plus government payments and crop salvage value (if losses are incurred). Each crop value is determined by multiplying actual harvested production times the national average market price (the regulation provides for adjustments for quality at the local level). For NAP crops, the national average market price cannot be greater than the NAP price.

The government payment sum equals 15% of direct payments plus 100% of all other payments— counter-cyclical payments, average crop revenue election payments, loan deficiency payments, marketing loan gains, net crop insurance payments (indemnities minus premiums), NAP payments, and other disaster payments. Including government payments prevents a farmer from receiving two payments for the same loss.

Payment Timing

Disaster payments under SURE will likely arrive well after the crop loss because some of the data needed to computed payment rates become available more than one year after harvest. Computing actual farm revenue requires season-average prices, which USDA publishes after the market year ends. For example, the 2008 corn crop was harvested in fall 2008. The 2008 corn marketing year ended on August 31, 2009, and USDA published the market year average price on September 29, 2009. After that date, revenue calculations could be determined for farms producing corn, assuming other data are also available. Thus, crop disaster payments in any year could be delayed for more than a year after the actual loss.

Income and Payment Limits

For 2008 crops, SURE payments are not available for persons or legal entities if their average adjusted gross income (AGI) for 2005, 2006, and 2007 exceeds $2.5 million, unless 75% or more of their AGI is from agriculture (AGI includes farm and nonfarm income). Beginning in crop year 2009, the limit is $500,000 for average adjusted gross nonfarm income.

Total payments per person may not exceed $100,000 for SURE and the three livestock-related disaster programs under the 2008 farm bill's Supplemental Agricultural Disaster Assistance programs.[7]

Changes to SURE since the 2008 Farm Bill

The authorizing statute for SURE has been amended twice since the 2008 farm bill was enacted. The first was on October 13, 2008, when P.L. 110-398 made a variety of technical corrections. It also extended the date by which producers were required to "buy-in" to crop insurance or NAP coverage for 2009 crops with closing dates prior to August 14, 2008. Producers would remain eligible for the 2009-crop SURE program by paying the applicable fees by January 12, 2009. (This affected producers with crops such as citrus, nursery, avocados, selected fresh vegetables, and macadamia nuts). Paying the administrative fees makes farmers eligible for SURE payments as if they had purchased crop insurance or NAP on time, but it does not provide the coverage itself.

The second change, which affects the 2008 crop year, was contained in the American Recovery and Reinvestment Act of 2009 (ARRA, P.L. 111-5). The enacted ARRA extended "buy-in" deadline for 2008 crops from September 16, 2008,[8] to May 18, 2009 (90 days after enactment of the conference agreement).[9] Additionally, the enacted law allows all producers to receive potentially higher SURE payments than they otherwise would have received by altering the payment formula.[10] SURE is expected to have greater participation because of the changes enacted under ARRA.

INTERACTION WITH OTHER GOVERNMENT PROGRAMS

The SURE program is designed to help fill gaps in other government commodity and risk management programs. The cost to the farmer is relatively low, and becoming eligible for SURE does not affect decisions for other programs.[11] As a result, interest in SURE is expected to increase demand for crop insurance and NAP coverage, resulting in a greater share of U.S. crops covered under crop insurance and NAP.[12]

Unlike previous ad-hoc disaster legislation, farmers now have a pre-determined program for dealing with crop disaster loss, at least during the life of the program through September 30, 2011. This certainty may be helpful for farmers when making business plans and securing financing, particularly for farms which have little diversification and are susceptible to significant variation in whole-farm revenue.

FUNDING SOURCE AND EXPECTED OUTLAYS

SURE and the four other disaster programs authorized in the 2008 farm bill are to receive funding through a newly authorized Agricultural Disaster Relief Trust Fund within the U.S. Treasury. The Trust Fund is to receive the equivalent of 3.08% of the amount received each year (FY2008-20 11) in U.S. Customs receipts collected on certain goods.

At the time of 2008 farm bill enactment, the Congressional Budget Office (CBO) estimated the combined total costs of the five programs to be $3.8 billion over the four-year life of the programs. Of this total, CBO estimated that supplemental crop revenue assistance would cost $1.7 billion over the four years, or an average of $425 million per year. Another $1.6 billion would cover increased crop insurance and NAP costs associated with the requirement that participants purchase either crop insurance or NAP coverage. The balance of $500 million would cover the combined estimated cost of the other four disaster programs, according to CBO. If the cost of the programs exceeds the level of funding provided through Customs receipts, the 2008 farm bill gives the Trust Fund the authority to borrow from the Treasury such sums as necessary to meet its obligations.[13]

SURE provisions in the American Recovery and Reinvestment Act of 2009 (ARRA, P.L. 111-5) are expected to cost an additional $674 million, according to CBO estimates. About $500-$600 million would be for higher SURE program benefits for the 2008 crop, with the remaining for the cost of crop insurance subsidies associated with additional policy purchases.

USDA estimates total SURE payments at $3.4 billion for 2008-2011, or $0.85 billion per year. This is less than average annual payments of $1.14 billion per year under previous ad hoc disaster programs (1998-2007). USDA says SURE is expected to cost less because losses will be lower when calculated at the farm level, with individual crop losses partially offset by crop insurance indemnities, NAP payments, and revenue from other crops. Also the SURE guarantee cap of 90% is 5 percentage points lower than previous ad hoc disaster programs.

PROGRAM IMPLEMENTATION ISSUES

On December 28, 2009, USDA issued regulations for SURE.[14] Previously, farm groups had been calling for their publication so that farmers could learn program details, sign up, and consider related business issues such as appropriate insurance coverage levels. Farmer signup for 2008 crop losses began January 4, 2010, and USDA began making payments shortly thereafter.

USDA officials say that SURE is the most complex program USDA's Farm Service Agency (FSA) has undertaken. It has faced a number of implementation challenges in terms of program administration. From a computational standpoint, a significant challenge for USDA is to create software for issuing producer payments. It requires loading, retrieval, and manipulation of a significant amount of data, including the collection of data from FSA county offices across the country, wherever a farmer may be operating. USDA intends to develop a Web-based system that will use data from its mainframe system in Kansas City and combine it with data located elsewhere. For example, NAP records are housed in each county office. The system will share data so that the "home" county office designated by the farmer has access to all of that producer's records. In order to expedite program delivery and payments, USDA began accepting and processing applications in January 2010 using an interim (manual) process until software that incorporates all SURE program rules can be developed. [15]

Along the same lines, the "farms" used for commodity program payments by USDA's Farm Service Agency (FSA) are different tracts of land than units used for FSA's NAP program and the Risk Management Agency's crop insurance program. Yields from all three may be needed in order to determine the appropriate yield for the SURE guarantee. This requires tabulating weighted average yields for a farmer across all farms in all counties. A significant amount of case-by-case attention may be required to ensure all data have been accounted for and used in the guarantee calculation.

Determining prices used in the guarantee and farm revenue calculations will also be challenging. USDA's National Agricultural Statistics Service publishes average prices for major crops and some specialty crops. For some additional specialty crops, USDA's Market News Service reports daily or weekly prices but does not tabulate average prices weighted by volume. For minor and/or thinly traded crops, USDA may find it difficult to gather enough data to determine average prices for the both the revenue and the guarantee calculation.[16] However, USDA reports that FSA's state committees have considerable experience developing prices for NAP crops, using a variety of sources such as extension agents.[17]

Another issue has been accounting for various insurance products when determining the farmer's guarantee level. The statutory language for the SURE calculation follows traditional yield-loss insurance in that a farmer selects a coverage level and price. However, some insurance products under the federal crop insurance program, such as adjusted gross revenue,[18] do not fit within this structure because there are no yields or prices in the policy on which to base the guarantee. In this case, to determine a farmer's revenue guarantee (on a crop-by-crop basis), USDA will use a combination of data from the individual (planted acres and insurance coverage level elected by the producer) and substitute data (county average yields and NAP prices). For "value loss" crops such as ornamental nursery, which are also covered by non-yield-based insurance policies, SURE payment eligibility will be determined by the inventory immediately before and after a disaster. This will help maintain consistency with insurance policies and NAP for these types of crops. USDA says daily inventory records required for NAP or crop insurance will typically be sufficient for documenting losses for SURE payment eligibility.

ISSUES FOR THE 111TH CONGRESS

In the next farm bill debate, Congress would likely be interested in program effectiveness. A major question would likely be whether the SURE program in fact eliminates the need for ad-hoc disaster legislation for crop farmers. Based on CBO and USDA cost estimates, annual SURE payments are expected to be less than the typical levels of ad-hoc disaster payments. These projected payment levels leave open the question of whether SURE will provide an acceptable level of disaster assistance.

Similarly, the reaction of farmers when they find out they might not qualify—for example, a freeze destroys a farmer's wheat crop but lost revenue is offset by corn revenue gains later in the season—would likely play a part in how SURE will be viewed by policymakers. For example, on diversified crop farms, the whole-farm revenue approach may pay fewer benefits than previous disaster programs, but in other cases farmers may see increased benefits if total crop revenue is adversely affected.

While SURE and other disaster programs authorized in the 2008 farm bill are meant to replace the need for ad hoc payments, Congress might pass additional emergency payments for producers, particularly for crop losses, because of the potential time lag between actual losses and government payments.[19] In fact, legislation introduced in late 2009 in both chambers (S. 2810 and H.R. 4177) would make emergency payments to producers for losses in calendar 2009.

Another question would be how well this whole-farm approach helps manage farm-level risk. It may take several years to determine how effective the program is for individual farmers. Some farmers have already complained that the whole-farm approach typically does not result in disaster payments for diversified operations because aggregating revenue across a farmer's entire operation substantially reduces the likelihood of receiving assistance.[20] Also, rice farmers have noted that SURE (like crop insurance) does not provide any coverage for increased harvested costs associated with "downed rice" following excessive rain or flooding immediately prior to harvest, which was a widespread problem in 2009.[21] In contrast, where farmers have qualified for payments, the initial reaction has been generally favorable. For example, farmers in North Dakota are reportedly fairly satisfied with SURE, in combination with benefits provided under crop insurance.[22]

One potential outcome of this program could be to inadvertently encourage some farmers to increase their farm business risk. Because SURE addresses whole-farm crop revenue risk, some analysts expect SURE to favor farmers with a single crop produced in a single county or counties with high yield variability. In contrast, planting multiple crops in multiple locations adds diversity to a farm, thereby reducing the chance that a farm would drop below its guaranteed revenue trigger. Consequently, in order to take advantage of SURE, farmers might eliminate crops from their rotations.[23] To the extent this happens, policymakers might consider ways to avoid incentives that encourage risky behavior or poor production practices.

End Notes

[1] Farm Service Agency, USDA, "Supplemental Revenue Assistance Payments Program," 74 *Federal Register* 68480- 68498, December 28, 2009. The regulation and other information on SURE are available from USDA at http://www.fsa.usda.gov/FSA/webapp?area=home&subject=diap&topic=sure.

[2] For an overview of disaster programs provided in 2008 farm bill, see CRS Report RS21212, *Agricultural Disaster Assistance*, by Dennis A. Shields and Ralph M. Chite.

[3] CRS Report RL3 1095, *Emergency Funding for Agriculture: A Brief History of Supplemental Appropriations, FY1989-FY2009*, by Ralph M. Chite.

[4] For software that estimates a farm's SURE payment, see USDA's program website at http://www.fsa.usda.gov/FSA/ webapp?area=home&subject=diap&topic=sure. Iowa State University Extension Service also provides software at http://www.extension.iastate.edu/agdm/crops

[5] The factors for 2008 crop guarantees are 1.20 and 1.25, respectively, as provided in the American Recovery and Reinvestment Act of 2009 (P.L. 111-5).

[6] When at least four years of history are available, the adjusted APH averages all years of historical yields and ignores yield "plugs" (substitute data when yields were affected by disaster). When less than four years are available, the yields are averaged after dropping the lowest plug yield.

[7] A separate limit of $100,000 applies for the Tree Assistance Program, as specified in the 2008 farm bill.

[8] The 2008 farm bill originally extended the buy-in date to September 16, 2008.

[9] The buy-in fee is $100 per crop. The maximum fee for insurable or noninsurable crops is $300 per county, per producer, not to exceed $900 for multi-county producers. Paying the fee does not provide the producer with crop insurance or NAP for the 2008 crop year; it merely permits the producer to become eligible for the 2008-crop disaster assistance programs. See "Agriculture Secretary Vilsack Announces Disaster Assistance for Producer: USDA extending buy-in waiver for those impacted by natural disasters," press release, March 17, 2008, http://www.usda.gov/ wps/portal/usdahome?contentidonly=true&contentid=2009/03/0062.xml.

[10] For 2008 crops, a producer's SURE calculation will be based on 70% yield crop insurance coverage (with 100% of price) even if less coverage was purchased. In addition, for farmers who met the original September 16, 2008, deadline, the guarantee for a 2008 crop is the greater of two calculated amounts based on (1) the 70/100 coverage or (2) increased payment factors, specifically 120% for crop insurance and 125% for NAP coverage instead of the 115% or 120% in current law.

[11] For catastrophic coverage, producers pay an administrative fee of $300 per crop per county. For NAP coverage, the fee is the lesser of $250/crop/county or $750/producer/county, not to exceed $1,875 for producers with farming interests in multiple counties.

[12] Crop insurance coverage is already relatively high. Policies covered 265 million acres in 2009 and 272 million acres in 2008 and 2007, according to USDA's Risk Management Agency. U.S.-harvested cropland totaled 310 million acres in 2007, according to the Census of Agriculture.

[13] This section is from CRS Report RL34207, *Crop Insurance and Disaster Assistance in the 2008 Farm Bill*, by Ralph M. Chite and Dennis A. Shields.

[14] Farm Service Agency, USDA, "Supplemental Revenue Assistance Payments Program," 74 *Federal Register* 68480- 68498, December 28, 2009.

[15] For the interim process, all producer information is manually loaded into a spreadsheet to calculate the SURE payment for a farmer. Given the potential for errors in the manual process, USDA implemented a plan in April 2010 to review SURE calculations for selected individuals.

[16] Technical corrections to the 2008 farm bill eliminated the requirement of using national prices, which some say is problematic because crop prices can vary significantly across the country. As specified in regulation, USDA will allow price adjustments by Farm Service Agency state committees to reflect regional variations consistent with prices established for crop insurance or NAP.

[17] FSA state committees review state office operations and make decisions on how programs are applied statewide.

[18] Adjusted gross revenue (AGR) insures revenue of the entire farm rather than an individual crop by guaranteeing a percentage of average gross farm revenue. To calculate the policy revenue guarantee, the plan uses a producer's Schedule F tax form and current-year expected farm revenue.

[19] In contrast to crop disaster payments under the 2008 farm bill, the method for determining loss under the livestock programs is more streamlined, and livestock payments arrive more quickly. Livestock death losses for individual producers immediately trigger Livestock Indemnity Program payments, while the weekly publication *U.S. Drought Monitor* is used to determine payments for grazing losses under the Livestock Forage Disaster Program. As of early January 2010, USDA had made more than $175 million in disaster payments under both programs.

[20] U.S. Congress, House Committee on Agriculture, *Testimony of Ronnie Holt*, hearing to review U.S. agriculture policy in advance of the 2012 farm bill, 111th Cong., 2nd sess., May 17, 2010, http://agriculture.house gov /hearings/ statements.html.

[21] U.S. Congress, House Committee on Agriculture, *Testimony of Joe Mencer*, hearing to review U.S. agriculture policy in advance of the 2012 farm bill, 111th Cong., 2nd sess., May 15, 2010,http://agriculture.house.gov/hearings/ statements.html.

[22] U.S. Congress, House Committee on Agriculture, hearing to review U.S. agriculture policy in advance of the 2012 farm bill, 111th Cong., 2nd sess., April 21, 2010, unofficial transcript of hearing available at http://www.farmpolicy.com/wp-content/uploads/2010/05/KGood042110-1.pdf.

[23] G.A. "Art" Barnaby Jr., "SURE Calculator (New Standing Disaster Aid)," Research paper, Kansas State University, Manhattan, Kansas, August 28, 2008, http://www.agmanager.info/crops ABSURE_CALC.pdf.

In: Agriculture Disaster and Crop Insurance: Background... ISBN: 978-1-61761-559-7
Editor: Angela M. Gil

Chapter 3

CROP INSURANCE AND DISASTER ASSISTANCE IN THE 2008 FARM BILL

Ralph M. Chite and Randy Schnepf

SUMMARY

The federal government has relied primarily on two policy tools in recent years to help mitigate the financial losses experienced by crop farmers as a result of natural disasters—a federal crop insurance program and congressionally mandated *ad-hoc* crop disaster payments. Congress has made several modifications to the crop insurance program since the 1980s, in an effort to forestall the demand for supplemental disaster payments. Although the scope of the crop insurance program has widened significantly over the past 25 years, the anticipated goal of crop insurance replacing disaster payments has not been achieved.

The federal crop insurance program is permanently authorized and hence does not require periodic reauthorization; however, some modifications were made to it in the context of the Food, Conservation, and Energy Act of 2008 (P.L. 110-246, the 2008 farm bill). Some policymakers viewed the projected baseline outlays for the crop insurance program as a potential target for program cost reductions, and proposed using these savings to fund new initiatives in various other titles of the farm bill. Consequently, many of the new crop insurance provisions are cost-saving measures. According to Congressional Budget Office estimates, the crop insurance provisions (Title XII) in the 2008 farm bill will reduce program baseline outlays by $3.9 billion over the five-year period of the bill (FY2008-FY20 12). Much of the savings ($2.8 billion) is achieved through a change in the timing of crop insurance payments and receipts that will not directly affect the final monetary amounts for participating farmers or insurance companies. The rest of the savings is generated through increased fees paid by farmers for catastrophic coverage and a reduction in reimbursements to the participating insurance companies for their operating expenses, among many other provisions. To address concerns about program waste, fraud, and abuse, the farm bill also authorizes up to $4 million annually for data mining activities beginning in FY2009.

Separately, Title XV of the 2008 farm bill authorizes a new trust fund with projected costs of $3.8 billion for providing agricultural disaster assistance available on an ongoing basis over the next four years through five new programs. The largest program is a supplemental revenue assistance payment program for crop producers that is designed to compensate eligible producers for a portion of crop losses that are not eligible for an indemnity payment under the crop insurance program. To be eligible for a payment, a producer must be either in or contiguous to a county that has been declared a disaster area by either the President or the Secretary of Agriculture. An eligible producer also is required to have purchased crop insurance in advance of a disaster. However, the statute makes an exception for the 2008 crop year by allowing uninsured producers to be eligible, as long as they pay the equivalent administrative fee for coverage within 90 days of enactment.

For a description of all crop insurance provisions in the enacted 2008 farm bill, and a comparison of the provisions with the House- and Senate-passed versions of the bill and previous law, see the Appendix at the end of this report.

Agriculture is generally viewed as an inherently risky enterprise. Farm production levels can vary significantly from year to year and by location, primarily because farmers operate at the mercy of nature, and frequently are subjected to weather-related and other natural disasters. Since the Great Depression, policymakers have decided that the federal government should absorb some portion of the weather-related production losses that otherwise would depress farm income and could alter farmers' decisions about what to produce in some high-risk locations.

Federal crop insurance is the primary ongoing crop loss assistance program. It is permanently authorized by the Federal Crop Insurance Act, as amended (7 U.S.C. 1501 *et seq.*), and is administered by the U.S. Department of Agriculture's Risk Management Agency (RMA). This is complemented with the Non-Insured Assistance Program, administered by the Farm Service Agency (FSA), which is available to producers not offered insurance coverage. Lack of insurance availability occurs in locations where there is insufficient production history to determine actuarial risks of a crop or in regions where production of a specific commodity is relatively small. Following a widespread and severe drought in 1988, Congress approved a large *ad hoc* disaster assistance program to supplement the ongoing disaster programs. Such *ad hoc* assistance subsequently has became routine. For more information on currently available agricultural disaster assistance, see CRS Report RS21212, *Agricultural Disaster Assistance*.

Since the federal crop insurance program is permanently authorized, it does not require periodic reauthorization in an omnibus farm bill. However, during the 2007-2008 farm bill debate, some policymakers expressed interest in revising the crop insurance program in the context of the farm bill with two goals: to score cost savings and/or to supplement it with a permanent disaster payment program. Ultimately, the 2008 farm bill (P.L. 110-246), enacted on June 18, 2008, contained provisions that accomplished both of those goals. This report provides background on the crop insurance program and describes in detail changes made to it as part of the 2008 farm bill.

CROP INSURANCE BACKGROUND

Federal crop insurance policies are marketed and serviced by private insurance companies. In purchasing a policy, a producer growing an insurable crop may select a level of crop yield and price coverage and pay a portion of the premium, which increases as the levels of yield and price coverage rise. The remainder of the premium is covered by the federal government. Coverage is made available through various insurance products, including crop-specific revenue insurance, which allows a participating producer to insure a target level of crop revenue rather than just production levels. According to the USDA, the federal crop insurance program provided coverage in 2007 to over 100 crops covering more than three-fourths of planted acreage in the country. Although the list of covered commodities has grown in recent years, 80% of total policy premiums (and federal subsidies) are accounted for by just four commodities—corn, soybeans, wheat, and cotton.

Table 1. Government Cost of Federal Crop Insurance (millions of dollars)

Fiscal Year	Program Losses or (Gains) [a]	Federal Premium Subsidy	Private Company Admin. Expense Reimbursements	Other Costs [b]	Total Gov't. Cost
1981	97	47	0	105	248
1982	(60)	91	18	110	160
1983	147	64	26	97	334
1984	211	98	76	102	487
1985	216	100	107	98	521
1986	216	90	101	97	504
1987	55	73	107	73	309
1988	609	103	155	78	945
1989	400	190	266	88	945
1990	234	213	272	87	806
1991	247	196	245	84	772
1992	232	197	246	88	764
1993	750	197	250	105	1,303
1994	(127)	247	292	78	489
1995	188	774	373	105	1,440
1996	88	978	490	64	1,621
1997	(373)	945	450	74	1,096
1998	(75)	940	427	82	1,374
1999	(74)	1,295	495	66	1,783
2000	196	1,353	540	86	2,175
2001	725	1,707	648	83	3,163
2002	1,182	1,513	656	114	3,466
2003	822	1,873	743	150	3,589
2004	(303)	2,387	899	142	3,125
2005	(591)	2,368	782	139	2,698
2006	(298)	2,782	960	126	3,571
2007	(1,344)	3,819	1,341	125	3,941

Source: USDA Office of Budget and Program Analysis. Totals may not add due to rounding.

a. The difference between total premiums (farmer and government paid) and total indemnity payments for crop losses, plus or minus any private company underwriting losses or gains.

b. Other costs primarily include federal salaries of USDA's Risk Management Agency and beginning in 2002, various research and development initiatives mandated by ARPA of 2000 (P.L. 106-224).

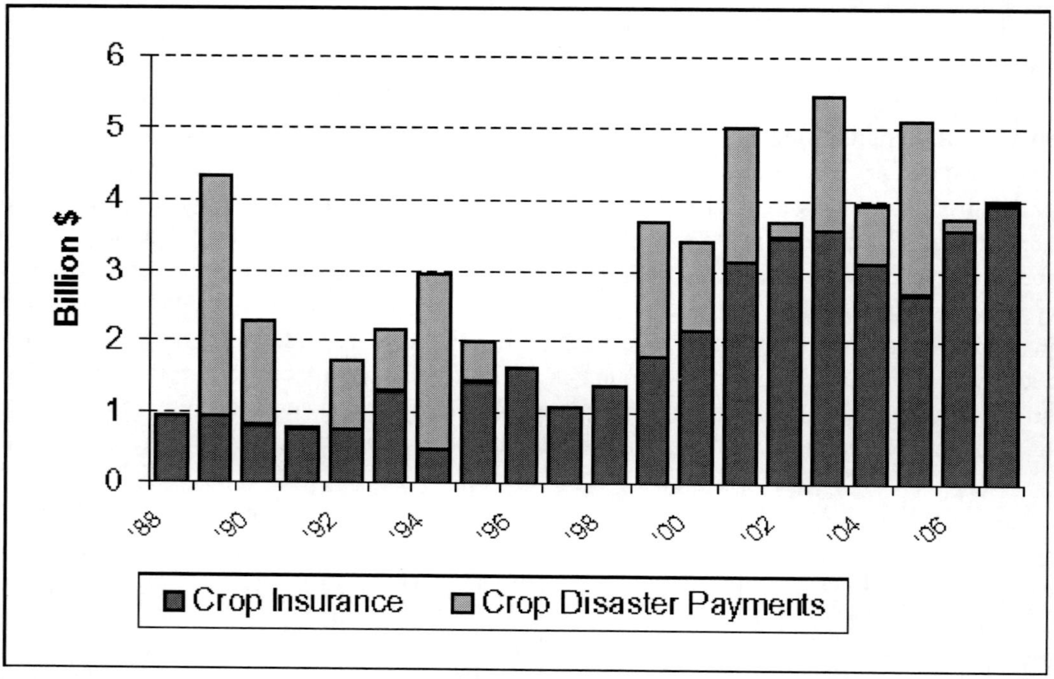

Source: Primary data are from USDA's Table 35, CCC Net Outlays by Commodity & Function for disaster payments, and USDA's Office of Budget & Program Analysis for crop insurance.

Figure 1. Crop Insurance and Disaster Payments: Total Federal Cost, by Fiscal Year

Because the program is not subject to periodic reauthorization, major changes to the crop insurance program usually are not addressed in the context of an omnibus farm bill. Over the past 25 years, the program has been subject to three major legislative enhancements (in 1980, 1994, and 2000),[1] each of which has pumped additional federal dollars into the program in order to enhance farmer participation levels in anticipation of precluding the demand for ad hoc disaster payments.

Since the last major modification in 2000, the federal subsidy to the crop insurance program has averaged about $3.25 billion per year, up from an annual average of $1.1 billion in the 1990s and about $500 million in the 1 980s. Nearly two-thirds of the current federal spending is used to subsidize insurance policy premiums, and the balance primarily covers the government share of program losses and reimburses participating private insurance companies for their administrative and operating expenses (see Table 1).

Although the scope of the program has widened significantly over the past 25 years, the anticipated goal of crop insurance replacing disaster payments has not been achieved. In virtually every crop year since 1988, Congress has provided *ad hoc* disaster payments to farmers with significant weather-related crop losses. These have been made available primarily through emergency supplemental appropriations, and, until recently, regardless of whether a producer had an active crop insurance policy. The exception to the historical pattern is the FY2007 supplemental appropriations act (P.L. 110-28, as amended by the FY2008 Consolidated Appropriations Act), which is expected to provide an estimated $2.4 billion in crop disaster payments for 2005, 2006, or 2007 crop losses, but only to those producers who held an active crop insurance policy or enrolled in the noninsured assistance program in the year of the crop loss.[2]

Since FY1989, total disaster payments have amounted to more than $20 billion, or just over $1 billion per year. Over the past six years (FY200 1 -FY2006), the federal cost of the crop insurance program combined with *ad hoc* supplemental disaster payments has averaged $4.5 billion per year (see Figure 1).

For a summary of all agricultural disaster assistance provided by Congress since 1988, see CRS Report RL3 1095, *Emergency Funding for Agriculture: A Brief History of Supplemental Appropriations, FY1989-FY2009*.

Crop Insurance and Disaster Provisions in the 2008 Farm Bill

The following sections review the major crop insurance and disaster assistance provisions of the enacted 2008 farm bill (P.L. 110-246) and the major issues that shaped the debate. See the Appendix, below, for a comparison of the crop insurance and disaster assistance provisions in the enacted 2008 farm bill, with the House- and Senate-passed versions of the farm bill and previous law.

Reducing Crop Insurance Program Costs

Because of the rising cost of the crop insurance program, many policymakers viewed the program as a potential target for spending reductions, whereby savings could be used to fund new initiatives in various other titles of the farm bill. Consequently, Title XII of the Food, Conservation, and Energy Act of 2008 (P.L. 110-246, the 2008 farm bill) contains several revisions to the crop insurance program, most of which are designed to reduce program costs. For all crop insurance provisions in Title XII, the Congressional Budget Office (CBO) estimates net budget outlay savings of $3.9 billion over 5 years (FY2008-FY2012), or $5.6 billion over 10 years (FY2008-FY2017), relative to the March 2007 baseline which was the official budget scoring benchmark for the bill.

Timing of Crop Insurance Payments

Approximately $2.8 billion of this estimated five-year savings is attributable to changes in the timing of premium receipts from farmers, and payments to the participating insurance companies. None of these revisions would directly affect the final monetary amounts for participating farmers or insurers, but would still be scored as savings within the five-year horizon of the bill. Essentially, these 2008 farm bill provisions (Sec. 12007 and Sec. 12015) will allow USDA to collect two crop years of premiums in 2012, and delay the 2012 payment of reimbursements and underwriting gains into the next fiscal year.

Insurance Company Reimbursements and Loss Sharing

Although crop insurance is sold and serviced by private insurance companies, the federal government absorbs a large portion of program losses and reimburses the companies for their administrative and operating (A&O) expenses. Loss sharing and A&O reimbursements currently are spelled out in a Standard Reinsurance Agreement (SRA) between USDA and the private companies.[3]

Under the SRA, the reimbursement rate for A&O expenses currently averages 22% to 24% of total premiums. The 2008 farm bill (Sec. 12016(E)) reduces the A&O reimbursement rate by 2.3 percentage points beginning with the 2009 reinsurance year (July 1, 2008). This reduction can be restored in any state that experiences a loss ratio of 1.2 or greater (i.e., when total indemnity payments to farmers are more than 20% greater than total premiums). The farm bill (Sec. 12016(F)) also reduces the A&O reimbursement rate to 12% for any plan of insurance that is based on area-wide losses. CBO estimates that these provisions will save $618 million over five years.

A House provision to require the insurance companies to share more of their underwriting gains with the federal government was not included in the final version of the bill. The conferees did adopt a provision (Sec. 12017) that allows USDA to renegotiate the SRA once every five years beginning with the 2010-2011 reinsurance year.

During the farm bill debate, the Administration and others contended that the private insurance companies should be required to absorb more of the program losses, and that the reimbursement rate for company A&O expenses needed to be reduced as a means of reducing federal costs. Proponents for change point out that A&O reimbursements to the companies have doubled over the last seven years (see **Table 1**), mainly because farmers have been buying up to higher levels of insurance coverage, causing total premiums to rise. Since A&O reimbursements are based on a percentage of total premiums (and premiums have been rising significantly in tandem with crop prices), the Administration contends that the companies are being overcompensated for their expenses. The private crop insurance companies contend that any reductions in the A&O reimbursement will negatively impact the financial health of the crop insurance industry and possibly jeopardize the delivery of crop insurance, particularly in high-risk areas.

Farmer Subsidy and Costs

Under the crop insurance program, farmers pay no premium for CAT coverage (which is 100% subsidized by the government), and are encouraged to purchase higher levels of coverage. On average, about 50% of the premium is subsidized by the government for this buy-up coverage. For farmers whose crops are not covered by crop insurance, they are offered the equivalent of CAT coverage under a separate Noninsured Assistance Program (NAP), and pay an administrative fee for this coverage.

A number of provisions are included in the 2008 farm bill that require participating farmers to share more in program costs, including (1) an increase in the fee paid by farmers for both catastrophic (CAT) coverage and NAP to $300 per crop per county, from the previous $100 fee (Sec. 12006); and (2) a 4 percentage point reduction in the rate of premium subsidy received by farmers for policies based on area-wide losses (Sec. 12012). The 2008 farm bill (Sec. 12003) also requires USDA to operate the crop insurance program so that the anticipated loss ratio is 1.0 (i.e., total indemnity payments equal to total premiums), compared with the then-current statutory loss ratio requirement of 1.075. To achieve the new lower ratio could mean somewhat higher premiums for farmers.

Crop Production on Native Sod

In an attempt to protect and preserve virgin prairie, the 2008 farm bill added a provision (Sec. 12020)[4] that declares that any parcel of native sod greater than 5 acres that is cultivated for production of an annual crop after May 22, 2008, is ineligible for federal crop insurance and noninsured crop disaster assistance during the first five crop years of planting. However, the governors for states within the Prairie Pothole National Priority Area[5] are given the discretion of electing whether this provision is effective for their state.[6]

Waste, Fraud, and Abuse

For many years, policymakers have been concerned about waste, fraud, and abuse within the federal crop insurance program. The Agricultural Risk Protection Act (ARPA) of 2000 (P.L. 106- 224) contained several provisions designed to enhance USDA's recognition of and response to challenges to program compliance and integrity. In response to the ARPA requirements, USDA used "data mining" techniques to compile an annual list of producers who either exhibit high loss ratios (i.e., high indemnity payments relative to total premiums), exhibit high frequency and severity of losses, or are suspected of poor farming practices that might contribute to production losses. USDA estimates that the use of the spot-check list has prevented between $70 million and $110 million each year in improper payments. Mandatory funding authorized by ARPA for data mining and other ARPA-related program integrity activities expired at the end of FY2005. A general provision in the FY2008 Consolidated Appropriations Act (P.L. 110-161) allows USDA to use up to $11.166 billion in mandatory funds in FY2008 to strengthen its ability to reduce waste, fraud, and abuse within the crop insurance program. However, future funding for this activity was uncertain.

The 2008 farm bill (Sec. 12021) authorizes up to $4 million annually for data mining activities beginning in FY2009, and authorizes $15 million annually for four years (FY2009-FY2013) to upgrade USDA's computer technology for crop insurance.

Agricultural Disaster Assistance

During the 2007-2008 farm bill debate, some policymakers wanted to make permanent in the farm bill some level of disaster payments to supplement the crop insurance program. Supporters say that ongoing farm disaster programs do not adequately address emergency needs when a major disaster strikes and that USDA should have at its disposal a permanent source of disaster funds in the same manner as the Federal Emergency Management Administration (FEMA). Questions in the debate included how such a program would be funded given current budget constraints, and whether the permanent availability of disaster payments would adversely affect participation in the crop insurance program, and possibly encourage production on high-risk lands.

Title XV (Sec. 15101) of the 2008 farm bill authorizes a series of new disaster programs through September 30, 2011, the largest of which is a supplemental revenue assistance payment program for crop producers.

Supplemental Crop Revenue Assistance Program (SURE)

The SURE program is designed to compensate eligible producers for a portion of crop losses that are not eligible for an indemnity payment under the crop insurance program (i.e., the portion of losses that is part of the deductible on the policy.) An eligible producer can receive a payment equal to 60% of the difference between a target level of revenue and the actual total farm revenue for the entire farm. The target level of revenue would be based on the level of crop insurance coverage selected by the farmer, thus increasing if a farmer opts for higher levels of coverage. (See the box in this report for a description of how the guarantee level and total farm revenue are defined by the statute.) To be eligible for a payment, a producer must be either in or contiguous to a county that has been declared a disaster area by either the President or the Secretary of Agriculture. Payments are limited so that the disaster program guarantee level cannot exceed 90% of what income likely would have been in the absence of a natural disaster.

The producer also must have at least the minimum level of crop insurance (CAT) coverage for insurable crops and participate in the NAP program for non-insurable crops. The statute made an exception for the 2008 crop year by allowing producers who did not purchase crop insurance or NAP coverage in advance to be eligible for the program, as long as they pay the equivalent administrative fee for coverage within 90 days of enactment.

Some farm groups have raised concerns about the delayed timing of payments under SURE. Final payments for crop losses cannot be determined until after the marketing year since a portion of the disaster payment formula is based on the national average market price of the commodity for the year in which the loss was incurred. For example, since the 2008 marketing year for corn and soybeans ends September 30, 2009, any eligible SURE payments for 2008 losses cannot be made until late October 2009 at the earliest. Consequently, some farm groups have asked USDA to make more timely payments under the new program by providing advance payments until the final payment levels can be determined. To date, program regulations have not been released.

Other Authorized Disaster Programs

In addition to the supplemental crop revenue assistance payment program described above, the 2008 farm bill also authorizes and funds four smaller disaster programs: (1) Livestock Indemnity Payments, which compensate ranchers at a rate of 75% of market value for livestock mortality caused by a disaster; (2) Livestock Forage Disaster Program, to assist ranchers who graze livestock on drought-affected pastureland or grazing land; (3) Emergency Assistance for Livestock, Honey Bess and Farm Raised Fish, which will provide up to $50 million to compensate these producers for disaster losses not covered under other disaster programs; and (4) Tree Assistance Program, for orchardists and nursery growers who can receive a payment to cover 70% of the cost of replanting trees or nursery stock following a disaster (up to $100,000 per year per producer).

SUPPLEMENTAL AGRICULTURAL DISASTER ASSISTANCE PAYMENT MECHANISM IN THE 2008 FARM BILL

Title XV of the 2008 farm bill (P.L. 110-246) authorizes a new crop disaster program for FY2008-FY2011. Eligible farmers must be in or contiguous to a disaster declared county, or have a 50% crop loss. They must have purchased crop insurance or Noninsured Assistance Program (NAP), where applicable.

I. Payment Formula

Eligible crop producers can receive a supplemental payment equal to: 60% of (Disaster Assistance Program Guarantee (DAPG) minus Total Farm Revenue (TFR)) Formula is based on the revenue of the entire farm. DAPG cannot exceed 90% of Expected Revenue

II. How to Calculate the Disaster Assistance Program Guarantee (DAPG)

A. Insurable Crops

DAPG = 115% of (Payment Rate X Payment Acres X Payment Yield)
Payment Rate = Crop Insurance Price Election
Payment Acres = Planted and Prevented Planting Acreage
Payment Yield = Selected Crop Insurance Coverage Level X Crop Insurance Yield

Hypothetical Corn Example:

Price Election = \$4.75; Planted Acres = 500; Coverage Level = 70%; Yield = 150 bushels per acre
DAPG = 1.15 (\$4.75 X 500 Acres X (.7(150 bushels per acre))) = \$286,781.25

B. Non-insurable Crops

120% of (Payment Rate X Payment Acres X Payment Yield)
Payment Rate = 100% of the Noninsured Assistance Program (NAP) Price
Payment Acres = Planted and Prevented Planting Acreage
Payment Yield = Adjusted NAP yield or Counter-Cyclical Payment (CCP) yield, whichever is higher

III. How to Calculate Total Farm Revenue (TFR)

TFR = Estimated Actual Value for each crop produced on the farm =

Value of Actual Crop Production + 15% of Direct Payments + CCP or Average Crop Revenue (ACRE) Payments + Loan Deficiency Payments (LDP) or Marketing Loan Gains (MLG) + Crop Insurance Indemnities + NAP Payments + Other Disaster Payments

Where the Value of Actual Crop Production = Actual Harvested Acreage X Estimated Actual Yield x Natl. Avg. Market Price

For NAP eligible crops, the National Average Market Price cannot be greater than 100% of NAP Price.

IV. How to Calculate Expected Revenue

DAPG cannot exceed 90% of Expected Revenue.

Expected Revenue = (Adjusted APH or CCP Yield X Planted and Prevented Acreage X Price Guarantee) + (Adjusted NAP Yield X Adjusted NAP Price)

Appendix. Major Crop Insurance and Disaster Assistance Provisions in the Enacted 2008 Farm Bill

Table A-1. Major Crop Insurance and Disaster Assistance Provisions in the Enacted 2008 Farm Bill: Comparison with Previous Law and House- and Senate-Passed Bills

Previous Law/Policy	House-Passed Farm Bill (H.R. 2419)	Senate-Passed Substitute Amendment (H.R. 2419)	Enacted 2008 Farm Bill (P.L. 110-246)
Title XII: Crop Insurance			
Timing of Crop Insurance Payments and Receipts			
The federal gove-rnment provides three levels of subsidies to the crop insur-ance program: (1) subsidizing a portion of the farmer-paid premium, (2) reimbursing the private crop insurance companies for most administrative and operating expe-nses, and (3) absorbing most of the program losses. *[7 USC 1501 et seq.]*	Changes the timing of crop insurance rece-ipts (premium collctions) and the timing of payments to the insurance companies, beginning with the 2012 reinsurance year (which starts July 1, 2011). Two insurance years of program receipts will be received in the same fiscal year (FY2012) and payments will be delayed until the next fiscal year, thus scoring budget savings in FY2012. *[Secs. 11001(c), 11001(e), and 11010]*	Similar, but not identical, language as the House bill, which effectively requires premiums to be collected from producers slightly earlier, and payments to the insurance companies to be made slightly later, beginning in the 2012 crop year, so that savings can be scored in the last year of the 5-year farm bill (FY2012). [Secs. 1906 and 1914]	Adopts the House provision that changes the premium billing date to August 15 [Sec. 12007], the Senate provisions that change the timing of reimbursements to the private companies for operating expenses to between October 1 and 31 [Sec. 12015] and underwr-iting gains to October 1 [Sec. 12018], thus allowing the scoring of budget savings in FY2012.
Reimbursement of Administrative and Operating Expenses			
Law prohibits co-mpanies from rec-eiving a reimbursement greater than 24.5% of total premiums. The previous Standard Reinsurance Agreement (SRA) established the reimbursement rate below the statutory maximum for all insura-nce plans, ranging from 18.1% to 24.2%. *[7 USC 1508(k)(4)(A)]*	Beginning in the 2009 reinsurance year, the reimbursement rate to the insurance companies for their admin-istrative and operating expenses for all poli-cies declines by 2.9 percentage points from the current rate. The range of reimbursement rates declines to between 15.2% to a maximum of 21.3%. *[Sec. 11001(d)(1)]*	Beginning in the 2009 reinsurance year, the reimbursement rate for additional coverage policies falls by 2 percentage points. An exception is any reinsurance year in any state that has a loss ratio greater than 1.2 (i.e., when indemnity payments exceed total premiums by more than 20%.)	Beginning in the 2009 reinsurance year, the reimbursement rate for additional coverage policies falls by 2.3 percentage points. Restores one-half of the reduction in states with a loss ratio Greater than 1.2. *[Sec. 12016]* The reimbursement rate for policies based on area-wide losses is reduced to 12% of total premiums. *[Sec. 12012]*

Table A-1. (Continued)

Previous Law/Policy	House-Passed Farm Bill (H.R. 2419)	Senate-Passed Substitute Amendment (H.R. 2419)	Enacted 2008 Farm Bill (P.L. 110-246)
		The reimbursement rate for policies based on area-wide losses is reduced to 17% of total premiums. *[Sec. 1912]*	
Premiums and Fees			
For catastrophic (CAT) coverage, producers paid no premium, but paid an administrative fee of $100 per crop per county. [*7 USC 1508(b)(5)(A)]* Growers of uninsurable crops were eligi-ble for a separate Noninsured Assi-stance Program (NAP) and paid a fee of $100 per crop, or $300 per producer per county, not to exceed $900 per producer. *[7 USC 7333(k)(1)]*	Increases the produ-cer-paid fee for catastrophic coverage to $200 per crop per county. For NAP, the fee also is raised to $200 per crop per county, or $600 per producer per county, not to exceed $1800 per producer. *[Secs. 11002 and 11009]*	Similar to the House bill for raising the CAT fee to $200. The NAP fee is increased to $200 per crop per county, or $600 per producer per county, not to exceed $1,500 per producer. *[Secs. 1905 and 1926]*	Raises the CAT fee to $300 per crop per county. [Sec.12006] Increases the NAP fee to $250 per crop per county, or $750 per producer per cou-nty, not to exceed $1,875 per producer. *[Sec. 12028]*
When permitted by state law, a cooperative or trade association could pay on beh-alf of its members, any or all of the administrative fee for CAT coverage. *[7 USC 1508(b)(5)(B)]* .	Limits the ability of associations to pay the CAT fee on behalf of a producer. *[Sec.11001(b)]* Prohibits insurance companies from paying or rebat-ing premiums, or making any induce-ments to purchase crop insurance. *[Sec. 11001(a)]*	Revises current law to clarify that the provision applies only to fees for CAT coverage. *[Sec. 1905]*	Adopts the provision in Sec. 1905 of the Senate bill which clarifies that coope-ratives and trade associations can pay only the fees for catastrophic cove-rage on behalf of their members. [Sec. 12006] Also adopts the provision in Sec. 11001(a) of the House bill that prohibits the rebating of premiums, with certain exceptions for entities that have already been approved for rebating. *[Sec. 12004]*
Authorized crop insurance comp-anies to offer customers a discount when the insurance companies adopted	Strikes authority for companies to offer a Premium Reduction Plan (PRP) or Prem-ium Rate Reduction Pilot program. *[Sec. 1101(f)]*	Strikes authority for PRP only, and requires USDA to commission a study on the feasibility of the PRP	Strikes authority for the PRP only. *[Sec. 12010]*

Table A-1. (Continued)

Previous Law/Policy	House-Passed Farm Bill (H.R. 2419)	Senate-Passed Substitute Amendment (H.R. 2419)	Enacted 2008 Farm Bill (P.L. 110-246)
efficiencies that reduced their administrative and operating costs. *[7 USC 1508(b)(5)(A)]*		within 18 months of enactment. [Sec. 1908]	
No comparable provision.	Reduces the premium subsidy for area risk plans by 4 percentage points. *[Sec. 11013]*	No comparable provision.	Adopts the House provision. *[Sec. 12012]*
Required USDA to set premiums so that the overall program loss ratio is 1.075. *[7 USC 1506(n)]*	No comparable provision	Reduces the statutory loss ratio to 1.0, meaning that total premiums should be established to equal expected total indemnity payments. *[Sec. 1903]*	Adopts the Senate provision. *[Sec. 12003]*
Authorized an Ag-ricultural Mana-gement Assistance (AMA) program to in part help certain states make better use of risk management tools. *[7 USC 1524(b)]*	No comparable provision	Allows USDA to use AMA funds to match state funds used to provide additional premium discounts to underserved states. *[Sec. 1923]*	No comparable provision.
Standard Reinsurance Agreement and Risk-Sharing			
The Standard Reinsurance Agreem-ent (SRA) between the federal government and private crop insu-rance companies determines levels of risk sharing. The current agreement requires companies to reinsure 5% of their retained premium with the government.	Requires the private insurance companies to reinsure at least 22% of their retained premiums with the government, and in return the government will provide a ceding commission of 2% to companies, allowing the government to receive some underwriting gains that would otherwise accrue to the companies. *[Sec. 11014]*	No comparable provision.	No comparable provision.
No comparable provision.	USDA can renegotiate the SRA starting with the 2012-13 reinsurance year, and once every 5 years thereafter. Insurance companies can confer with	Similar to the House bill, except that USDA has discretion to renegotiate the SRA more frequently than every 5 years,	Allows USDA to renegotiate the SRA beginning with the 2010-11 reinsurance year and once every 5 years thereafter.

Table A-1. (Continued)

Previous Law/Policy	House-Passed Farm Bill (H.R. 2419)	Senate-Passed Substitute Amendment (H.R. 2419)	Enacted 2008 Farm Bill (P.L. 110-246)
	each other during the process. *[Sec. 11001(d)(2)]*	with congressional notification of such action. Allows crop insurance companies to confer with each other and collectively with USDA during the renegotiation process. *[Sec. 1913]*	Adopts the Senate provision to allow companies to confer with each other and collectively with USDA during renegotiation. SRA can be renegotiated more than once in a 5-year period if one of the changes is required by law, and Congress is notified. *[Sec. 12017]*
Program Integrity (Waste, Fraud, and Abuse)			
Annual mandatory funds of $23 million for data mining and pro-gram integrity activities expired at the end of FY2005. *[7 USC 1516(k)]* Annual appropriations acts provided $3.6 million in annual discretionary funds (FY2006, FY2007). FY2008 appropriations act authorized mandatory funds of $11.2 million.	Authorizes mandatory funding of $11 mill-ion in FY2008, and $7 million in FY2009 and subsequent years for crop insurance program compliance and integrity activeies, including data mining. *[Sec. 11008]*	Requires USDA to establish a program whereby crop insur-ance companies pay USDA a fee for access to its data mining system, and USDA uses proceeds for its data system. *[Sec. 1915]* Prohibits farmers from collecting commissions as agents on policies in which their family has a substantial interest. *[Sec. 1904]*	Provides mandatory funding of up to $4 million per year beginning in FY2009 for data mining, and requires periodic competition for the funds. Also, adds a new subsection to provide mandatory funds of up to $15 million per year over 4 years (FY2009-13) to upgrade USDA's computer technology for crop insurance. [Sec. 12021] Adopts the Senate provision that prohibits farmers from collecting com-missions as agents on policies in which their family has an interest, with modifications to the definitions of "family" and "comp-ensation." *[Sec. 12005]*
Risk Management Research and Development			
USDA is required to reimburse an applicant for the R&D costs associated with developing a new plan of crop insurance that is approved by USDA *[7 USC 1522]* and with developing crop	Authorizes USDA to use no more than $30 million annually in mandatory funds for grants for R&D and education and information programs, of which $5 million is for underserved states. Stipulates criteria for which grants will be awarded.	Reduces annual mandatory funding for R&D from $15 million to $7.5 million, and for contracting and partnerships from $25 million to $12.5 million. Prohibits a surcharge on premiums for organic crops, unless greater loss history is confirmed.	Adopts the Senate provision to reduce mandatory funding for R&D from $15 million to $7.5 mill-ion and for contrac-ting and partnerships from $25 million to $12.5 million. [*Sec. 12024]* Applicants with approved concept papers for a new policy can receive up to 50% of expenses in advance, and the balance

Table A-1. (Continued)

Previous Law/Policy	House-Passed Farm Bill (H.R. 2419)	Senate-Passed Substitute Amendment (H.R. 2419)	Enacted 2008 Farm Bill (P.L. 110-246)
insurance edu-cation programs. *[7 USC 1524]* Annual mandatory funding was $15 million for R&D reimbursements and $25 million for contracting and partnerships. *[7 USC 1522(e)]*	Requires USDA to enter into contracts to improve coverage for organic crops, and to address the needs of beginning and minority farmers. *[Secs. 11003-11006]*	Establishes an alternative reimbursement grant process. Requires USDA to enter into contracts to expand coverage for organic crops, aquaculture, energy crops such as switchgrass, and to address the needs of beginning and minority farmers. *[Secs. 1917-1919, 1907]*	upon approval. *[Sec. 12022]* Adopts the House provision to enter into contracts to improve coverage for organic crops, and Senate provisions for energy crops and aquaculture, and other new provisions for poultry, beekeep-ers, and beginning farmers. *[Sec. 12023]* Requires USDA to emphasize the devel-opment of risk man-agement education programs for begin-ning, immigrant, soc-ially disadvantaged, retiring, and transiti-oning farmers. *[Sec. 12026]*
Other Crop Insurance Provisions			
No comparable provision.	Establishes a National Drought Council within USDA and national drought pre-paredness plans, including a Drought Assistance Fund to provide technical and financial assistance to states for mitigating drought risk. *[Sec. 11012]*	No comparable provision.	No comparable provision.
Adhoc emergency disaster payments are ava-ilable to producers who experienced significant losses to a 2005, 2006, or 2007 crop. (Sec. 9001 of P.L. 110-28, as amended by P.L. 110-161).	Prohibits USDA from using production data from the sweet potato crop insurance pilot program in determining crop disaster payments for 2005 and 2006. *[Sec. 11016]*	Similar to the House bill. Also requires USDA to extend the disaster application deadline for sweet potato growers, if necessary, to implement this provision. *[Sec. 1927]*	Adopts the Senate provision. *[Sec. 12029]*
Authorizes USDA to create crop insurance pilot programs. *[7 USC 1523]*	Mandates a sesame insurance pilot program for Texas. *[Sec. 11011]*	Creates pilot prog-rams for sesame *[Sec. 1921]*, camelina *[Sec. 1920]*, and enterprise/ whole farm units *[Sec. 1909]*.	Authorizes separate insurance pilot pro-grams for sesame, camelina, grass seed *[Sec. 12025]* and for enterprise and whole farm units (with some modifications to the Senate provision) *[Sec. 12011]*

Table A-1. (Continued)

Previous Law/Policy	House-Passed Farm Bill (H.R. 2419)	Senate-Passed Substitute Amendment (H.R. 2419)	Enacted 2008 Farm Bill (P.L. 110-246)
No comparable provision.	Non-cropland (including native grassland and pastureland) planted to an insurable crop ineligible for crop insurance for the first 4 years of planting. *[Sec. 11007]*	Makes native sods planted to an insura-ble crop (over 5 acres) ineligible for crop ins-urance and the nonin-sured crop disaster assistance program. Directs USDA to report within 180 days of enactment, and annually ther-eafter, on changes in cropland acreage, by county, since 1995. *[Sec. 2608]*	Makes native sods planted to an insu-rable crop (over 5 acres) ineligible for crop insurance and the noninsured crop disaster assistance program for the first 5 years of planting. May apply to virgin prairie converted to cropland in the Prai-rie Pothole National Priority Area, if elected by the state. *[Sec. 12020]*
No comparable provision.	No comparable provision.	Makes contract livestock producers eligible for crop insu-rance, if not covered by other policies. [Sec. 1916] Requires a USDA report within 180 days of enactme-nt on issues regarding declining crop insurance yields, especially for perennials. *[Sec. 1928]*	No provision adder-ssing the eligibility of contract livestock producers. Adopts the requirement that USDA report on declining yield issues. *[Sec. 12030]*
No comparable provision.	No comparable provision.	An organic crop is defined as any agricultural commodity that is organically produced consistent with section 2103 of the Organic Foods Production Act of 1990 (7 U.S.C. 6502). *[Sec. 1901]*	Adopts the Senate provision. *[Sec. 12001]*
Title XV: Supplemental Agriculture Disaster Assistance			
Congress periodically provides ad-hoc emergency disaster payments to crop and live-stock growers to supplement income following a natural disaster.	No comparable provision.	Authorizes a permanent agricultural disaster trust fund that will fund a series of disaster programs that provide payments to crop and livestock growers who experience significant production	Adopts a variation of the Senate provision. For FY2008-11, five new disaster programs are authorized and funded through a transfer of 3.08% of annual customs receipts. The five new programs are: (1) Supplemental

Table A-1. (Continued)

Previous Law/Policy	House-Passed Farm Bill (H.R. 2419)	Senate-Passed Substitute Amendment (H.R. 2419)	Enacted 2008 Farm Bill (P.L. 110-246)
Most recently, Congress provided emergency supplemental assistance for 2005, 2006, or 2007 production losses. *[Sec. 9001 of P.L. 110-28, as amended by P.L. 110-161].*		losses in a USDA-declared disaster area. For FY2008-12, the program is funded through a transfer of 3.34% of annual customs receipts from the U.S. Treasury. Payments are made under four new programs: (1) Supplemental Revenue Assistance Payments (for crops); (2) Livestock Indemnity Payments; (3) Eme-rgency Assistance for Livestock, Honeybees, and Farm-Raised Catfish; and; (4) Tree Assistance Program. *[Sec. 12101]*	Revenue Assistance Payments (for crops); (2) Livestock Indemnity Payments; (3) Livestock Forage Disaster Program; (4) Emergency Assistance for Livestock, Honeybees, and Farm-Raised Catfish; and (5) Tree Assista-nce Program. *[Sec. 15101]*

Disaster Program Funding

All five of these farm bill disaster programs will receive funding through a newly authorized Agricultural Disaster Relief Trust Fund within the U.S. Treasury. The Trust Fund will receive the equivalent of 3.08% of the amount received each year (FY2008-2011) in U.S. Customs receipts collected on certain goods. The Congressional Budget Office (CBO) estimates the combined total costs to be $3.8 billion over the four-year life of the programs, relative to the March 2007 budget baseline. Of this total, CBO estimates that supplemental crop revenue assistance will cost $1.7 billion over the four years, or an average of $425 million per year. Another $1.6 billion would cover increased crop insurance and NAP costs associated with the crop insurance and NAP purchase requirement. The balance of $500 million would cover the combined estimated cost of the other four disaster programs. If the cost of the programs exceeds the level of funding provided through Customs receipts, the 2008 farm bill gives the Trust Fund the authority to borrow from the Treasury such sums as necessary to meet its obligations.

End Notes

1 Federal Crop Insurance Act of 1980 (P.L. 96-365), Federal Crop Insurance Reform Act of 1994 (P.L. 103-354), Agriculture Risk Protection Act (ARPA) of 2000 (P.L. 106-224). For information on ARPA of 2000, see CRS Report RL30739, *Federal Crop Insurance and the Agriculture Risk Protection Act of 2000* (P.L. 106-224), by Ralph M. Chite.

2 This assistance was provided in Title IX, Section 9001 of the FY2007 Iraq War Supplemental Act (P.L. 110-28). The projected spending of $1.5 billion for 2005, 2006 and early 2007 crop losses will be made in FY2008. For a description of this and other types of agricultural assistance made available in P.L. 110-28, see CRS Report RS21212, *Agricultural Disaster Assistance*, by Ralph M. Chite.

3 For more background and for the text of the SRA, see http://www.rma.usda.gov/pubs/ra/.

4 The 2008 farm bill provision Sec. 12020 was written into law as Sec. 508(o) of the Federal Crop Insurance Act.

5 The Prairie Pothole National Priority Area encompasses specific counties within the five northernmost states of the northern Great Plains—Iowa, Minnesota, South and North Dakota, and Montana—that contain thousands of shallow wetlands known as potholes.

6 If the governor makes this election for any state, RMA will announce the election via a Manager's Bulletin and at the website http://www.rma.usda.gov/data/pothole/.

In: Agriculture Disaster and Crop Insurance: Background... ISBN: 978-1-61761-559-7
Editor: Angela M. Gil

Chapter 4

FEDERAL CROP INSURANCE: BACKGROUND AND ISSUES

Dennis A. Shields

SUMMARY

The 111th Congress is considering the effectiveness and operations of the federal crop insurance program. The House Committee on Agriculture has been seeking input from farmers and others on the program in advance of the next farm bill debate. Meanwhile, concern about the federal budget deficit is coinciding with the rising cost of the federal crop insurance program. This report provides a primer on the federal crop insurance program and discusses related issues.

The federal crop insurance program began in 1938 when Congress authorized the Federal Crop Insurance Corporation. The current program, which is administered by the U.S. Department of Agriculture's Risk Management Agency (RMA), provides producers with risk management tools to address crop yield and/or revenue losses on their farms. In purchasing a policy, a producer growing an insurable crop selects a level of coverage and pays a portion of the premium—or none of it in the case of catastrophic coverage—which increases as the level of coverage rises. The federal government pays the rest of the premium (averaging nearly 60% of the total).

Insurance policies are sold and completely serviced through 15 approved private insurance companies. The insurance companies' losses are reinsured by USDA, and their administrative and operating costs are reimbursed by the federal government.

In 2009, federal crop insurance policies covered 265 million acres. Major crops are covered in most counties where they are grown. Four crops—corn, cotton, soybeans, and wheat—accounted for 73% of total acres enrolled in crop insurance. Most crop insurance policies are either yield- based or revenue-based. For yield-based policies, a producer can receive an indemnity if there is a yield loss relative to the farmer's "normal" (historical) yield. Revenue-based policies protect against crop revenue loss resulting from declines in yield, price, or both. The most recent addition has been insurance products that protect against losses in whole farm revenue rather than just for an individual crop.

Government costs for crop insurance have increased substantially in recent years. After ranging between $2.1 and $3.6 billion during FY2000-FY2006, costs rose to $5.7 billion in FY2008 and $7.3 billion in FY2009 as higher policy premiums from rising crop prices drove up premium subsidies to farmers and expense reimbursements (which are based on total premiums) to private insurance companies. Reimbursements and risk-sharing between USDA and private insurance companies are spelled out in a Standard Reinsurance Agreement (SRA), which plays a large role in determining program costs. USDA is currently renegotiating the SRA for the 2011 reinsurance year (which begins July 1, 2010) to address issues such as the calculation of reimbursements.

Insurance companies, farm groups, and some Members of Congress remain concerned that significant reductions in federal support, including possible cuts stemming from the new SRA, will negatively impact the financial health of the crop insurance industry and possibly jeopardize the delivery of crop insurance. The crop insurance industry argues that cuts to the program were already made in the 2008 farm bill, and additional cuts would be unfair. Others point to recent increases in operating expense reimbursements and underwriting gains, questioning whether these higher levels are necessary for maintaining a viable crop insurance industry. A main concern for most would likely be saving federal dollars without adversely affecting farmer participation, policy coverage, or industry interest in selling and servicing crop insurance products to farmers.

The 111th Congress is considering the effectiveness and operations of the federal crop insurance program. The House Committee on Agriculture has been seeking input from farmers and others on the program and how it fits with other farm programs in advance of the next farm bill debate. Meanwhile, concern about the federal budget deficit is coinciding with the rising cost of the federal crop insurance program, and the U.S. Department of Agriculture is renegotiating the Standard Reinsurance Agreement with the crop insurance companies; the agreement governs many aspects of the program and plays a central role in determining program costs. This report provides a primer on the federal crop insurance program and discusses related issues.

Crop Insurance History

Farming is generally regarded as a financially risky enterprise. Most agricultural production is subject to the vagaries of weather, and the nature of agricultural supply and demand often results in volatile market prices. Farm financial risk, periods of low returns, and the importance of agriculture in the nation's economy during the early to mid-1900s led to the development of federal policies that financially supported farmers, primarily through commodity price mechanisms. Today's farm commodity policies—authorized in the 2008 farm bill—have their roots in the 1930s.[1]

During the same era, Congress also first authorized federal crop insurance as an experiment to address the effects of the Great Depression and crop losses seen in the Dust Bowl. In 1938, the Federal Crop Insurance Corporation (FCIC) was created to carry out the program, which focused on major crops in major producing regions. The federal crop insurance program remained limited until passage of the Federal Crop Insurance Act of 1980 (P.L. 96-365), which expanded crop insurance to many more crops and regions of the country. Congress enhanced the crop insurance program in 1994 and again in 2000 in order to encourage greater participation. The changes also expanded the role of the private sector in developing new products that would help farmers manage their risks.[2]

The federal crop insurance program is permanently authorized by the Federal Crop Insurance Act, as amended (7 U.S.C. 1501 et seq.). It is periodically modified, most recently in the 2008 farm bill (P.L. 110-246). Congress chose to revise the legislation in the 2008 farm bill to achieve budget savings and to supplement crop insurance with a permanent disaster payment program.[3] The U.S. Department of Agriculture's (USDA's) Risk Management Agency (RMA) operates and manages the FCIC.

PROGRAM BASICS

The federal crop insurance program provides producers with risk management tools to address crop yield and/or revenue losses on their farms.[4] Insurance policies are sold and completely serviced through 15 approved private insurance companies. Independent insurance agents are paid sales commissions by the companies. The insurance companies' losses are reinsured by USDA, and their administrative and operating costs are reimbursed by the federal government (see "Federal Program Costs," below).

In purchasing a policy, a producer growing an insurable crop selects a level of coverage and pays a portion of the premium, which increases as the level of coverage rises. The remainder of the premium is covered by the federal government (nearly 60% of total premium, on average, is paid by the government).[5] In the case of catastrophic coverage, the government pays the full premium. In the absence of subsidies, farmer participation in the crop insurance program would be substantially lower.

In 2009, crop insurance policies covered 265 million acres (**Figure 1**). Major crops are covered in most counties where they are grown. Four crops—corn, cotton, soybeans, and wheat—accounted for more 73% of total enrolled acres. For these major crops, a large share of plantings is covered by crop insurance: corn at 83% of plantings; cotton, 94%; soybeans, 83%; and wheat, 82%.

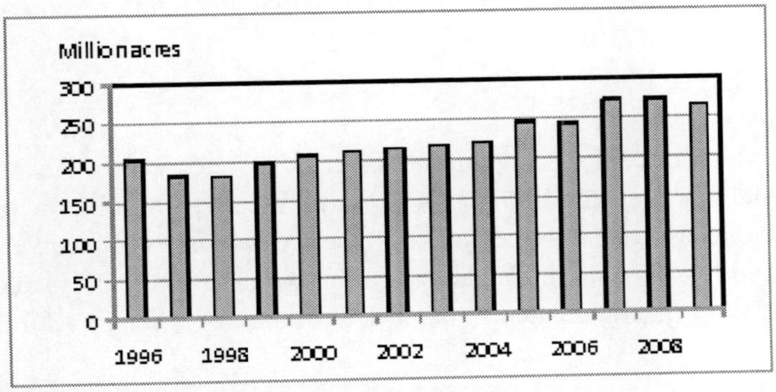

Source: U.S. Department of Agriculture, Risk Management Agency.

Figure 1. Insured Acres

Policies for less widely produced crops are available in primary growing areas. Examples include dry peas, blueberries, citrus, and walnuts. In total, policies are available for more than 100 crops (including coverage on a variety of fruit trees, nursery crops, pasture, rangeland, and forage).[6] Many specialty crop producers depend on crop insurance as the only "safety net" for their operation, unlike field crop producers who are also eligible for farm commodity program payments (see "Intersection with Other Government Programs").[7]

Crop insurance is not necessarily limited to crops; livestock coverage has recently become available. Relatively new or pilot programs protect livestock and dairy producers from loss of gross margin or price declines.

The availability of crop insurance for a particular crop in a particular region is an administrative decision made by USDA. The decision is made on a crop-by-crop and county-by-county basis, based on farmer demand for coverage and the level of risk associated with the crop in the region, among other factors. In areas where a policy is not available, farmers may request that RMA expand the program to their county. The process usually starts with a pilot program in order for RMA to gain experience and test the program components before it becomes more widely available.

Current law requires that RMA strive for actuarial soundness for the entire federal crop insurance program (that is, indemnities paid out should equal total premiums, including premium subsidies).[8]

Types of Insurance

Federal crop insurance policies are generally either yield-based or revenue-based. For most yield- based policies, a producer can receive an indemnity if there is a yield loss relative to the farmer's "normal" (historical) yield. Revenue-based policies were developed in the mid-1990s to protect against crop revenue loss resulting from declines in yield, price, or both. The most recent addition has been products that protect against losses in whole farm revenue rather than just for an individual crop. These two basic forms—yield-based and revenue-based—are discussed below. The text boxes below entitled "Crop Insurance Examples: Yield-Based vs. Revenue-Based" and "Federal Crop Insurance: Range of Coverage and Policies" explain program operation within these two broad categories.

Two million crop insurance policies were sold in 2009, with yield-based policies accounting for 48% of the total (**Figure 2**), and the remainder being revenue-based policies.

Yield-Based Insurance

When purchasing a crop insurance policy, a producer is assigned (1) a "normal" crop yield based on the producer's actual production history, and (2) a price for his commodity based on estimated market conditions. The producer can then select a percentage of his normal yield to be insured and a percentage of the price he wishes to receive when crop losses exceed the selected loss threshold. The level of crop yield coverage is viewed by farmers as a critical feature of crop insurance, and a major determinant of whether a farmer will purchase insurance.[9]

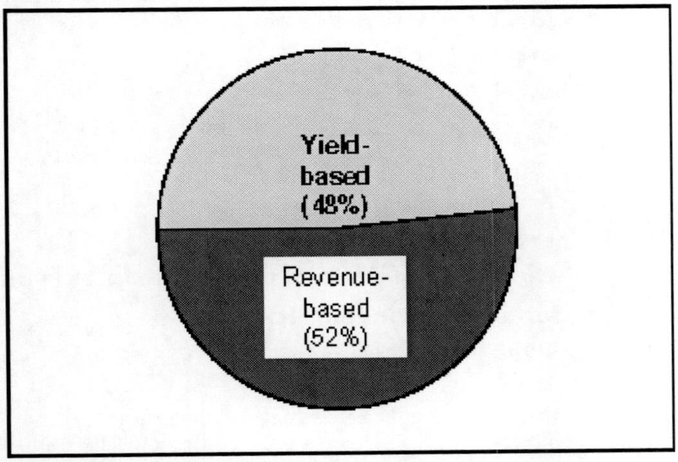

Source: U.S. Department of Agriculture, Risk Management Agency.

Figure 2. Types of Crop Insurance Policies (total policies sold in 2009 = 2.05 million)

In determining what a normal production level is for an insurable farmer, USDA requires the producer to present actual annual crop yields (usually stated on a bushel-per-acre basis) for the last 4 to 10 years. The simple average of a producer's annual crop yield over this time period then serves as the producer's actual production history (APH). If a farmer does not have adequate records, he can be assigned a transition yield (T-yield) for each missing year of data, which is based on average county yields for the crop.

The most basic policy is called catastrophic (CAT) coverage. The premium for this level of coverage is completely subsidized by the federal government. The farmer pays an administrative fee for CAT coverage ($300 per crop per county under the 2008 farm bill, up from $100 previously), and in return can receive a payment on losses in excess of 50% of normal yield, equal to 55% of the estimated market price of the crop (called 50/5 5 coverage).

Crop Insurance Examples: Yield-Based vs. Revenue-Based

Two basic forms of crop insurance are yield-based and revenue-based. Yield-based insurance provides an indemnity when the actual yield falls below the guarantee level. Revenue-based insurance provides an indemnity when the revenue (actual yield x price) falls below the guarantee.

Actual Production History (APH) Example:

A loss occurs when the bushels of soybeans produced for the insurance unit (insurable acreage) fall below the production guarantee as a result of damage from a covered cause of loss. Assumptions: "normal" production = 48 bushels / acre; yield coverage level = 75%; established price coverage = 100%; price election = $9.90 / bushel; actual production = 20 bushels per acre.

48	bushels per acre APH yield
x .75	coverage level
36.0	bushel / acre guarantee
- 20.0	bushels / acre actually produced
16.0	bushels / acre of covered loss
x $9.90	per-bushel price election
$158.40	per-acre gross indemnity payment
- $6.00	estimated producer-paid premium per acre (varies)
$152.40	**per-acre net indemnity**

Revenue Product Example:

36.0	bushels / acre guarantee (see prior example)
x $11.00	per-bushel base price (announced in March)
$396.00	per-acre guarantee
20	bushels / acre actually produced
x $10.00	per-bushel harvest price (announced in November)
$200.00	per-acre revenue
$196.00	per-acre gross indemnity payment ($396.00 - $200.00)
- $13.00	estimated producer-paid premium (varies)
$183.00	**per-acre net indemnity**

Source: U.S. Department of Agriculture, Risk Management Agency, *2009 Commodity Insurance Fact Sheet - Soybeans - Iowa*, January 2009, http://www.rma.usda.gov/fields/mn_rso/2009/2009iasoybeans.pdf.

Federal Crop Insurance: Range of Coverage and Policies

I. Catastrophic Coverage (CAT) pays 55% of the established price of the commodity on crop losses in excess of 50%. The premium on CAT coverage is paid by the federal government; however, producers must pay a $300 administrative fee (as of the 2008 farm bill, up from $100) for each crop insured in each county. Limited-resource farmers may have this fee waived. CAT coverage is not available on all types of policies.

II. Buy-up Coverage (any coverage level higher than CAT)

Yield-based policies:

Actual Production History (APH) policies insure producers against yield losses due to natural causes such as drought, excessive moisture, hail, wind, frost, insects, and disease. The farmer selects the amount of average yield he or she wishes to insure; from 50% to 85%. The farmer also selects the percentage of the projected price he or she wants to insure; between 55% and 100% of the crop price established annually by RMA. If the harvest is less than the yield insured, the farmer is paid an indemnity based on the difference. Indemnities are calculated by multiplying this difference by the insured percentage of the established price selected when crop insurance was purchased.

Group Risk Plan (GRP) insures against widespread loss of production based on county average yields. When the county yield for the insured crop, as determined by the National Agricultural Statistics Service (NASS), falls below the trigger level chosen by the farmer, an indemnity is paid regardless of the individual farmer's actual yield. Yield levels are available for up to 90% of the expected county yield. GRP protection involves less paperwork and costs less than the farm-level coverage described above. However, individual crop losses may not be covered if the county yield does not suffer a similar level of loss. This insurance is most often selected by farmers whose crop losses typically follow the county pattern.

Dollar Plan provides protection against declining value due to damage that causes a yield shortfall. (Crop examples include cherries, chili peppers, and citrus.) Amount of insurance is based on the cost of growing a crop in a specific area. A loss occurs when the annual crop value is less than the amount of insurance. The maximum dollar amount of insurance is stated on the actuarial document. The insured may select a percentage of the maximum dollar amount equal to CAT (catastrophic level of coverage), or additional coverage levels.

The **Vegetation Index and Rainfall Index** do not measure direct production or loss; rather the farmer is insuring against a rainfall or vegetation index that is expected to estimate production. The Pasture, Rangeland, and Forage (PRF) pilot program and the Apiculture pilot program (for beekeepers) use each index for different parts of the country.

Revenue-based policies:

Crop Revenue Coverage (CRC) provides revenue protection based on price and yield expectations by paying for losses below the guarantee at the higher of an early-season price or the harvest price. CRC is similar to RA (below) except that CRC uses an earlier period for its harvest price (October instead of November), and CRC limits how much the harvest price can vary from its base price (generated before planting time) while RA does not.

Revenue Assurance (RA) provides dollar-denominated coverage by the producer selecting a dollar amount of target revenue from a range defined by 65%-75% of expected revenue.

Income Protection (IP) protects producers against reductions in gross income when either a crop's price or its yield declines from early-season expectations. IP is similar to CRC and RA (with fall harvest price option) except that it does not use a harvest price as part of the guarantee.

Group Risk Income Protection (GRIP) makes indemnity payments only when the average county revenue for the insured crop falls below the revenue chosen by the farmer.

Adjusted Gross Revenue (AGR) insures revenue of the entire farm rather than an individual crop by guaranteeing a percentage of average gross farm revenue, including a small amount of livestock revenue. The plan uses information from a producer's Schedule F tax forms, and current-year expected farm revenue, to calculate the policy revenue guarantee.

Source: USDA's Risk Management Agency, http://www.rma.usda.gov/policies/.

Coverage levels that are higher than CAT are called "buy-up" or "additional" coverage.[10] For an additional premium paid by the producer, and partially subsidized by the government, a producer can "buy up" the 50/55 catastrophic coverage to any equivalent level of coverage between 50/100 and 75/100 (i.e., up to 75% of "normal" crop yield and 100% of the estimated market price). In limited areas, production can be insured up to the 85/100 level of coverage.

The producer's premium increases as the levels of insurable yield and price coverage rise, and the premium on buy-up coverage is subsidized by the government at amounts ranging from 38% to 67%, depending on the coverage level (**Table 1**). The subsidy rate declines as the coverage level rises, but the total premium subsidy in dollars increases because the policies are more expensive.

APH policies account for more than 90% of yield-based policies sold. The remaining policies, including the Group Risk Plan and Dollar Plan (see box on page 5), are not widely used but can be important for certain crops. Some of these policies use an area-wide index—county-level yield in the case of the Group Risk Plan—to measure losses.

Revenue-Based Insurance

Revenue insurance is another major type of crop insurance, accounting for just over one-half of all crop insurance policies. It began in 1997 as a buy-up option on a pilot basis for major crops. By 2003, acreage under revenue-based insurance exceeded acreage covered by APH policies. Revenue insurance combines the production guarantee component of crop insurance with a price guarantee to create a target revenue guarantee.

Under revenue insurance programs, participating producers are assigned a target level of revenue based on market prices for the commodity and the producer's production history. A farmer who opts for revenue insurance can receive an indemnity payment when his actual farm revenue (crop- specific or entire farm, depending on the policy) falls below a certain percentage of the target level of revenue, regardless of whether the shortfall is caused by low prices or low production levels. The two most popular revenue plans are Revenue Assurance and Crop Revenue Coverage, which together account for slightly more than one-half of all yield- and revenue-based policies sold (**Figure 2**).

After years of development, USDA's Risk Management Agency issued the "COMBO" rule in late March 2010 to consolidate several crop insurance plans into a single "Common Crop Insurance Policy" beginning with the 2011 crop year.[11] Yield-based plans (APH) continue, but current revenue products (Crop Revenue Coverage, Income Protection, Indexed Income Protection and Revenue Assurance) will be offered as single revenue product for crops where revenue products are currently offered.[12] RMA expects the move to greatly simplify the insurance process for agents and promote better understanding of the options available for producers.

Geographic Distribution of Indemnities

With widespread use of crop insurance products for major crops (corn, cotton, soybeans, and wheat), the geographic distribution of acreage enrolled in crop insurance mirrors that of major producing areas (**Figure 3**). Crop insurance indemnities follow the same pattern, but with an emphasis in producing areas with less rainfall and more variable crop-weather conditions. For example, **Figure 4** shows crop insurance indemnities by county. In 2009, relatively high indemnities were paid in the Great Plains, a region with generally low but variable rainfall.[13] In other years, the distribution of indemnities is similar, especially with respect to payments across the Great Plains. However, the concentration of payments shifts within major producing areas, primarily depending upon the prevalence of local weather problems.

Table 1. Crop Insurance Premium Subsidies on Yield- and Revenue-Based Coverage (Government-Paid Portion of Premium as a Percent of Total Premium, 2009 Crops)

Yield coverage level (%)	CAT	50	55	60	65	70	75	80	85
Premium subsidy (%)	100	67	64	64	59	59	55	48	38

Source: USDA, Risk Management Agency (http://www.rma.usda.gov/data/premium.html).

Notes: Schedule applies to all plans of insurance except for Group Risk Plan, Group Risk Income Protection, and livestock (separate schedules apply).

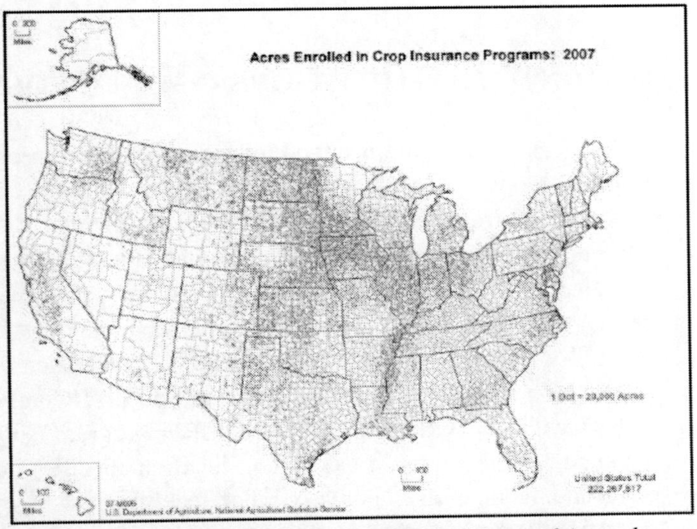

Source: USDA, National Agricultural Statistics Service, *2007 Census of Agriculture*.

Figure 3. Acres Enrolled in Crop Insurance, 2007

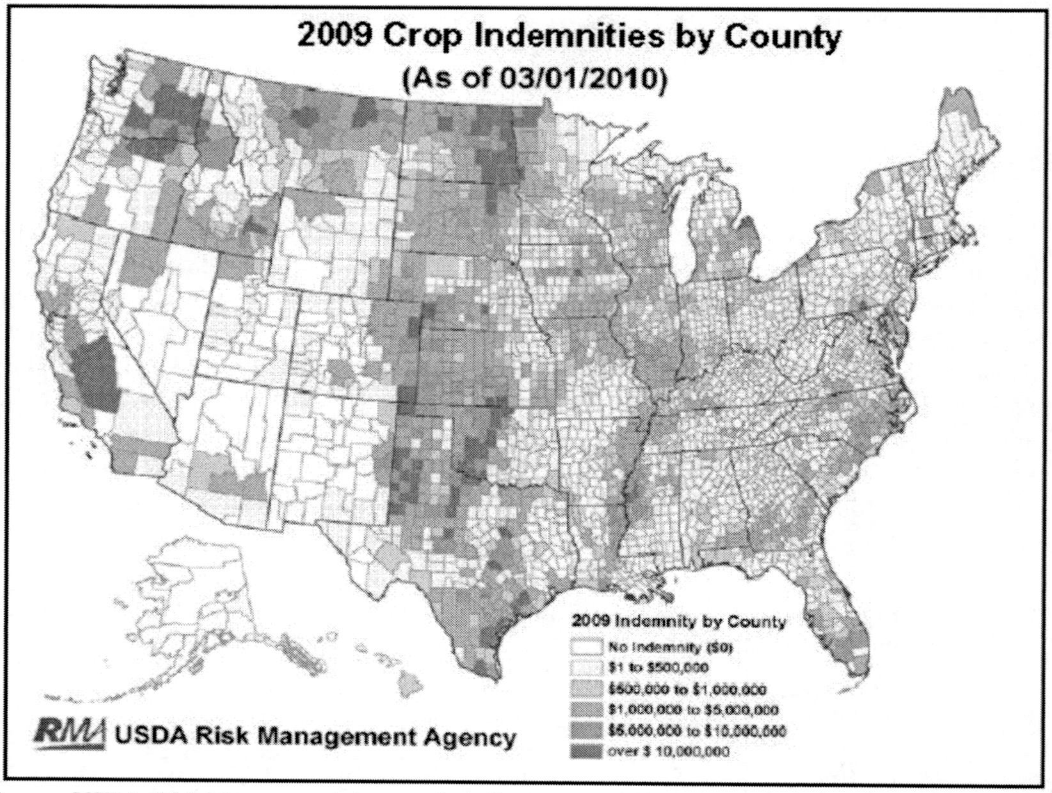

Source: USDA, Risk Management Agency, http://www.rma.usda.gov/data/indemnity/.

Figure 4. Crop Insurance Indemnities

Intersection with Other Government Programs

The intersection between crop insurance and other government programs varies by commodity. For "program crops" such as wheat, corn, and soybeans, eligible producers receive government payments from several programs. These include the direct/counter-cyclical payment program (with fixed payment rates/price-dependent rates, respectively), the average crop revenue election (ACRE) program (revenue-dependent), and the marketing assistance loan program (pricedependent).[14] These programs have elements of risk reduction (i.e., reducing the variability of farm income or the "effective" farm price of a commodity). They can also enhance farm income for participating producers. Compared with these national farm programs, with the exception of the ACRE program and its state yield component, crop insurance provides a more exact (i.e., location-specific) benefit to farmers trying to manage price and income risk. For crops not receiving payments under federal commodity programs, crop insurance serves as a primary risk management tool for farmers, particularly with respect to losses in yields.[15]

Crop insurance and other government programs for farmers are also linked via disaster programs. The Supplemental Revenue Assistance Payments Program (SURE) requires the purchase of crop insurance for program eligibility.[16] Generally, ad-hoc disaster bills in the past (except the most recent one) have not required crop insurance for eligibility, although most required future crop insurance purchases (or participation in the noninsured assistance program) and/or linked payment rates to crop insurance participation. For participation in commodity programs listed above, there is no crop insurance requirement.

When crop insurance is not available, USDA's noninsured crop disaster assistance program (NAP) provides coverage. To be eligible for a NAP payment, a producer first must apply for coverage under the program by the application closing date, which varies by crop, but is generally about 30 days prior to the final planting date for an annual crop. Like catastrophic crop insurance, NAP applicants pay an administrative fee (currently $250 per crop).

For the other major farm programs (direct/counter-cyclical and marketing assistance loan), payments are made independent from crop insurance indemnities, but the same market factors may play a role in triggering payments in some instances.

FEDERAL PROGRAM COSTS

The annual agriculture appropriations bill traditionally makes two separate appropriations for the federal crop insurance program. It provides discretionary funding for the salaries and expenses of the RMA. It also provides "such sums as are necessary" for the Federal Crop Insurance Fund, which finances all other expenses of the program, including premium subsidies, indemnity payments, and reimbursements to the private insurance companies.

Government costs for crop insurance have increased substantially in recent years. After ranging between $2.1 and $3.6 billion during FY2000-FY2006, costs rose to $5.7 billion in FY2008 and $7.3 billion in FY2009 as higher policy premiums from rising crop prices drove up premium subsidies and expense reimbursements to private insurance companies. Expenditures in a particular fiscal year mainly reflect the previous crop year (since fall harvest overlaps with the beginning of the fiscal year).

In FY2009, the largest government cost was the subsidy on policy premiums for producers, totaling $5.2 billion (**Table 2**). The next largest component—$1.6 billion—was reimbursement of administrative and operating (A&O) expenses to private insurance companies. With premiums reflecting only costs associated with policy risk, the A&O reimbursement is meant to pay delivery costs. In recent years, the federal government also has realized underwriting gains (premiums received in excess of indemnities), which has partially reduced total government costs. The underwriting gains (or losses) are derived in part from the federal government's role in providing the first level of reinsurance—that is, insurance for insurance companies.

RISK SHARING AND PRIVATE COMPANY EXPENSE REIMBURSEMENT

Risk sharing between USDA and the private companies and A&O reimbursements to the companies are spelled out in a Standard Reinsurance Agreement (SRA), which plays a large role in determining program costs. The current SRA was completed in June 2004.

Table 2. Government Cost of Federal Crop Insurance (Millions of Dollars)

Fiscal Year	Program Losses or (Gains)[a]	Federal Premium Subsidy	Private Company A&O Expense Reimbursements[b]	Other Costs[c]	Total Government Cost
2000	196	1,353	540	86	2,175
2001	725	1,707	648	82	3,162
2002	1,182	1,513	656	115	3,466
2003	822	1,874	743	149	3,588
2004	(305)	2,387	900	143	3,125
2005	(293)	2,070	783	139	2,699
2006	(31)	2,517	960	125	3,571
2007	(1,068)	3,544	1,341	123	3,940
2008	(1,717)	5,301	2,016	137	5,737
2009	340	5,198	1,602	131	7,271
2010 (forecast)	682	5,201	1,546	155	7,584

Source: U.S. Department of Agriculture, Risk Management Agency.

a. Government's underwriting loss (gain if negative) = the difference between total indemnity payments for crop losses and total premiums (farmer and government paid), plus or minus any private company underwriting losses or gains.

b. A&O = administrative and operating.

c. Other costs primarily include federal salaries of USDA's Risk Management Agency and, beginning in 2002, various research and development initiatives mandated by the Agriculture Risk Protection Act of 2000 (P.L. 106-224).

The 2008 farm bill allows USDA to renegotiate the SRA once every five years starting with the 2011 reinsurance year (the 12-month period beginning July 1, 2010). USDA is currently renegotiating the SRA for the 2011 reinsurance year to address issues such as the calculation of reimbursements. For more information on the proposed SRA and related issues, see CRS Report R40966, *Renegotiation of the Standard Reinsurance Agreement (SRA) for Federal Crop Insurance*, by Dennis A. Shields.

Standard Reinsurance Agreement (SRA)

Under the SRA and cuts specified in the 2008 farm bill, the reimbursement rate for A&O expenses averaged 18% of total premiums in 2009.[17] This means that for every $100 in premiums collected, the companies receive an administrative payment of $18 from the federal government. The reimbursement rate varies by insurance product, depending on whether it is for a yield-based or a revenue insurance product.

The SRA also defines risk-sharing between the government and private insurance companies. Under the SRA, insurance companies may transfer some liability associated with riskier policies to the government and retain profits/losses from less risky policies.[18] This transfer of risk is accomplished through a set of reinsurance funds maintained by FCIC. Within 30 days of the sales closing dates for each crop, companies allocate each policy they sell to one of three funds: assigned risk, developmental, or commercial. The developmental and commercial funds are further subdivided by insurance product type (CAT, buy-up, and revenue). Each company then decides what proportion of premiums (and potential for losses/gains) to retain within each reinsurance fund, subject to required minimum retention limits of individual funds. The ceded (i.e., not retained) portion goes to the government.

The assigned risk fund is used for policies believed to be high-risk; it helps ensure that benefits of the federal crop insurance program are extended to all eligible farmers, regardless of risk. Depending on the state where the policy is sold, companies retain only 15% to 25% of their business as specified in the SRA. Consequently, the federal government assumes a large portion of liability associated with high-risk policies. The SRA also specifies limits on the proportion of a company's business that may be placed in the assigned risk fund.

When the assigned risk designation limit is reached, companies allocate policies—particularly medium-risk policies and pilot programs—to the developmental fund. Each company decides what proportion of its business (by plan type and state) to retain, ranging from 35% to 100%.

The commercial fund is for policies for which companies expect to have only a small amount of losses. The companies select to retain (by plan type and state) between 50% and 100% of premium and associated liability of policies in the commercial fund. In 2008, about 20% of total premium value was placed in assigned risk, 10% in developmental, and 70% in commercial.

Following the allocation of policies to one of the three funds, the gain/loss sharing for a company's retained business is based on loss ratios (indemnities paid divided by premiums collected) as established in the SRA. As a general rule, the higher the loss ratio (i.e., potential for loss), the lower the company share of gains or losses (and vice versa).[19]

The final risk-sharing component of the SRA is the "net book quota share." Once a company's net gain or loss is calculated over its entire "book of business," the company must cede a 5% share of its cumulative underwriting gains/losses to the government. As a result, the government receives a portion of underwriting gains from a company's retained business (but will also pay a portion of the losses, if realized). Since the company's total book includes a higher proportion of policies with lower risk, this portion is generally a positive value, which offsets part of the government costs of the program.

Trends in A&O Reimbursement and Underwriting Gains

Since A&O reimbursements are based on a percentage of premiums, the dollar amount of A&O reimbursement has risen sharply in recent years as premiums have risen to reflect higher crop prices. The A&O reimbursement increased from an average of $881 million during 2004-2006 to $2.0 billion in 2008. A&O reimbursements declined to $1.6 billion in FY2009 following a decline in crop prices. RMA data also indicate that A&O reimbursement per policy increased from $750 in 2004-2006 to $1,749 in 2008 and $1,373 in 2009.[20] Similarly, company underwriting gains (the amount by which a company's share of retained premiums exceeds its indemnities) have increased substantially in recent years as weather has been generally favorable for growing crops (**Table 3**). During this period, increases in insured acreage and higher crop prices have also increased gross liability. Liability represents total exposure of the program, meaning that if all participating farmers suffer losses to the full extent of coverage, program indemnities would be the total liability.

Some observers argue that the reimbursement rate should be pegged to something other than premium value, such as the number of policies sold, to better reflect actual costs and to help reduce federal expenditures. If premiums are actuarially sound, the administrative costs of writing a policy are likely not proportional to the value of the policy (e.g., whether 10 acres or 1,000 acres, or $3 per bushel or $9 per bushel). The private crop insurance companies contend that any reductions in the A&O reimbursement will negatively affect the crop insurance industry and possibly jeopardize the delivery of crop insurance, particularly in high-risk areas.

In 2009, the Government Accountability Office (GAO) released a study on costs associated with administering the crop insurance program.[21] GAO concluded that the current structure of A&O reimbursements "present[s] an opportunity to reduce government spending without compromising the crop insurance program's safety net for farmers." According to GAO, the method for calculating the A&O reimbursement should be redesigned to better reflect reasonable business expenses, in terms of dollars per policy, rather than crop prices. The current approach using crop prices, GAO says, has generated a "kind of windfall" for many insurance agencies/agents as insurance companies, using funds from increased levels of A&O reimbursements, pay higher commissions to compete for each other's "book of business" and associated underwriting gains. In response to GAO's recommendations, USDA's Risk Management Agency has proposed to alter the A&O calculation method in its current draft of the next SRA.[22] The crop insurance industry contends that overall agent compensation is consistent with compensation paid in related insurance industries.[23]

Table 3. Federal Crop Insurance Program and Company Data

Reinsurance Year	Gross Premium[a] ($ million)	Gross Liability[b] ($ million)	Gross Loss Ratio[c]	Private Company Loss Ratio[c]	Private Company Underwriting Gain (Loss)[d] ($ million)
2000	2,538	34,000	1.02	0.70	282
2001	2,979	37,000	1.00	0.73	346
2002	2,911	37,000	1.39	0.91	(47)
2003	3,436	41,000	0.95	0.76	381
2004	4,087	47,000	0.79	0.62	691
2005	3,945	44,000	0.52	0.43	917
2006	4,709	55,000	0.75	0.54	819
2007	6,548	67,000	0.53	0.49	1,572
2008	9,832	89,000	0.88	0.85	1,102
2009 (est.)	8,942	79,000	0.66	0.59	2,194

Source: U.S. Department of Agriculture, Risk Management Agency.

a. Farmer-paid premium plus government-paid premium subsidy.

b. Liability represents total exposure of the program, meaning that if all participating farmers suffered losses to the full extent of coverage, program indemnities would be the total liability.

c. Indemnities divided by premiums. Gross loss ratio is for the program in total (government plus private companies).

d. The underwriting gains represent the amount by which the company's share of retained premiums exceeds its indemnities (vice versa for underwriting losses).

FARMER CONCERNS WITH CROP INSURANCE

The House Agriculture Committee held hearings in spring 2010 to review agricultural policy ahead of the next farm bill debate. Comments on crops insurance surfaced as farmers, academics, other panelists, and Members discussed the farm safety net and the role of crop insurance. Previously, on April 22, 2009, the Subcommittee on General Farm Commodities and Risk Management of the House Agriculture Committee held a hearing to receive input on the crop insurance program from farmers. Based on the testimony, farmers appear to be generally satisfied with the overall crop insurance program and do not seek major changes. However, the producer groups represented at the hearings listed several issues that need attention.

Rice and Other Crops Produced in the South

While the crop insurance program receives favorable marks from farmers in general, producers of some crops, such as rice, contend that current policies are of little value to them. According to rice producers in California and the southern United States, drawbacks include high premiums relative to the insurance guarantee levels and low historical yields that adversely affect guarantees. Also, rice producers say crop insurance does not protect them against one of their biggest risks—fluctuations in the cost of energy-related inputs, particularly fertilizer, fuel, and irrigation pumping. The rice industry is working with RMA to develop a policy to address input risk.[24]

Some farmers in southern U.S. producing regions and elsewhere also contend that their insurance guarantees are too low because the calculation uses 10 years of data, which gives insufficient weight to recent yield gains or the potential for such gains given improved seeds or management practices. As a result, producers say insurance does not fully cover total production, and they must self-insure the remainder.[25]

More Affordable Premiums

Southern producers also feel that premiums for buy-up coverage or revenue products are not affordable, leaving catastrophic policies (with minimal coverage) as the only viable option for many farmers. More broadly, in the April 2009 hearing, some farm groups requested that current subsidies be maintained or increased so premiums would be more affordable.[26] Some groups specifically urged Congress to use caution when making program changes in the SRA negotiations so that farmer participation does not slip. Corn producers want their premiums reduced because the loss ratio has been reportedly only 0.58 (indemnities paid divided by premiums). On a positive note, producers said they appreciate the recently reduced premiums under the 2008 farm bill for policies with enterprise units (coverage for groups of fields instead of individual fields).

Nursery Products

Similar to organizations representing field crop producers, the American Nursery and Landscape Association said that the nursery industry considers the federal crop insurance program to be a valuable component of risk management practices. According to the association, incremental program enhancements have been made in recent years, including the use of a grower's wholesale price list for the basis of coverage. However, they contend that the program falls short of adequately addressing the extreme diversity and unique situations found in the industry because production practices are less uniform than for major field crops. Producers say there is a great degree of variation in program management across the country, depending upon agents' and claim adjustors' familiarity with industry practices. A certification program would be helpful, they say.

"Shallow" Losses and Other Concerns

Congress heard from national farm organizations representing a cross-section of American agriculture. The American Farm Bureau Federation (AFBF) would like USDA to address shallow losses, which occur when losses are significant for the farmer but not enough to trigger an indemnity.[27] Also, the group points out a need to address declines in actual production history (APH), which is used for determining the insurance guarantee. Some farmers are subject to a declining insurance guarantee because of recent repeated disasters. (The American Sugar Cane League commented on the inadequacy of the APH for sugar cane because it is adversely affected by an old variety that is no longer being planted.)

Another broad-based farm organization, the National Farmers Union (NFU), contends that crop insurance remains inadequate for those with multi-year disasters, and that crop quality loss discounts applied in insurance contracts do not reflect realities of the marketplace. The organization also wants insurance companies to offer coverage in all areas and not "cherry pick" regions that are most profitable. Finally, the organization requests a revised auditing procedure that could avoid duplicative reviews of records. Currently, RMA requires an automatic review if a farmer receives an indemnity exceeding $100,000.

Farm groups identified the need for better information management. The National Association of Wheat Growers wants streamlined acreage reporting between crop insurance and other USDA farm programs, while the AFBF has asked Congress to push for USDA's completion of the Comprehensive Information Management System (CIMS) project. The project is designed to manage data used for both crop insurance and farm commodity programs, thereby reducing duplicative efforts by both producers and USDA personnel.

Issues the for 111th Congress

Given concerns about the federal deficit, reductions in funding for crop insurance were included in the Administration's FY2010 budget proposal (proposed cuts of $500 million per year) and FY2011 budget proposal (proposed cuts of $800 million per year).[28] The Administration's FY2010 proposal called for three specific cuts: (1) reduce subsidies on the premiums that producers pay for policies by five percentage points on all coverage levels, (2) increase the federal government's share on underwriting gains to 20% from 5%, and (3) reduce the premium for CAT coverage by 25% and charge a sliding scale fee for CAT coverage from $300 to $5,000, depending on the crop value. No changes were suggested for the reimbursement rate for private company operating expenses. According to the Administration, the proposed subsidy reductions were justified because new risk management programs created in the 2008 farm bill (ACRE and SURE) reduce the need for continuing the same level of crop insurance subsidies. Moreover, the Administration says the proposal would control "crop insurance costs [that] have ballooned in recent years" while reducing "a corporate subsidy that has grown disproportionately as participation has increased since 2001."[29]

In response to the Administration's proposal, Congress took no action on crop insurance. The FY2010 budget resolution conference report (S.Con.Res. 13) did not contain cuts related to crop insurance.[30] The FY20 10 Agriculture appropriations bill was enacted on October 21, 2009. None of the proposed cuts to crop insurance were included in the final bill.

In the Administration's FY20 11 budget proposal, the savings would be generated from changes in the Standard Reinsurance Agreement through the SRA renegotiation process that has been underway with insurance companies since late 2009. USDA is renegotiating the Standard Reinsurance Agreement beginning with the 2011 season (which starts July 1, 2010), as provided under the 2008 farm bill. The proposed savings reflected USDA's first draft of the new SRA in December 2009. Subsequent drafts by USDA has reduced the savings amounts. The final draft requires ultimate approval by participating companies. The crop insurance industry and insurance agents are particularly concerned with changes that would reduce A&O reimbursements.

Insurance companies, farm groups, and some Members of Congress remain concerned that significant reductions in federal support, including any cuts stemming from the new SRA, will negatively impact the financial health of the crop insurance industry and possibly jeopardize the delivery of crop insurance, particularly in high-risk areas. The crop insurance industry argues that cuts to the program were already made in the 2008 farm bill, and additional cuts would be unfair.[31] Others point to recent increases in operating expense reimbursements and underwriting gains, questioning whether these higher levels are necessary for maintaining a viable crop insurance industry.

In addition to concern with proposed cuts and their potential impact on the crop insurance program, some Members of Congress, including the chairman of the House Committee on Agriculture, are concerned that any reductions would lower baseline funding levels for crop insurance, which could have a negative effect on spending for the next farm bill. If concerns about the federal budget deficit lead to a call for reduction in mandatory spending, including funds for agriculture, cuts made administratively by USDA (i.e., through the new SRA) would not count as savings for agriculture spending that the House and Senate Agriculture Committees would need to make.

Previous renegotiations of the SRA generated criticism from the crop insurance industry. When USDA's Risk Management Agency released its final version of the current SRA on June 10, 2004, the revised SRA was criticized by the crop insurance industry and various farmer groups as being detrimental to the program and the industry. According to USDA estimates, the changes were expected to reduce federal costs (and consequently industry revenue) by $22 million in the first year and $36 million in the second and subsequent years.

Despite these changes, expense reimbursement and underwriting gains have increased sharply since 2005. The crop insurance industry argues that generally good weather, which limited widespread crop losses, and higher crop prices (and related premium levels) contributed to these gains to the industry, and such conditions will not necessarily continue.

For policymakers, a main concern when contemplating financial changes to the crop insurance program would likely be saving federal dollars without adversely affecting farmer participation, policy coverage, or industry interest in selling and servicing crop insurance products to farmers. For many farmers, crop insurance is the most important component of the farm safety net, given the breadth of commodity coverage and, compared with previous periods, less protection from a decline in prices because other farm program parameters remain generally below market prices (which reduces the potential for farm payments when prices decline).

One general policy question for crop insurance is whether or not there is overlap in payments with other farm programs. The potential for overpayment is reduced in SURE by including crop insurance indemnities (and other program payments) in its farm revenue calculation for individual producers. In contrast, the ACRE program includes producer-paid crop insurance premiums in the producer's farm benchmark revenue guarantee. This helps trigger a payment earlier than would otherwise occur, but does not alter the program payment rate, which is based on state-level yields and national prices. In addition, some observers have noted that ACRE and crop insurance provide duplicate coverage and question why taxpayers should fund both programs.[32]

End Notes

[1] For details on farm programs, see CRS Report RL34594, *Farm Commodity Programs in the 2008 Farm Bill*, by Jim Monke.

[2] For more on the history of federal crop insurance, see http://www.rma.usda.gov/aboutrma/what/history.html. Law citations are the Federal Crop Insurance Act of 1980 (P.L. 96-3 65), the Federal Crop Insurance Reform Act of 1994 (P.L. 103-354), and the Agriculture Risk Protection Act (ARPA) of 2000 (P.L. 106-224).

[3] For more information, see CRS Report RL34207, *Crop Insurance and Disaster Assistance in the 2008 Farm Bill*, by Ralph M. Chite and Dennis A. Shields, and CRS Report R40452, *A Whole-Farm Crop Disaster Program: Supplemental Revenue Assistance Payments (SURE)*, by Dennis A. Shields.

[4] Portions of this section are from CRS Report RL3 0739, *Federal Crop Insurance and the Agriculture Risk Protection Act of 2000 (P.L. 106-224)*, by Ralph M. Chite.

[5] In practice, the crop insurance company bills the farmer for the producer's portion of the premium (i.e., excluding the government portion). The company then sends the entire producer-paid premium to RMA. When a producer files a claim and the company pays an indemnity, RMA reimburses the company in full for the loss. At the end of the reinsurance year, there is an annual settlement where the company's proportion of any underwriting gain or loss is determined and paid.

[6] A complete list of 2010 crops is available at http://www.rma.usda.gov/policies/2010policy.html#3. For previous years, see http://www.rma.usda.gov/policies/08croplist.html.

[7] Carey Frick, "Frick: Not So Peachy," *The State*, May 26,2010, http://www.thestate.com/2010/05/26/1302654/ fricknot-so-peachy.html.

[8] U.S. Department of Agriculture, Risk Management Agency, http://www.rma.usda.gov/help/faq/basics.html.

[9] A number of university and Extension Service offices provide information to farmers when making crop insurance decisions. Some examples include http://www.agmanager.info/crops http://www.ag.ndsu.nodak.edu/aginfo/cropmkt/cic.htm,http://www.farmdoc.uiuc.edu/cropins/index.asp,andhttp://extension.umaine.edu/c rop insurance/default.htm.

[10] Participation at the CAT level has steadily decreased, particularly since subsidies on buy-up levels were increased in the Agriculture Risk Protection Act (ARPA) of 2000. In 2008, only about 11% of insured acres were insured at the CAT level.

[11] USDA, Risk Management Agency, "RMA Releases New Common Crop Insurance Policy Basic Provisions," press release, March 31, 2010, http://www.rma.usda.gov/news/2010/03/combo.html.

[12] Crop are barley, canola, corn, cotton, grain sorghum, rapeseed, rice, soybeans, sunflowers, and wheat.

[13] In some North Dakota counties in 2009, for example, the cause of loss was drought for some wheat policies, while it was excess moisture for other wheat policies.

[14] For more on USDA commodity programs, see CRS Report RL34594 , *Farm Commodity Programs in the 2008 Farm Bill*, by Jim Monke; and CRS Report R40422, *A New Farm Program Option: Average Crop Revenue Election (ACRE)*, by Dennis A. Shields.

[15] In some cases, a farmer's price risk can also be managed by contracting production with buyers or by using the futures market to lock in selling prices.

[16] For more details on agricultural disaster programs, see CRS Report RS21212, *Agricultural Disaster Assistance*, by Dennis A. Shields and Ralph M. Chite, and CRS Report R40452, *A Whole-Farm Crop Disaster Program: Supplemental Revenue Assistance Payments (SURE)*, by Dennis A. Shields.

[17] The 2008 farm bill (Sec. 12016(E)) reduced the A&O reimbursement by 2.3 percentage points beginning with the 2009 reinsurance year (July 1, 2008). Also, the farm bill reduced the A&O reimbursement rate to 12% for any plan of insurance that is based on area-wide losses. The farm bill also reduced the target loss ratio (indemnities paid divided by premiums collected) from 1.075 to 1.00.

[18] Dmitry V. Vedenov et al., "Portfolio Allocation and Alternative Structures of the Standard Reinsurance Agreement," vol. 31, no. 1 (April 2006), pp. 57-73, http://ageconsearch.umn.edu/bitstream/10145/1/31010057.pdf.

[19] The exception is, at very low loss ratios, the company share of gains declines.

[20] USDA, Risk Management Agency, "Federal Crop Insurance Program History" data sheet, Washington, DC, March 1, 2010.

[21] U.S. Government Accountability Office, *Crop Insurance—Opportunities Exist to Reduce the Costs of Administering the Program*, Washington, DC, April 2009, http://www.gao.gov/new.items/d09445.pdf.

[22] For more information on the SRA renegotiation, see CRS Report R40966, *Renegotiation of the Standard Reinsurance Agreement (SRA) for Federal Crop Insurance*, by Dennis A. Shields.

[23] On June 1, 2009, 14 organizations affiliated with the crop insurance industry wrote to Congress to comment on the crop insurance program performance and the need for maintaining current subsidies and A&Oreimbursements.Seehttp://www.farmpolicy.com/wp-content/uploads/2009/06/gaocropinsurance letter.pdf.

[24] U.S. Congress, House Committee on Agriculture, *Testimony of Frank Rehermann*, hearing to review U.S. agriculture policy in advance of the 2012 farm bill, 111th Cong., 2nd sess., May 3, 2010, http://agriculture.house.gov/ testimony/11 1/h0503 10/Rehermann.pdf.

[25] U.S. Congress, House Committee on Agriculture, *Testimony of David Waide*, hearing to review U.S. agriculture policy in advance of the 2012 farm bill, 111th Cong., 2nd sess., May 15, 2010, http://agriculture.house.gov/ testimony/ 11 1/h051510/Waide.pdf.

[26] Statements from witnesses are available at http://agriculture. U.S. Congress, House Committee on Agriculture, Subcommittee on General Farm Commodities and Risk Management, hearing to review producers' views on the effectiveness and operations of the federal crop insurance program, 11 1th Cong., 1st sess., April 22, 2009.

[27] Under the 2008 farm bill, the new Supplemental Revenue Assistance Payments Program (SURE) has provisions to partially address the shallow loss problem, at least at the whole-farm level, by applying factors to the individual farm program guarantee level (115% of insured value of each insurable commodity and 120% of value of non-insurable commodity).

[28] Office of Management and Budget, "A New Era of Responsibility: Renewing America's Promise," February 26, 2009, http://www.gpoaccess.gov/usbudget/fy10/pdf/fy10-newera.pdf; and "Budget of the United States Government, Fiscal Year 2011," February 1, 2010, http://www.whitehouse.gov/omb /budget/fy2011/assets

[29] Office of Management and Budget, *Terminations, Reductions, and Savings - Budget of the U.S. Government Fiscal Year 2010*, Washington, DC, 2009, http://wwwwhitehouse.gov/omb/budget /fy2010/ assets

[30] Note that the Senate-passed budget resolution had assumed crop insurance reductions of $70 million per year over five years.

[31] Philip Brasher, "Proposed Ag Subsidy Cuts Dropped," *Des Moines Register*, April 8, 2009. For farm bill changes, see CRS Report RL34207, *Crop Insurance and Disaster Assistance in the 2008 Farm Bill*, by Ralph M. Chite and Dennis A. Shields.

[32] U.S. Congress, House Committee on Agriculture, *Testimony of Bruce A. Babcock*, hearing to review U.S. agriculture policy in advance of the 2012 farm bill, 111th Cong., 2nd sess., May 13, 2010, http://agriculture.house.gov/testimony/11 1/h051310/Babcock.pdf.

In: Agriculture Disaster and Crop Insurance: Background... ISBN: 978-1-61761-559-7
Editor: Angela M. Gil

Chapter 5

RENEGOTIATION OF THE STANDARD REINSURANCE AGREEMENT (SRA) FOR FEDERAL CROP INSURANCE

Dennis A. Shields

SUMMARY

Under the federal crop insurance program, farmers can purchase crop insurance policies to manage financial risks associated with declines in crop yields and/or revenue. The program covers more than 100 crops and is administered by the U.S. Department of Agriculture's (USDA's) Risk Management Agency (RMA), which acts as both regulator and reinsurer. To encourage farmer participation and reduce the need for ad hoc disaster assistance, the federal government subsidizes the purchase of crop insurance policies, which are sold and serviced through 15 approved private insurance companies. Insurance company losses are reinsured by USDA, and their administrative and operating (A&O) costs are reimbursed by the government.

A Standard Reinsurance Agreement (SRA) between USDA and the private companies spells out expense reimbursements and risk-sharing by the government, including the terms under which the government provides subsidies and reinsurance (i.e., insurance for insurance companies) on eligible crop insurance contracts sold or reinsured by insurance companies. As a result, the SRA plays a central role in determining program costs. The SRA does not affect policy premiums paid by farmers, which are based on RMA's estimates of risk and on subsides set in statute.

RMA is in the process of renegotiating the SRA that has been in effect since 2004. Some have criticized it as being too generous for insurance companies following a significant increase in government costs in recent years. Although Congress does not directly approve any new agreement, Congress has been interested in its oversight capacity, particularly with respect to cost-effectiveness and effects on farmer participation, the industry's selling and servicing of crop insurance products to farmers, and baseline funding levels for the next farm bill.

Since A&O reimbursements under the current SRA are based on a percentage of premiums, their dollar amount has risen sharply in recent years as premiums have risen to reflect higher crop prices. The A&O reimbursement increased from an average of $881 million during FY2004- FY2006 to $1.6 billion in 2009. Some observers argue that reimbursements should be pegged to something other than premiums, such as a flat fee per policy sold, to better reflect actual costs and to help reduce federal expenditures. The insurance industry contends that reimbursements are currently less than actual delivery expenses.

Similarly, company underwriting gains (the amount by which a company's share of retained premiums exceeds its indemnities) have increased substantially in recent years, as weather has been generally favorable for growing crops. Some have argued that if the government share of gains is increased in exchange for a larger government share of losses, average taxpayer costs would decline. The insurance industry contends that a certain provision of the current SRA ("net book quota share") is a tax on underwriting income and crowds out private reinsurance.

RMA released its first draft of the 2011 SRA on December 4, 2009, a second draft in mid- February 2010, and a "final" draft on June 10, 2010. The most recent draft places a cap on A&O reimbursements to control costs, and limits a company's expenditures on agent commissions. Among the proposed changes to underwriting provisions, the final draft improves profit potential and reduces company risk in higher-risk states. The draft also directs proceeds from an increase in the net book quota share to companies operating in "underserved states." Throughout the negotiations, the industry has been concerned that overall funding reductions are excessive. RMA expects that most companies will sign the agreement in time for it to take effect in July 2010. The new SRA will cover crops with policy closing dates after July 1, 2010 (e.g., 2011-crop corn).

INTRODUCTION

Under the federal crop insurance program, farmers can purchase crop insurance policies to manage financial risks associated with declines in crop yields and/or revenue. The program, which began in 1938 when Congress authorized the Federal Crop Insurance Corporation (FCIC) and now covers more than 100 crops, is administered by the U.S. Department of Agriculture's (USDA's) Risk Management Agency (RMA), which acts as both regulator and reinsurer.

A Standard Reinsurance Agreement (SRA) between USDA and the private companies spells out expense reimbursements and risk-sharing by the federal government, including the terms under which FCIC provides subsidies and reinsurance (i.e., insurance for insurance companies) on eligible crop insurance contracts sold or reinsured by insurance companies. As a result, the SRA plays a central role in determining program costs.

RMA is in the process of renegotiating the SRA that has been in effect since 2004. Some have criticized it as being too generous for insurance companies following a significant increase in government costs in recent years, driven in part by rising crop prices. The 2008 farm bill (P.L. 110-246) allows USDA to renegotiate the SRA once every five years starting with the 2011 reinsurance year (which runs from July 1, 2010, through June 30, 2011).[1]

The negotiation process involves USDA developing a draft agreement, meeting separately with the insurance companies, and responding to the comments, concerns, and suggestions of the insurance companies and the public. On June 10, 2010, RMA issued what it calls the final draft of a new SRA to cover the 2011 reinsurance year and subsequent years.[2] Following any technical corrections, RMA expects the agreement to be signed separately by insurance companies and put into effect in July 2010. Typically, the Department of Justice monitors the negotiations to assure that antitrust guidelines are followed.

This report discusses federal crop insurance costs, the SRA that has been in effect for the 2010 reinsurance year, and issues related to the renegotiation of the SRA. Although Congress does not directly approve any new agreement, Congress has been interested in the SRA negotiation in an oversight capacity, particularly with respect to cost-effectiveness and changes that might affect farmer participation, policy coverage, or industry interest in selling crop insurance to farmers.[3] Another congressional concern is how cuts in crop insurance expenditures stemming from a new SRA might affect baseline spending levels used for determining funding for the next farm bill.[4]

Crop Insurance Background

Congress first authorized federal crop insurance as an experiment to address the effects of the Great Depression and crop losses in the Dust Bowl. In 1938, the Federal Crop Insurance Corporation (FCIC) was created to carry out the program, which focused on major crops in major producing regions. The federal crop insurance program remained limited until passage of the Federal Crop Insurance Act of 1980 (P.L. 96-365), which expanded crop insurance to many more crops and regions of the country. Congress enhanced the crop insurance program in 1994 and again in 2000 to encourage greater participation. The changes also expanded the role of the private sector in developing new products that would help farmers manage their risks.

To encourage farmer participation and reduce the need for ad hoc disaster assistance, the federal government subsidizes the purchase of crop insurance policies, which are sold and completely serviced through 15 approved private insurance companies. Independent insurance agents are paid sales commissions by the companies. Insurance company losses are reinsured by USDA, and their administrative and operating costs are reimbursed by the federal government. These costs include payroll, rent, commissions to agents, and expenses for adjusting claims (e.g., traveling to farmers' fields).

The SRA does not affect policy premiums paid by farmers, which are based on RMA's estimates of risk and on subsides set in statute. The premiums depend in part on crop price levels, coverage levels that producers select, and policy type (e.g., yield-based or revenue-based). The expense reimbursement is currently calculated as a share of policy premiums. For more information on crop insurance policies, see CRS Report R40532, *Federal Crop Insurance: Background and Issues*, by Dennis A. Shields.

FEDERAL PROGRAM COSTS

Federal program costs for crop insurance fall into one of four main categories: premium subsidies, administrative and operating (A&O) expense reimbursement, program losses (or gains), and other (**Table 1**). The SRA essentially defines the parameters that eventually determine A&O expense reimbursements and program losses (or gains). Premium subsidies are specified in the Federal Crop Insurance Act of 1980 (P.L. 110-365), as amended. Periodic legislation can also affect federal outlays (see "A&O Reimbursement," below).

The largest cost category is premium subsidies, which lower the cost to farmers of purchasing insurance policies. When purchasing a policy, a producer growing an insurable crop selects a level of coverage and pays a portion of the premium. The remainder of the premium is covered by the federal government. Nearly 60% of total premium, on average, is paid by the government. As with other insurance, premiums increase with additional coverage, in terms of greater price protection or yield protection (or both).

The second-largest cost category is A&O expense reimbursement. Unlike some other insurance products, premiums for crop insurance are not "expense loaded." For crop insurance, the entire premium covers only the liability associated with payment of crop losses and excludes expenses for delivery of the product. Currently, expense reimbursement for insurance companies is directly related to the value of the premiums. Therefore, as premiums rise, so does the A&O expense reimbursement, even if other factors, such as the number of policies sold, remain unchanged.

Table 1. Government Cost of Federal Crop Insurance (Millions of Dollars)

Fiscal Year	Federal Premium Subsidy	Private Company A&O Expense Reimbursements[a]	Program Losses or (Gains)[b]	Other Costs[c]	Total Government Cost
2000	1,353	540	196	86	2,175
2001	1,707	648	725	82	3,162
2002	1,513	656	1,182	115	3,466
2003	1,874	743	822	149	3,588
2004	2,387	900	(305)	143	3,125
2005	2,070	783	(293)	139	2,699
2006	2,517	960	(31)	125	3,571
2007	3,544	1,341	(1,068)	123	3,940
2008	5,301	2,016	(1,717)	137	5,737
2009	5,198	1,602	340	131	7,271
2010 (forecast)	5,201	1,546	682	155	7,584

Source: U.S. Department of Agriculture, Risk Management Agency.

a. A&O = administrative and operating.

b. Government's underwriting loss (gain if negative) = the difference between total indemnity payments for crop losses and total premiums (farmer- and government-paid), plus or minus any private company underwriting losses or gains.

c. Other costs primarily include federal salaries of USDA's Risk Management Agency and, beginning in 2002, various research and development initiatives mandated by the Agriculture Risk Protection Act of 2000 (P.L. 106-224).

The third category is program losses. As a reinsurer, the federal government is liable for insured losses as agreed to in the current SRA. In a number of recent years, the government has received a gain because of relatively favorable weather.

The fourth category is other expenses such as RMA salaries and benefits or costs associated with research and development activities, which typically account for a small portion of total costs.

In recent years, government costs for crop insurance have increased substantially (**Figure 1**). After ranging between $2.1 and $3.6 billion annually during FY2000-FY2006, costs rose to $5.7 billion in FY2008 and more than $7 billion in FY2009 as higher policy premiums from rising crop prices drove up premium subsidies for farmers and expense reimbursements to private insurance companies.[5]

Major Provisions in the Standard Reinsurance Agreement for 2010

The Standard Reinsurance Agreement is a cooperative financial agreement between FCIC and each of the approved crop insurance companies to deliver eligible crop insurance contracts. It becomes effective upon its execution and FCIC's approval of the company's plan of operations for the applicable reinsurance year.

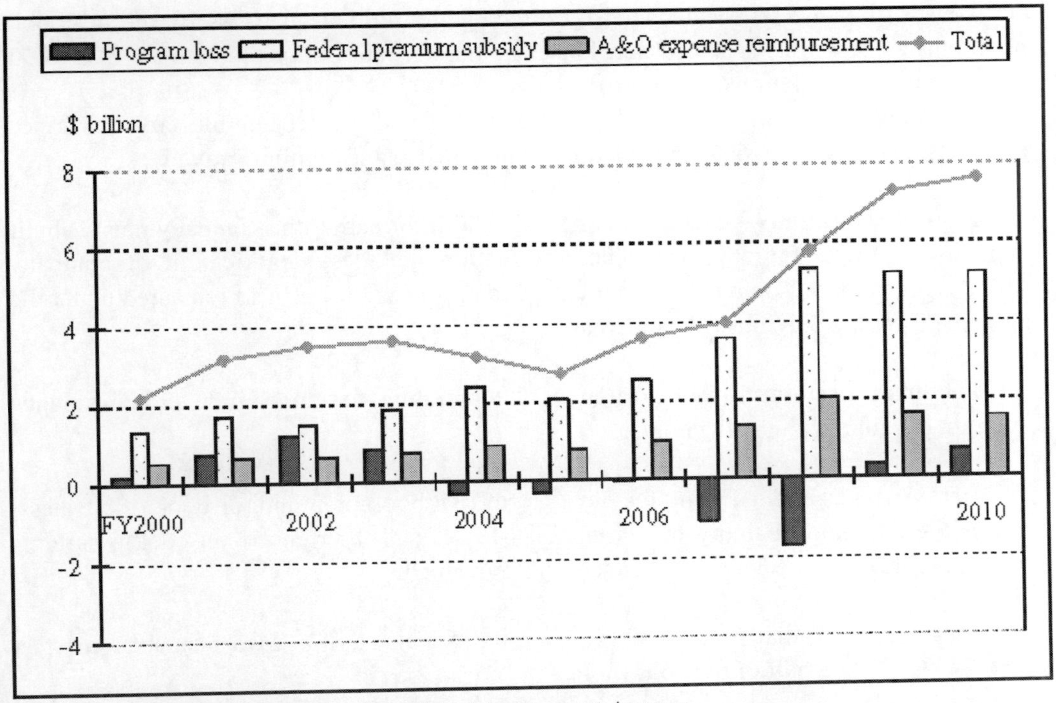

Source: U.S. Department of Agriculture, Risk Management Agency.

Notes: 20 10 forecast. Total includes small amounts of "other" costs. For program losses, a negative number indicates an underwriting gain, which reduces total government costs.

Figure 1. Government Costs for Crop Insurance Have Increased Sharply

Selected Terms Defined in the Standard Reinsurance Agreement

A&O subsidy—the subsidy for the administrative and operating expenses paid by FCIC on behalf of the policyholder to the company for eligible crop insurance contracts.

Administrative fee—the processing fee the policyholder must pay under an eligible crop insurance contract.

Book of business—the aggregation of all eligible crop insurance contracts in force between the company and its policyholders that have a sales closing date within the reinsurance year and are eligible to be reinsured under the SRA.

Cede—to pass to another all or part of the net book premium and associated liability for ultimate net losses on eligible crop insurance contracts.

Eligible producer—a person who has an insurable interest in an agricultural commodity, who has not been determined ineligible to participate in the federal crop insurance program, and who possesses a U.S.-issued social security number (SSN) or employer identification number (EIN).

Loss ratio—the ratio calculated by dividing the ultimate net loss by the net book premium, expressed as a percentage. For example, the ratio of $1 ultimate net loss to 50 cents net book premium would be expressed as 200%.

Net book premium—the total premium calculated for all eligible crop insurance contracts, less A&O subsidy, cancellations, adjustments, and administrative fees.

Plan of operations—documents and financial information the company must submit annually to FCIC for approval. The information includes identification of company officials, declarations on retention amounts, and expenses for business reinsured under the agreement for the previous calendar year.

Producer premium—that portion of the premium for an eligible crop insurance contract payable by the policyholder.

Retained—as applied to ultimate net losses, net book premium, or book of business, means the remaining liability for ultimate net losses and the right to net book premiums after all reinsurance ceded to FCIC under this agreement.

Risk subsidy—that portion of the premium for an eligible crop insurance contract paid by FCIC on behalf of the policyholder.

Ultimate net loss—the amount paid by a company under any eligible crop insurance contract reinsured under the SRA in settlement of any claim, less any recovery or salvage by the company.

Underwriting—the determination of the terms and conditions by which the company will accept the risk for an eligible crop insurance contract.

Underwriting gain (loss)—the amount by which a company's share of retained net book premium exceeds (falls short of) its retained ultimate net losses.

Source: U.S. Department of Agriculture, Risk Management Agency, *Standard Reinsurance Agreement between the Federal Crop Insurance Corporation and the (Insurance Company Name) (City and State)*, http://www.rma.usda.gov/pubs/ra/ 05sra_final.pdf.

The SRA for the 2010 reinsurance year (ending June 30, 2010) contains four sections: definitions (see box, "Selected Terms Defined in the Standard Reinsurance Agreement"), reinsurance, A&O expense reimbursement, and general provisions.[6]

Reinsurance

The SRA establishes terms for the type of insurance contracts that will be reinsured and subsidized. In general, in order to prevent companies from "cherry-picking" the most profitable policies, an insurance company must offer and market all plans of insurance for all crops in any state in which the company writes a crop insurance contract, provided that RMA actuarial documents are available in that state.[7] A company must also accept and approve applications from all eligible producers, and it is prohibited from providing a rebate (money, goods, or any other benefit) in exchange for purchasing a policy. Employees and agents of the company must also be properly licensed by the state in which they are doing business, if required by the state. Only the amount of net book premium—defined as the total premium calculated for all eligible crop insurance contracts, less A&O subsidy and fees—in the company's approved plan of operations may be reinsured and subsidized under the agreement.

The SRA defines risk-sharing between the government and private insurance companies. Under the SRA, insurance companies may transfer some liability associated with riskier policies to the government and retain profits/losses from less risky policies. This transfer of risk is accomplished through a set of reinsurance funds maintained by FCIC. Within 30 days of the sales closing dates for each crop, companies assign each policy they sell to one of three funds—assigned risk, developmental, or commercial—for each state. Each company then decides what proportion of premiums (and potential for losses/gains) to retain within each reinsurance fund, subject to required minimum retention limits of individual funds.[8] The ceded (i.e., not retained) portion goes to the government. Overall, a company must retain at least 35% of its book of business.

Assigned Risk Fund

The assigned risk fund is used for policies believed to be high-risk; it helps ensure that benefits of the federal crop insurance program are extended to all eligible farmers, regardless of risk. Depending on the state where the policy is sold, companies may retain as little as 15%

to 25% of their highest-risk business, as specified in the SRA. Consequently, the federal government assumes a large portion of liability associated with high-risk policies. The SRA also specifies limits on the proportion of a company's business that may be placed in the assigned risk fund.

Developmental Fund

When the assigned risk designation limit is reached, companies allocate policies—particularly medium-risk policies and pilot programs—to the developmental fund. Each company decides what proportion of its business (by plan type and state) to retain, ranging from 35% to 100%.

Commercial Fund

The commercial fund is for policies for which companies expect to have only a small amount of losses. The companies select to retain (by plan type and state) between 50% and 100% of premium and associated liability of policies in the commercial fund. In 2008, about 20% of total premium value was placed in assigned risk, 10% in developmental, and 70% in commercial.

Following the allocation of policies to one of the three funds, the actual gain/loss sharing for a company's retained business is based on loss ratios (indemnities paid divided by premiums collected) as established in the SRA. As a general rule, for underwriting losses, the higher the loss ratio, the lower the company share of losses (calculated separately for each fund within each state). This provision limits overall losses, with the government paying increasing amounts as losses mount. For example, FCIC assumes 100% of the underwriting loss for portions incurred when a company's loss ratio exceeds 500% (indemnities are five times greater than total premiums). Similarly, when there are underwriting gains, a company's share of gains declines (and the government's share increases) when the loss ratio is relatively low.

A company's shares of gains and losses also vary by fund. They are greatest in the commercial fund and the least in the assigned risk fund. Company exposure and potential gains are much greater in the commercial fund than in the assigned risk fund.

The final risk-sharing component of the SRA is the "net book quota share." Once a company's net gain or loss is calculated over its entire "book of business," the company must cede a 5% share of its cumulative underwriting gains/losses to the government. As a result, the government receives a portion of underwriting gains from a company's retained business (but will also pay a portion of the losses, if realized). Since the company's total book includes a higher proportion of policies with lower risk, this portion is generally a positive value, which offsets part of the government costs of the program (See Table 1, above, and "Cost Control and Financial Viability of Crop Insurance Companies," below).

A&O Reimbursement

The SRA establishes the reimbursement rate for administrative and operating (A&O) expenses to private insurance companies. During 2006-2008, the reimbursement rate—defined as a percentage of net book premiums—ranged from 18.1% to 24.2%, with higher rates associated with lower levels of insurance coverage.[9] This means that for every $100 in premiums collected, the companies received an administrative payment of $18.10 to $24.20 from the federal government.

To generate cost savings, Congress mandated a reduction in reimbursement rates in the Food, Conservation, and Energy Act of 2008 (P.L. 110-246, the 2008 farm bill, Sec. 12016(E)).[10] Beginning with the 2009 reinsurance year (July 1, 2008), the A&O reimbursement was reduced for most crop insurance policies by 2.3 percentage points, with the resultant rates ranging from 15.8% to 21.9%.[11] For a discussion on recent trends in the A&O reimbursement, see "Cost Control and Financial Viability of Crop Insurance Companies," below.

General Provisions

An insurance company is required to collect and provide to FCIC data on policyholders, as well as producer premiums and administrative fees collected by the company. Monetary penalties are applied if the required information is not submitted timely or accurately. The company must also provide policyholders with a summary of coverage and a billing statement that prominently displays the policy premium, the FCIC-paid portion, and the administrative and operating (A&O) reimbursement paid by FCIC. The company must also follow FCIC regulations and procedures for a host of activities, including verification of yields and other information used to establish insurance guarantees and indemnity payments.

STUDIES ON RATES OF RETURN

As part of USDA's preparation for renegotiating the SRA, the department hired a firm to calculate rates of return for crop insurers. In a two-part study, Milliman, Inc., estimated historical rates of return on equity for crop insurers and "reasonable" rates of return in order to determine if crop insurers are being over- or undercompensated by the government.[12] The reasonable rate of return was defined as the "cost of capital" or, in this case, the returns received by property and casualty insurers, which was considered to be an investment of equivalent risk.

The study concluded that the historical returns on equity for crop insurers averaged 16.6% during 1989 to 2008, or 3.8% above the average "reasonable" rate of return over the same period, which was estimated at 12.8%. In addition, during the 20-year period under examination, the calculated historical rate of return was above the calculated "reasonable" rate in all but three years, with historical returns negative in only one year (1993) because of massive flooding. If a second catastrophic year had occurred during the period, the study notes, the average historical rate of return would have declined to 15.6%. The crop insurance industry has criticized the Milliman study for failing to consider reinsurance and actual A&O costs.

The crop insurance industry completed its own analysis, which defined profitability relative to premiums or "sales" rather than relative to equity. The study, conducted by Grant Thorton LLP, measured profitability as pre-tax net income as a percentage of net retained premium. [13] The ratio for the 1992-2008 period averaged 14.2% for the crop insurance industry, compared with 17.5% for the property and casualty industry. USDA has criticized the Grant Thorton study for ignoring investment income on policyholder surplus when assessing returns on crop insurance.

Issues in the SRA Renegotiation

The new SRA is expected to address several issues raised by policymakers, the agriculture community, and the crop insurance industry. These include control of government costs and financial viability of the crop insurance industry, crop insurance availability and farmer participation, and uncertainties after completion of the SRA renegotiation.

Any cost reductions imposed by the new SRA would be in addition to reductions mandated under the 2008 farm bill. These changes resulted in net budget outlay savings of $3.9 billion over five years (FY2008-FY2012), or $5.6 billion over 10 years (FY2008-FY2017), relative to the March 2007 baseline, according to the Congressional Budget Office. Approximately $2.8 billion of this estimated five-year savings was attributable to changes in the timing of premium receipts from farmers, and payments to the participating insurance companies.

Cost Control and Financial Viability of Crop Insurance Companies

A&O Reimbursements

Since A&O reimbursements are based on a percentage of premiums, the dollar amount of A&O reimbursement has risen sharply in recent years as premiums have risen to reflect higher crop prices. The A&O reimbursement increased from an average of $881 million during FY2004- FY2006 to $1.6 billion in FY2009, after reaching $1.3 billion in FY2007 and $2.0 billion in FY2008. RMA data also indicate that A&O reimbursement per policy more than doubled from $750 during 2004-2006 to $1,748 in 2008.

Some observers argue that the reimbursement rate should be pegged to something other than premium value, such as a flat fee per policy sold, to better reflect actual costs and to help reduce federal expenditures. If policies are actuarially sound, critics say, the administrative costs of writing and servicing a policy are generally not proportional to the value of the policy (e.g., whether 10 acres or 1,000 acres, or $3 per bushel or $9 per bushel).

The Government Accountability Office (GAO) released a study in April 2009 on costs associated with administering the crop insurance program. [14] GAO concluded that the current structure of A&O reimbursements "present[s] an opportunity to reduce government spending without compromising the crop insurance program's safety net for farmers." The current approach using crop prices, GAO says, has generated a "kind of windfall" for many insurance agencies and agents, as the companies, using funds from increased levels of A&O reimbursements, pay higher commissions to compete for each other's "book of business" and associated underwriting gains.

GAO reported that crop insurance companies have spent a large share of their higher A&O reimbursements on commission payments, partly in an effort to compete for business from other insurance agencies. Since the federal government, through RMA and FCIC, sets policy premiums and determines which products can be offered, insurance companies do not compete on product quality or price. Rather, they can offer independent insurance agents, who sell policies through multiple companies, higher commissions to increase the company's market share. Some argue that increases in agent commissions in recent years amount to "excessive compensation" that is directly attributable to additional subsidies paid to crop insurance companies, and their absence would not have reduced the level of service provided by the industry.[15]

The private crop insurance companies contend that any reductions in the A&O reimbursement will negatively affect the industry and possibly jeopardize the delivery of crop insurance, particularly in high-risk areas. Analysis conducted on behalf of the National Crop Insurance Services, Inc., a not-for-profit organization representing more than 60 crop insurance companies, concluded that, although companies have cut expenses over time through efficiencies, A&O reimbursements have been consistently below actual expenses incurred by private insurers, with a shortfall of 1-2 percentage points in 2008. (Moreover, with crop prices declining from highs in recent years, A&O expense reimbursements declined in FY2009 and are projected to decline again in FY20 10.) The analysis states that the inadequacy of the A&O reimbursements is absorbed through a reduction in company profits.[16] To address the volatile nature of A&O reimbursements and policy premiums resulting from fluctuating crop prices, the crop insurance industry has proposed "smoothing" commodity prices for use in calculating reimbursement expenses.[17]

Underwriting

Similarly, company underwriting gains (the amount by which a company's share of retained premiums exceeds its indemnities) have increased substantially in recent years, as weather has been generally favorable for growing crops. During this period, increases in insured acreage and higher crop prices have also increased gross liability. Liability represents total exposure of the program, meaning that if all participating farmers suffer losses to the full extent of coverage, program indemnities would be the total liability.

To reduce government costs of the program, some have suggested that the new SRA could alter the amount of underwriting gains that companies return to the government.[18] They say that if the government share of gains is increased in exchange for a larger government share of the losses in loss years, average taxpayer costs would decline. The insurance industry contends that the net book quota share provision of the SRA is equivalent to a tax on underwriting income and crowds out private reinsurance. The industry wants to see it eliminated and wants the general underwriting gain and loss provisions to be revised to reduce the potential for unusually large gains or losses. The industry expects this approach to reduce disincentives for insurers to offer insurance in less profitable (high loss) states.

Insurance companies point out that since they do not set rates (RMA does), crop insurers cannot respond to underwriting losses by increasing their rates in subsequent years or limiting coverage as is done in the property and casualty insurance industry. Generally higher policyholder surplus requirements also have implications for the level of required reserves and the amount of retained underwriting gains for insurance companies.

Crop Insurance Availability and Farmer Participation

A major concern for policymakers is maintaining crop insurance availability and farmer participation in the crop insurance program. Crop insurance is an important risk management tool for many of the nation's farmers, and it complements to some extent other federal programs, such as direct and counter-cyclical payments.[19] Policies are offered for major crops in most counties where they are grown, and in 2009, federal crop insurance policies covered 265 million acres.

The crop insurance industry warns that in order to preserve both crop insurance availability and farmer participation, the basic structure of the SRA—for example, the number and operation of the existing reinsurance funds and minimum retention percentages—should remain unchanged. Stability in design is also desired, insurance companies say, so they and their reinsurers will remain interested in participating in the program. In contrast, some say that there is room for cuts without risking declines in company and farmer participation, because reimbursements, when adjusted for inflation, are substantially above levels of the recent past.

In some states, particularly those with small agricultural sectors such as Utah, Wyoming, and several states in the Northeast, relatively few companies offer policies because overhead costs (per policyholder) are relatively high and the opportunity for growth in sales is limited. To improve availability in these states, the crop insurance industry recommends considering a shift of A&O reimbursements toward underserved states and promotion of additional education programs for farmers.

Uncertainties after Completion of SRA Renegotiation

The crop insurance industry contends that several developments not directly related to the SRA could create uncertainties for the industry. One issue is payment timing. In order to score savings in FY20 12, the 2008 farm bill pushed back the date for government payments to companies for A&O reimbursements and pulled forward the date for producers' premium bills, which means that companies may need to secure additional short-term financing during the late summer/early fall period.

Another issue is general demand for crop insurance and the combined effect of lower commodity prices and reduced crop insurance acreage in 2009, which followed strong prices and increased plantings the previous year. The industry points to these declines and prospects for uncertain demand recovery with concern that expense reimbursement is already headed downward, along with reductions mandated in the 2008 farm bill, even without changes in the SRA.

Finally, RMA is currently reviewing its methodology for premium rate determination.[20] The industry is concerned that any change from the current method has the potential to alter the industry's profitability under the new SRA. Without knowing the final outcome of rate determinations, the crop insurance industry is reluctant to embrace changes to the SRA that have the potential to adversely affect their operation and profitability. RMA counters that it strives to ensure that the policies are actuarially sound and in the best interest of the federal crop insurance program.

DEVELOPING THE 2011 SRA

On December 4, 2009, USDA's Risk Management Agency (RMA) released it first draft of the 2011 SRA.[21] It was designed to serve as the starting point for negotiations with the crop insurance companies. Following industry feedback, USDA issued a second draft in mid-February. USDA expects to issue a final draft in April, with interested companies signing the agreement before the 2011 reinsurance year begins on July 1, 2010. The 2011 reinsurance year covers crops with policy closing dates after July 1, 2010 (e.g., 2011-crop corn and soybeans).

USDA's First Draft SRA

USDA's initial draft (December 4, 2009) provided a new method for calculating administrative and operating (A&O) expenses, which RMA expects would save federal money and reduce volatility in the level of reimbursements received by insurance companies. Rather than tying A&O reimbursements to the value of current premiums (and current crop prices), the new method would use 10-year average farm prices (fixed period of 1999-2008) for seven major commodities as published by USDA.[22] According to USDA, the new approach would result in A&O reimbursement levels comparable to those in 2005 and 2006 (i.e., before the major price run-up), which the department contends were adequate for delivering the program.

The draft also made significant changes in the underwriting provisions. First, at the operational level, the number of reinsurance funds under the draft would decline. According to the draft agreement, companies would place policies into either the "residual" fund for riskier policies (as designated by the insurance companies) or the "commercial" fund for less risky policies. The move would eliminate the marginally used developmental fund and three sub-funds in the commercial fund under the 2010 SRA (see "Major Provisions in the Standard Reinsurance Agreement for 2010," above). Importantly, the draft made the residual fund a nationwide fund, in contrast with the current assigned risk fund, which is state-based. By consolidating the highest- risk policies into a single national pool shared by all crop insurance companies, USDA would expect the loss performance to be more stable for the residual fund than for the current assigned risk fund. An individual company's share of the fund would depend on its share of total premiums.

For the commercial fund under the draft agreement, a significant change in the first draft was to group states with similar levels of risk (e.g., low or high frequency of loss).[23] According to USDA, the alignment as well as new risk-sharing provisions—which vary by state group—would increase opportunities for gains by private insurance companies in high-risk states (e.g., Plains states) while decreasing opportunities for gains in low-risk states (e.g., Corn Belt states). Overall, the changes were intended to increase competition in states that historically have been less profitable and are considered "underserved." Also, RMA said that it would assume a greater share of extreme losses (and gains), which would protect insurance companies from potentially catastrophic losses.

The initial draft also changed the "net book quota share"—the portion of overall company gain or loss that the government retains. The new amount proposed was 10%, up from 5% in the current SRA. USDA intends to return some of the additional underwriting gains to companies that reach underserved producers and areas. USDA says it does not need additional authority to reallocate underwriting gains.

According to USDA, the first draft would save $4 billion over five years. The Administration's FY2010 budget proposal, which incorporates USDA's first draft of the SRA as an assumption for baseline projections, claimed savings of $8 billion over 10 years.[24]

Industry Response to USDA's First Draft

In response to USDA's first draft, the crop insurance industry immediately voiced concerns that the initial proposal "is way beyond the ability of most insurance companies to stay in business and will force companies to reduce staff and service to farmers."[25] Subsequently, on January 20, 2010, National Crop Insurance Services, Inc.(NCIS), issued a lengthy written response to USDA's initial proposal.[26] In commenting on the draft proposal, the industry stated a variety of concerns, primarily about proposed changes to A&O reimbursements and the underwriting provisions. NCIS believes that the overall funding reductions implied by the initial draft SRA are excessive and unacceptable to the industry, and that cuts in delivery expenses and underwriting gains would reduce industry returns well below the long-term average. Moreover, the industry said the proposed changes would sharply reduce the ability of insurance companies to serve all producers, particularly those in "underserved states," and result in job loss in the crop insurance industry.

According to the industry, the proposed "fixed" formula for calculating A&O reimbursements does not account for current delivery costs or those incurred under the SRA in the coming years, such as additional computer and data reporting requirements. Aside from the level of A&O cuts, NCIS claims that USDA does not have discretion to negotiate lower A&O rates because the 2008 farm bill "fixed" them. In its formal response, NCIS stated that A&O reimbursements must remain as provided in statute, although the industry indicated elsewhere that they are continuing to work with USDA to arrive at A&O cuts that are acceptable to both parties.

Regarding changes to provisions for underwriting gains and losses, the industry does not want the government to take on additional risk—specifically by RMA taking a larger portion of the gains and losses for the most profitable states [27]—and "crowd out" commercial reinsurance. In addition, the draft proposal, according to the industry, would have only a limited improvement in potential underwriting gains for low-return states. The overall effect of the proposed changes, according to the industry, would be a sharp reduction in potential net underwriting gains by the insurance companies and in incentives to expand in underserved markets, and a potential increase in the cost of reinsurance for crop insurance companies.

In its response, the industry proposed two options for changing the underwriting provisions. Both options retain the current assigned risk fund and provide for a commercial fund with gain/loss share provisions that would differ for each of two state groups (group 1 is Illinois, Indiana, Iowa, Minnesota, and Nebraska; group 2 is all other states). Option A would eliminate quota share and alter both the company share of risk (which would increase for group 1 and decrease for group 2) and the company share of gain (which would be reduced for group 1 and increased for group 2). Option B would increase quota share to 10% and increase (relative to Option A) the company share of gains in both groups, particularly group 2. The industry estimated that both proposals would reduce expected underwriting gains by about $100 million annually.

Another industry concern is "regulatory risk." According to the industry, the proposal mandates items such as data reporting and other activities, yet procedures for them are not thoroughly defined in the draft agreement. The concern is that companies could be subject to severe penalties, including loss of A&O reimbursements and/or reinsurance, if procedures are not followed.

USDA's Second Draft SRA

On February 17, 2010, USDA issued a news release announcing the second draft of the Standard Reinsurance Agreement.[28] USDA said that the second draft, identified with the date of February 23, 2010, contained significant changes that reflected negotiations between RMA and the participating crop insurance companies, particularly with respect to the structure of A&O reimbursements and risk-sharing terms.

Regarding A&O reimbursements, USDA inserted a two-year phase-in period for the proposed changes for using historical crop prices when calculating reimbursement levels. Rather than shifting immediately to the historical prices series, crop prices would be increased by 10 percentage points in the first year of the SRA and by five percentage points in the second year. Also, companies would receive an additional 5% in A&O reimbursements for operations in lower-served and/or higher-risk states. In an attempt to assert some control over agent commissions and to avoid instability in an insurance company's financial prospects, USDA also proposed a "soft cap" on agent commissions equal to no more than 80% of A&O reimbursements. The agreement would, however, allow profit sharing from underwriting gains.

In response to industry concerns that the commercial fund should be streamlined, the risk-sharing provisions in the second draft essentially reduced the number of state groups to only two—one for Corn Belt states and another group for all other states. Also, at the request of the crop insurance companies, the second draft provided more profit/loss sharing for policies in the commercial fund. For the residual fund (containing the highest-risk policies), USDA shifted its proposal from a nationwide, all-company pool to individual company pools so that companies would not be exposed to liability associated with policies sold by other companies. Finally, the net book quota share, which had been set at 10% in USDA's first draft, was set at 7.5%, compared with the current level of 5%. Under the second draft, up to 2.5% of any net book quota share would be distributed to companies operating in underserved states.

Together, these changes, according to USDA, would move the expected rate of return for insurance companies from 12% in the first draft to 14% in the second draft, but still below the historical level of more than 16%.

Budget Implications

USDA estimated that the second draft would reduce federal crop insurance expenditures by $6.9 billion over 10 years, or about 20% less than the savings estimated under the first draft. The initial feedback from the industry was mixed, noting that USDA had listened to the industry "to some extent," but arguing that the cost savings and associated impacts on the industry were still too great.[29]

Some Members of Congress, including the Chairman of the House Committee on Agriculture, remain concerned that any cuts would reduce baseline funding levels for crop insurance, which could have a negative effect on spending for the next farm bill. If concerns about the federal budget deficit lead to a call for reduction in mandatory spending, including funds for agriculture, cuts made administratively by USDA would not count as savings for agriculture spending that the House and Senate Agriculture Committees would need to make. Following precedence for reflecting a portion of budget savings due to "rulemaking" or similar administrative action, some cost savings based on USDA's first draft of the SRA have already been incorporated in the current estimate of baseline spending.

The Congressional Budget Office's (CBO's) baseline budget estimates will serve as the official benchmark for scoring the budgetary impacts of the next farm bill. (CBO's March 2007 baseline was used to score the 2008 farm bill.) CBO's baseline projections typically assume continuation of current farm bill policies under expected economic conditions, as well as ongoing rulemaking and administrative changes. In the most recent CBO baseline (March 2010), spending on crop insurance totals $77.2 billion during FY2011-FY2020.

While CBO's estimates of the SRA impacts can change, it is possible that the final SRA will not appreciably alter baseline spending levels beyond what is already embedded in the current CBO baseline, particularly if the gap between proposed cuts by USDA ($690 million per year in the second draft) and by industry ($100 million) narrows. CBO could revise its estimate of changes to the SRA in its next baseline or in a subsequent baseline that may be used to score the next farm bill.

USDA's "Final" Draft SRA

On June 10, 2010, USDA announced the release of what it calls the final draft agreement.[30] USDA's RMA expects that most companies will sign the agreement and that it will go into effect in July 2010.

To control costs, the final draft places a cap on A&O reimbursements of $1.3 billion per year. The cap is adjusted annually for inflation, reaching $1.37 billion in 2015. The reference price concept proposed in earlier drafts was eliminated, and the A&O reimbursement is to be calculated using market prices as in the current SRA. To ensure company financial solvency and to control what some consider excessive commissions, particularly in the Midwest, the final draft limits a company's expenditures on agent commissions to 80% of the A&O reimbursement in each state. Companies can supplement commissions with profit sharing, but total agent compensation will be limited to 100% of A&O reimbursements. According to USDA, under the current SRA, average commissions are 108% of A&O reimbursements, which reportedly can put companies at financial risk if they encounter significant losses.

Among the proposed changes to underwriting provisions, the final draft is designed to make crop insurance delivery more attractive in higher-risk states. The commercial fund state groupings remain the same as in the second draft, but risk-sharing terms for higher-risk states are altered to provide increased profit potential and reduced share of loss. Also, for the highest-risk policies, USDA has shifted back to an assigned risk fund for each state (and company) so companies can maintain stop-loss protection for major disasters in individual states, as provided under the current SRA. Finally, the net book quota share, which had been set at 10% in USDA's first draft, would be set at 6.5%, compared with the current level of 5%. Under the final draft, 1.5% of any net book quota share would be distributed to companies operating in underserved states.

USDA estimates that the final draft would reduce federal crop insurance expenditures by $6 billion over 10 years, using the Administration's February 2010 baseline.[31] The department states that $4 billion of the savings would be used for deficit reduction and $2 billion for risk management and conservation programs, including expansion of the Pasture, Rangeland, and Forage crop insurance program and a "good experience" discount for producers.

End Notes

[1] The reinsurance year for a crop insurance policy is determined by its sales closing date. For example, a policy for 2010-crop corn is covered under the 2010 standard reinsurance agreement because the sales closing date is March 15, 2010 (in most cases).

[2] U.S. Department of Agriculture, "USDA Releases Final Draft Crop Insurance Agreement," press release, June 10, 2010, http://www.usda.gov/wps/portal/usda/usdahome?contentidonly=true&contentid=2010/06/0316.xml.

[3] Office of Senator Blanche Lincoln, "Lincoln, Chambliss Urge USDA to Revisit Crop Insurance Changes," press release, January 20, 2010. See also Office of U.S. Representative Stephanie Herseth Sandlin, "Herseth Sandlin Works to Ensure Producer Access to Crop Insurance," press release, January 22, 2010.

[4] Jerry Hagstrom, "Peterson Floats Reconciliation for Farm Bill," *CongressDaily*, February 16, 2010, http://www.nationaljournal.com/congressdaily/cop_20100216_5206.php.

[5] Expenditures in a particular fiscal year mainly reflect the expenditures associated with the previous crop year (since fall harvest overlaps with the beginning of the fiscal year).

[6] U.S. Department of Agriculture, Risk Management Agency, *Standard Reinsurance Agreement between the Federal Crop Insurance Corporation and the (Insurance Company Name) (City and State)*, http://www.rma.usda.gov/pubs/ra/ 05sra_final.pdf.

[7] However, companies reportedly steer agents to more profitable business through commissions.

[8] The developmental and commercial funds are further subdivided by insurance product type—catastrophic, buy-up, and revenue. (Retention percentages for each of the sub-categories may differ within a state.) For information on these policies, see CRS Report R40532, *Federal Crop Insurance: Background and Issues*, by Dennis A. Shields.

[9] See table 1 in U.S. Government Accountability Office, *Crop Insurance—Opportunities Exist to Reduce the Costs of Administering the Program*, Washington, DC, April 2009, http://www.gao.govnew.items/d09445.pdf.

[10] CRS Report RL34207, *Crop Insurance and Disaster Assistance in the 2008 Farm Bill*, by Ralph M. Chite and Dennis A. Shields.

[11] U.S. Department of Agriculture, Risk Management Agency, *Amendment No. 1 to the Standard Reinsurance Agreement Effective Beginning with the 2009 Reinsurance Year*, http://www.rma.usda.gov/pubs/ra/ sraarchives/ 09sraamendment1.pdf. Note that, for catastrophic (CAT) policies, the A&O reimbursement rate is zero, but FCIC pays companies an amount equal to 6% of net book premium for CAT polices for loss adjustment expenses. The farm bill also reduced (1) the A&O reimbursement rate to 12% for any plan of insurance that is based on area-wide losses, and (2) the target loss ratio (indemnities paid divided by premiums collected) from 1.075 to 1.00. In states with a gross loss ratio of 120% in any year, the A&O reduction is 1.15%, not the full 2.3%. This is presumably intended to cover additional costs of servicing additional claims in that state.

[12] Milliman, Inc., *Historical Rate of Return Analysis*, August 18, 2009, http://www.rma.usda.gov/pubs/2009/millimanhistoricalrate.pdf (numbers cited in text above reflect revised data reported at http://www.rma.usda.gov/pubs/ 2009/millimanhistoricalratetable8.pdf); and Milliman, Inc., *Rate of Return Update—2008: Reasonable Rate of Return*, Task Order #20692, June 23, 2009, http://www.rma.usda.gov/pubs/2009/millimanreasonablerate.pdf.

[13] Grant Thorton LLP, *Federal Crop Insurance Program Profitability and Effectiveness Analysis*, prepared on behalf of National Crop Insurance Services, Inc., October 2, 2009, http://www.ag-risk.org/NCISPUBS/SpecRPTS/ GrantThornton/Grant_Thornton_Report-2009_FINAL.pdf.

[14] U.S. Government Accountability Office, *Crop Insurance—Opportunities Exist to Reduce the Costs of Administering the Program*, Washington, DC, April 2009, http://www.gao.govnew.items/d09445.pdf.

[15] Bruce A. Babcock, "Examining the Health of the U.S. Crop Insurance Industry," *Iowa Ag Review*, vol. 15, no. 4 (Fall 2009), http://www.card.iastate.edu/iowa_ag_review/fall_09/article1.aspx.

[16] Grant Thorton LLP, *Federal Crop Insurance Program Profitability and Effectiveness Analysis*, prepared on behalf of National Crop Insurance Services, Inc. , October 2, 2009, http://www.ag-risk.org/NCISPUBS/SpecRPTS/ GrantThornton/Grant_Thornton_Report-2009_FINAL.pdf.

[17] National Crop Insurance Services, Inc., *Recommendations for the Standard Reinsurance Agreement*, Overland Park, KS, October 19, 2009, http://www.ag-risk.org/NCISPUBS/SpecRPTS/Recommendations _for _the _Standard _Reinsurance _Agreement.pdf.

[18] Bruce A. Babcock, "Examining the Health of the U.S. Crop Insurance Industry," *Iowa Ag Review*, vol. 15, no. 4 (Fall 2009), http://www.card.iastate.edu/iowa_ag_review/fall_09/article1.aspx.

[19] For details on farm commodity programs, see CRS Report RL34594 , *Farm Commodity Programs in the 2008 Farm Bill*, by Jim Monke.

[20] On November 30, 2009, USDA's Risk Management Agency released a draft of a periodic review of RMA's premium rating methodology. The final report, dated March 15, 2010, "A Comprehensive Review of the RMA APH and COMBO Rating Methodology Final Report," and other studies are available at http://www rma .usda.gov/pubs/.

[21] The first draft and a side-by-side comparison with the 2010 SRA are available at http://www.rma.usda.gov/news/2009/12/sra.html.

[22] The seven commodities are wheat, corn, soybeans, grain sorghum, barley, upland cotton, and rice. Current (not historical) prices would be used to calculate reimbursement rates for all other commodities.

[23] State groups are based on each state's historical underwriting performance, with group 1 having the best performance. The first draft defines state groups as: 1 = Illinois, Indiana, Iowa, Minnesota, and Nebraska; 2 = California; 3 = Kentucky, Ohio, Oregon, Tennessee, Washington, and Wisconsin; 4 = all other states.

[24] Office of Management and Budget, *Budget of the United States Government, Fiscal Year 2011*, Washington, DC, February 1, 2010, p. 48, http://www.whitehouse.gov/omb/budget/fy2011/assets. Subsequently, USDA officials revised their estimate of savings to $8.4 billion over 10 years.

[25] "New Crop Insurance Plan: Less for Companies, More for Underserved," *Agri-Pulse*, December 9, 2009, p. 8.

[26] National Crop Insurance Services, Inc., "Response to the Risk Management Agency's Draft Standard Reinsurance Agreement Issued on December 4, 2009," Overland Park, KS, January 20, 2010, http://www.ag-risk.org/. See also National Crop Insurance Services, "Fundamental Problems Exist with the USDA's Proposed 2011 Standard Reinsurance Agreement," press release, January 20, 2010, http://www.ag-risk.org/PressRel/2010/NCIS01202010.htm. See also comments by Keith Collins on FarmPolicy.com published February 2, 2010.

[27] These states are Illinois, Indiana, Iowa, Minnesota, and Nebraska (called "Group 1" in both USDA's proposal and NCIS's counterproposal).

[28] U.S. Department of Agriculture, "USDA Releases Second Draft of Proposed Crop Insurance Agreements," press release, February17, 2010,http://www.usda.gov/wps/portal/usdahome?contentidonly=true&contentid=2010/02/0064.xml. The second draft and a side-by-side comparison are available at http://www.rma.usda gov/news/2009/12/ sra.html.

[29] Jerry Hagstrom, "USDA Pitches Smaller Cut in Crop Insurance," *CongressDaily*, February 17, 2010, http://www.nationaljournal.com/congressdaily/cop_20100217_1193.php.

[30] The final draft, related documents, and a side-by-side comparison with the 2010 SRA and earlier drafts are available at http://www.rma.usda.gov/news/2009/12/sra.html.

[31] USDA estimates savings at $5.3 billion relative to the 2009 baseline, which was used for cost estimates of earlier SRA drafts.

In: Agriculture Disaster and Crop Insurance: Background... ISBN: 978-1-61761-559-7
Editor: Angela M. Gil

Chapter 6

USDA Crop Disaster Programs: Lessons Learned Can Improve Implementation of New Crop Assistance Program

United States Government Accountability Office

Why GAO Did This Study

The U.S. Department of Agriculture's (USDA) Farm Service Agency (FSA) provides programs to help farmers recover financially from natural disasters. Congress has historically supplemented these programs with ad hoc programs that pay farmers who experienced crop losses. The 2008 farm bill established a program through 2011 to pay farmers who lose crops. To receive these payments, farmers must purchase coverage under federal crop insurance or the Noninsured Crop Disaster Assistance Program, and receive claims payments for losses.

GAO was asked to evaluate (1) how FSA administered the crop disaster programs for losses from 2001 through 2007 and the results of payments under these programs and (2) what lessons FSA can learn from the previous crop disaster programs to manage its new crop disaster program. GAO reviewed statutes, regulations, and guidance; analyzed USDA data; and interviewed USDA officials.

What GAO Recommends

GAO recommends that, among other things, USDA implement procedures to notify FSA county officials at the time of crop insurance claims for disaster-related losses so they can verify loss eligibility. In commenting on a draft of this report, USDA disagreed with some findings as well as the wording of this recommendation and provided technical comments. GAO revised the recommendation and made other changes as appropriate.

What GAO Found

FSA largely used crop insurance data from USDA's Risk Management Agency (RMA) to calculate nearly $7 billion in crop disaster payments under the 2001 through 2007 ad hoc crop disaster programs. FSA made about $395 million in payments under these programs to 8,463 farmers who RMA identified as having received suspicious crop insurance claims payments in those same years. Almost half of crop disaster payments for farmers RMA identified as having suspicious crop insurance claims payments were in five states. RMA provides its annual list of suspicious claims payments to FSA state and county offices and to the insurance company selling the policy to the farmer for appropriate follow-up action. However, GAO previously reported that few suspicious claims payments resulted in a conviction for fraud. As reported, the factors considered when accepting a case for investigation and prosecution include sufficiency of the evidence, complexity of the case, whether the fraudulent activity is part of a pattern or scheme, and workload and resources that would be needed to investigate and prosecute the case.

For 2001 through 2007, GAO could not use FSA's electronic data files to determine whether crop disaster payments complied with a statutory cap because the reliability of these files is undetermined for the purpose of assessing whether a crop disaster payment was in compliance with the cap. However, in using hard copy files to determine compliance with the cap, GAO found that payments to selected farmers were in compliance. Furthermore, FSA officials did not provide systems documentation, such as specifications and business rules on how FSA used data in its systems to calculate crop disaster payments.

FSA's experience with ad hoc crop disaster programs shows that a lag—as much as 4 years—between the occurrence of a disaster-related crop loss and the application for a disaster payment for that loss prevented FSA county officials from verifying the cause of the loss. Under the new program, there will still be a lag before farmers can apply for a payment; in contrast, farmers have to file a crop insurance claim immediately after a loss and be subject to insurance verification. Without more timely eligibility determinations for the new crop disaster program, FSA county officials will be unable to verify that applicants experienced losses due to an eligible cause. In addition, insufficient documentation of the data systems FSA used for calculating and issuing payments under the ad hoc programs makes it difficult to validate the accuracy of those payments. A similar lack of documentation under the new program could hamper FSA officials' efforts to track payments and ensure the payments adhere to statutes, regulations, and FSA guidelines.

Abbreviations

FSA	Farm Service Agency
RMA	Risk Management Agency
USDA	U.S. Department of Agriculture

June 4, 2010

The Honorable Paul Ryan
Ranking Member
Committee on the Budget
House of Representatives

The Honorable Jeff Flake
House of Representatives

The U.S. Department of Agriculture (USDA) provides a safety net of permanently authorized and regularly funded programs, including federally subsidized crop insurance and emergency disaster loans, to help farmers recover financially from natural disasters. Congress has historically supplemented these ongoing programs in an ad hoc manner by providing one-time payments through crop disaster programs that compensate farmers for disaster-related crop losses they sustained. Most recently, under three separate congressionally authorized ad hoc crop disaster programs, USDA provided $7 billion in disaster payments to farmers whose crops were damaged or destroyed by natural disasters from 2001 through 2007.[1,2] The Food, Conservation, and Energy Act of 2008 (the 2008 farm bill) established and funded a $3.8 billion permanent trust fund, and directed the Secretary of Agriculture to make crop disaster assistance payments to eligible producers who suffer crop losses on or before September 30, 2011, under a new program—the Supplemental Revenue Assistance Payments Program. Under this new program, USDA—through its Farm Service Agency (FSA)—began making payments in early 2010 for crop losses incurred in 2008. Crop disaster payments are largely based on data from USDA's Risk Management Agency (RMA), which is responsible for administering the federally subsidized crop insurance program. In addition to crop disaster payments, farmers may also receive federal assistance through crop subsidy programs and the crop insurance program.

You asked us to review USDA's ad hoc crop disaster assistance programs, as well as the new crop disaster program. Accordingly, we determined (1) how FSA administered its three crop disaster programs for crop losses from 2001 through 2007 and the results of payments made under these programs and (2) what lessons FSA can learn from its experience with the previous three crop disaster programs for managing its new crop disaster program.

To determine how FSA administered its crop disaster programs for crop losses from 2001 through 2007 (the period covered by the three programs), we reviewed statutes, regulations, and guidance related to the programs. We also obtained and analyzed electronic data files from FSA to determine how FSA applied statutes, regulations, and guidance in administering the programs. To assess the reliability of the data in these files, we performed electronic testing of the required data elements, reviewed existing information, and interviewed knowledgeable FSA officials about the data and the systems that produced them. We determined that the payment data in the files were sufficiently reliable for the purpose of determining the distribution of crop disaster payments by state, program, and type of recipient. However, the reliability of FSA's electronic data files is undetermined for the purpose of assessing whether a crop disaster payment complied with a statutory cap. In addition, to develop nongeneralizeable examples of farmers receiving disaster payments for crop losses, we first identified the four states with the highest amount of total crop disaster program payments for all three programs: Kansas, North Dakota, South Dakota, and Texas. We also selected North Carolina, another state with high payment levels, to expand the geographic dispersion of our review. We identified the 27 counties comprising the top 20 percent of the crop disaster payments FSA administered in each of those five states. For these 27 counties, we interviewed FSA officials about their experiences administering crop disaster programs. In addition, we reviewed hard copy payment files for 75 selected farmers who received disaster payments from among the 10 percent of farmers receiving the largest payments under all three programs (i.e., 15 farmers from each county that received the largest disaster payments under all three programs in each of these five states).

Because FSA bases its disaster assistance payments largely on RMA data, we also obtained information on crop insurance claims payments from RMA. We interviewed RMA officials and reviewed relevant documentation to assess the reliability of the RMA data and determined the data to be sufficiently reliable for the purposes of our report. To determine what lessons FSA can learn from its experience with past crop disaster programs for managing the new crop disaster program, we reviewed statutes, regulations, and guidance related to the new program. We also interviewed FSA officials responsible for administering crop disaster programs and FSA data experts responsible for developing the crop disaster payment systems. A more detailed description of our scope and methodology is presented in appendix I.

We conducted this performance audit from November 2008 through June 2010, in accordance with generally accepted government auditing standards. Those standards require that we plan and perform the audit to obtain sufficient, appropriate evidence to provide a reasonable basis for our findings and conclusions based on our audit objectives. We believe that the evidence obtained provides a reasonable basis for our findings and conclusions based on our audit objectives.

BACKGROUND

FSA has overall responsibility for administering crop disaster programs, including ensuring that recipients meet eligibility requirements and do not receive payments that exceed program limitations. FSA guidance directs the agency to annually notify every farming operation—whether an individual farmer or an entity, such as a corporation or a partnership—that it must file documents, including a farm operating plan and an acreage report, with its local FSA county office if the operation is seeking farm program payments. These documents record farming information, such as which crops are planted on each field, the farming practices used, and the name of each individual with an interest in the farming operation. FSA uses this information to determine farm program payments, including payments for various agriculture disaster assistance programs.

According to USDA documents, agriculture-related disasters are common: one-half to two-thirds of the counties in the United States have been designated as disaster areas in each of the past several years. As shown in figure 1, many counties received disaster designations for multiple years from 2001 through 2007.

In order for a county to qualify for a USDA secretarial disaster designation, a disaster must have caused a minimum loss of 30 percent of production of at least one crop in the county. The secretarial disaster designation process begins when an eligible disaster event, such as hail or drought, occurs in a county. After monitoring and recording the disaster conditions, local officials, including FSA county officials, contact their governor to request a disaster designation for the county. Next, the governor submits a written disaster designation request to the Secretary of Agriculture. As a result of this request, FSA directs its county officials to complete a damage assessment report to show whether the minimum loss requirement was met. A state emergency board reviews the report, and if the report is approved, it is forwarded to FSA's national headquarters for the Secretary of Agriculture's approval or disapproval of the request. The approved counties are designated as disaster counties.

RMA's Role in Federal Crop Insurance

RMA has overall responsibility for administering the federal crop insurance program, through the Federal Crop Insurance Corporation, and in partnership with private insurance companies that share a percentage of the risk of loss or opportunity for gain associated with each insurance policy written. RMA is also to address program compliance issues, including protecting the program against fraud, waste, and abuse. Under the Agricultural Risk Protection Act of 2000, RMA uses information technologies, such as data mining, to identify anomalous patterns of crop insurance claims payments that are consistent with actions farmers could take to obtain personal benefit through fraud or abuse of the crop insurance program. RMA has identified 45 patterns of crop insurance payments that it defines as anomalous, such as receiving payments while experiencing high frequency of losses or high severity of losses in comparison with surrounding farming operations; using poor farming practices; or exhibiting irregular behavior with insurance agents or adjusters that suggests collusion. RMA's data mining does not identify specific instances of fraud or abuse of the crop insurance program; rather, it identifies anomalous patterns of crop insurance claims payments that are consistent with the potential for fraud and abuse and considers these payments as "suspicious." RMA places farmers who exhibit such patterns on an annual list, after the year in which the crop insurance claims payments are made, to monitor their current or future farming practices. Farmers may be on the list for multiple anomalous patterns in 1 year.

RMA provides its annual list to the appropriate FSA state offices for distribution to FSA county offices, as well as to the insurance company selling the policy to the farmer. Staff in FSA county offices advise the selected farmers that they have been identified for an inspection as a result of data mining and conduct field inspections during the growing season. In conducting these inspections, FSA inspectors are to determine, among other things, the tillage method used; weed control practices; type and amount of fertilizer applied; weather conditions; and how the inspected crop compares with others in the area. As a result of these inspections and other information, RMA reported total cost savings from 2001 through 2007 of $564 million, primarily in the form of estimated claims payments avoided: $140 million in 2005, $27 million in 2006, and $85 million in 2007.

RMA has the authority to impose sanctions against farmers, agents, loss adjusters, and insurance companies that willfully and intentionally provide false or inaccurate information to RMA or to insurance companies. RMA also has the authority to disqualify farmers who have committed a violation not only from the insurance program but also from most other farm programs for up to 5 years. RMA also can refer suspicious crop insurance claims payments to USDA's Office of Inspector General, which can open investigations and, when warranted, refer cases to the Department of Justice for prosecution.

Ad Hoc Crop Disaster Programs, 2001 through 2007

Through supplemental appropriations, Congress authorized three multiyear crop disaster programs for 2001 through 2007. The first program provided financial assistance for crop losses that occurred in crop year 2001 or 2002.[3] The second program provided assistance for losses in 2003 or 2004 or for losses in 2005 that resulted from a hurricane or tropical storm during the 2004 hurricane season. The third program provided assistance for crop losses in 2005, 2006, or 2007. Generally, under each program, crop losses were eligible for crop disaster payments if the losses resulted from any of the following: (1) damaging weather, such as drought, excessive moisture, hail, freeze, tornado, or hurricane; (2) an adverse natural occurrence, such as an earthquake; or (3) a condition related to damaging weather or an adverse natural occurrence such as saltwater intrusion, rationing of irrigation water, disease, or insect infestation.

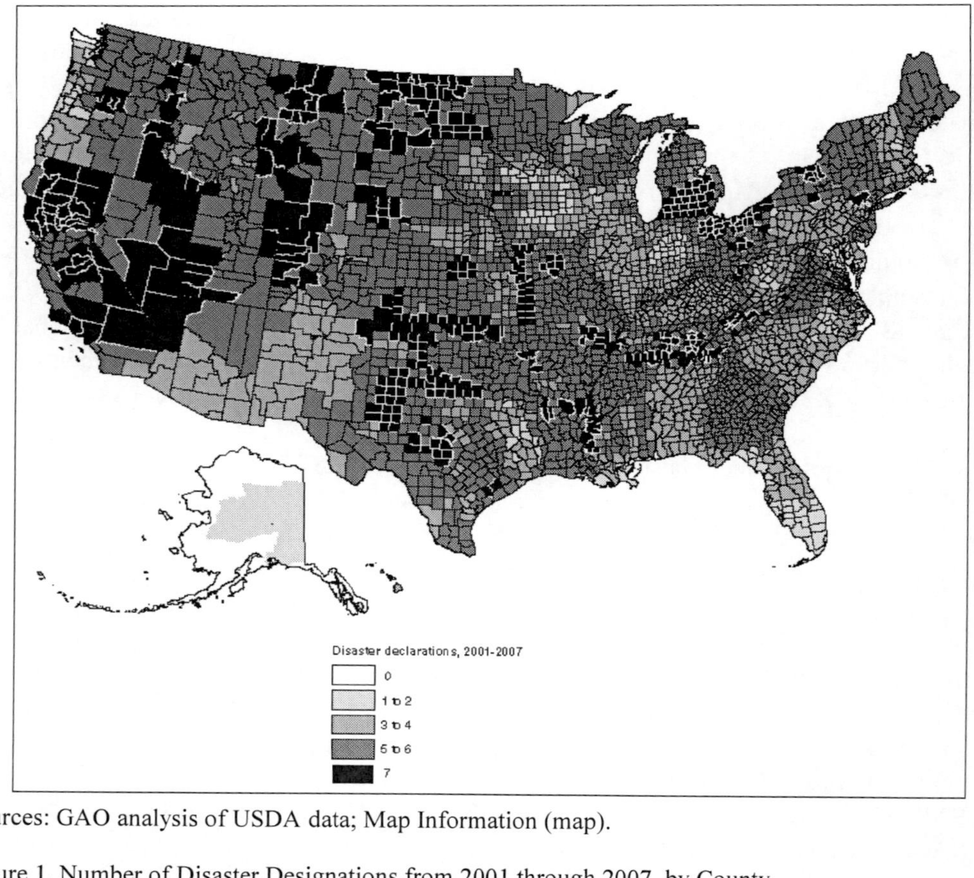

Sources: GAO analysis of USDA data; Map Information (map).

Figure 1. Number of Disaster Designations from 2001 through 2007, by County

The authorizing statutes and program regulations established payment limitations and eligibility requirements for the three crop disaster programs. For example, the statutes prohibited producers—who we refer to as farmers in this report—from receiving a payment for more than 1 year for each of the multiyear disaster programs. In addition, USDA regulations prohibited an individual farmer or member of a farming operation from receiving a crop disaster payment greater than $80,000. Regarding eligibility requirements, the statutes provided that farmers were only eligible to receive crop disaster payments if they had previously obtained federal crop insurance or coverage through FSA's Noninsured Crop Disaster Assistance Program for the crop that suffered weather-related damage.[4] Specifically, for crops covered by the federal crop insurance program (insured crops), farmers must have obtained crop insurance coverage through that program. For crops for which insurance was not available in the county where the crops were farmed (noninsurable crops),[5] farmers must have obtained coverage through the Noninsured Crop Disaster Assistance Program. "Uninsured crops," for the purposes of this report, refers to crops for which coverage was available in the county under either the federal crop insurance program or the Noninsured Crop Disaster Assistance Program, but the farmer did not purchase it. Not all uninsured crops were eligible for payment under the crop disaster programs. Furthermore, a statutory payment cap prohibited USDA from paying an individual or a farming operation for more than 95 percent of what the value of the crop would have been in the absence of the loss (expected value). Specifically, the sum of the disaster payment, the value of the salvageable crops, and any crop insurance payments could not exceed 95 percent of the crop's expected value in the absence of a disaster.

Provisions under the Supplemental Revenue Assistance Payments Program

The 2008 farm bill authorized and funded a new disaster program for losses in crop years 2008 through 2011.[6] This new program provides funds that will be available to assist farmers when disasters occur, without the need for further congressional action. While the past crop disaster programs separately considered each individual field,[7] the new disaster program considers aggregate losses on an entire farming operation, which includes all land in all counties where a farmer planted or intended to plant crops for harvest. To be eligible under the new program, a farming operation must

- be located in or contiguous to counties that received a USDA secretarial disaster designation and have lost at least 10 percent of production on at least one crop of economic significance;[8] or
- incur eligible total crop losses of greater than 50 percent of the normal production, including a loss of at least 10 percent of production on at least one crop of economic significance.

Furthermore, farmers must have purchased either federal crop insurance coverage or be covered under the Noninsured Crop Disaster Assistance Program for all crops of economic significance on their farming operation in order to qualify for a disaster payment. In addition, the 2008 farm bill prohibits any individual or member of a farming operation from receiving more than $100,000 per year in combined payments from the new crop disaster program and other disaster programs for livestock and specialty crops. See appendix II for additional information on the Supplemental Revenue Assistance Payments Program.

Concerns about Potential Waste and Abuse in Federal Farm Programs Have Been Raised in the Past

USDA's Office of Inspector General identified problems under the past crop disaster programs. For example, in 2006, the Office of Inspector General reported reviewing three FSA county offices, one of which issued $103,065 in crop disaster payments to farmers who did not meet program eligibility requirements under the 2001 through 2002 crop disaster program.[9] The Office of Inspector General found that in that county office, FSA relied on verbal statements from some farmers to determine their eligibility for crop disaster program payments. The Office of Inspector General also found weaknesses in FSA's management controls for the crop disaster programs in all three FSA county offices in its review. For example, the Office of Inspector General found that the three FSA county offices were not following the program guidance for verifying the accuracy of crop disaster payments—which states that FSA county offices are to perform three types of reviews to ensure the accuracy of payments—nor consistently interpreting or using data from RMA's crop insurance program when calculating crop disaster payments. The Office of Inspector General recommended that FSA improve its training of county office employees.

In addition, we and others have long raised concerns about the potential for waste and abuse in the federal crop insurance program. For example, in 2005, we reported that while RMA strengthened procedures for preventing questionable crop insurance claims, the federal crop insurance program remains vulnerable to abuse.[10] We recommended that RMA inform FSA's inspectors on the details of claims that they are to investigate, including the type of suspected fraudulent behavior. RMA concurred with this recommendation and in 2006 took actions to implement it. Specifically, RMA now provides detailed information to FSA's inspectors on the nature of each suspicious claim.

In 2008, we also identified strengthening the integrity and efficiency of federal farm programs, including the crop insurance program, as a major cost-saving opportunity for Congress and the administration.[11] More recently, USDA's Office of Inspector General reported that RMA needs to strengthen its quality assurance and compliance activities under the federal crop insurance program to ensure compliance with program requirements.[12]

FSA Largely Based Crop Disaster Payments on RMA Data, Resulting in about $395 Million to Farmers RMA Identified as Having Received Suspicious Crop Insurance Payments

FSA largely used RMA crop insurance payment data to calculate nearly $7 billion in crop disaster payments under the three crop disaster programs from 2001 through 2007. Of these crop disaster payments, about $395 million (almost 6 percent) were issued by FSA to individuals or entities that RMA had identified as having received suspicious crop insurance claims payments from 2001 through 2007.

FSA Relied Largely on RMA Data to Calculate Crop Disaster Payments

Under the three crop disaster programs from 2001 through 2007, FSA calculated and issued crop disaster payments largely based on crop insurance data from RMA for these years, but also information on farm operating plans and production records from the farmers requesting payment. According to the program guidelines, each FSA county office received information from RMA that listed all individuals and entities who had purchased insurance on a crop in that county. For the insured crops, the disaster payment system used RMA data to prefill information on the damaged crops, including the crop name, amount of damaged acres, and value of any salvageable crops. For noninsurable crops and uninsured crops, FSA employees used the farm operating plans and production records to manually enter data into the system. Using the prefilled RMA data or the manually entered data, the system in each county office calculated an estimated crop disaster payment for each applicant. Specifically, the system

- determined the amount of the lost or damaged crops on each of the payment applicant's fields;
- multiplied the amount of the lost or damaged crops on each field by a payment rate—determined by whether the damaged crops were insured, noninsurable, or uninsured—to calculate the maximum payment for each field;
- compared this maximum payment for each field with the statutory percentage cap to ensure that the payment complied with this cap; and
- combined all payments for each field and compared this maximum allowable crop disaster payment with the $80,000 payment limit to ensure payments complied with this limitation.

Once the FSA county office system determined the estimated maximum allowable payment, the system transmitted the payment information to FSA's Application Development Center. According to staff at this center, systems at the center then verified the payment amount by performing a series of checks that ensured the payment did not exceed the statutory payment cap and complied with applicable eligibility requirements and payment limitations. If errors were found in the payment calculation or if the payment did not comply with applicable eligibility requirements or payment limitations, FSA Application Development Center staff said that the payment amount was adjusted accordingly before FSA issued the final payment.

Table 1 shows the number of recipients and the amount of payments for each of the three programs.

We found that FSA data about the farming structure of the 2001 through 2007 crop disaster program payment recipients shows that the majority of recipients were individuals. According to our analysis, individuals received a total of about $4.9 billion in payments while entities received about $2.1 billion under the three crop disaster programs. See appendix III for additional information on the distribution of payments under the 2001 through 2007 crop disaster programs.

Crop Disaster Programs Resulted in Payments to Farmers RMA Identified as Having Received Suspicious Crop Insurance Payments

Of the nearly $7 billion in payments made under the 2001 through 2007 crop disaster assistance programs, we found that FSA made about $395 million in crop disaster payments to farmers or entities that were identified by RMA's data mining as having received suspicious crop insurance claims payments during that same period of time. In addition, our review of hard copy files found that payments to 75 farmers in the five selected states we reviewed complied with the statutory cap of 95 percent of the expected crop value.

FSA Paid About $395 Million to Farmers under the 2001 through 2007 Crop Disaster Programs Largely on the Basis of Crop Insurance Payments RMA Had Identified as Suspicious

For crop losses from 2001 through 2007, FSA made about $395 million in crop disaster payments to 8,463 individuals and entities that RMA identified, through data mining, as having received payments for suspicious crop insurance claims during the same time period. However, in a 2005 report, we found that few suspicious claims payments resulted in a conviction for fraud.[13] We reported that while the number of USDA Office of Inspector General referrals to the Department of Justice on suspicious crop insurance claims payments had increased, the Department of Justice declined more cases than it had accepted since 2000. According to Department of Justice officials, the factors considered when accepting a case include sufficiency of the evidence, complexity of the case, whether the fraudulent activity is part of a pattern or scheme, and workload and resources that would be needed to investigate and prosecute the case.[14] We also reported that insurance agents and company officials we contacted believed that RMA needs to more aggressively penalize those who abuse the program. Table 2 shows the five states with the largest dollar amounts of crop disaster payments for recipients listed as having suspicious crop insurance claims payments from 2001 through 2007. These five states represent about 47 percent of the crop disaster payments to farmers that RMA identified as receiving suspicious crop insurance payments from 2001 through 2007.

Table 1. Recipients and Payments for 2001 through 2007 Crop Disaster Programs, by Program

Crop disaster program	Number of recipients	Payments
2001-2002 program	381,029	$2,563,838,885
2003-2005 program	329,997	2,446,167,967
2005-2007 program	300,341	1,938,383,603
Total	[a]	**$6,948,390,455**

Source: GAO analysis of FSA data.

[a] The number of recipients is not additive because some individuals and entities may have received payments in multiple programs.

Table 2. Crop Disaster Payments to Recipients Identified by RMA as Receiving Payments for Suspicious Crop Insurance Claims in Top Five States, 2001 through 2007

State	Number of recipients	Payments	Percent of payments
Texas	1,222	$66,758,006	16.9
North Dakota	963	46,578,801	11.8
South Dakota	487	30,216,141	7.6
Kansas	424	21,075,987	5.3
North Carolina	378	20,990,788	5.3
Subtotal	**3,474**	**185,619,724**	**46.9**
Remaining 45 states	4,989	209,861,716	53.1
Total	**8,463**	**$395,481,440**	**100.0**

Source: GAO analysis of FSA and RMA data.

Note: The payments in this table represent the crop disaster program payments for 2001 through 2007 that FSA made to recipients RMA identified as receiving suspicious crop insurance claims payments for the crop years covered by the crop disaster program under which they received payments.

By comparing RMA's crop insurance data on suspicious payments with FSA's crop disaster payments, we identified payments made under the crop disaster programs to farmers RMA identified as having received suspicious crop insurance payments. The following are examples of farmers who received crop disaster payments from 2001 through 2007 and were identified by RMA as receiving suspicious crop insurance claims payments:

- In South Dakota, a farmer received almost $900,000 in crop disaster payments that were based on suspicious crop insurance claims payments. RMA put this farmer's operation on its annual list because the farmer received crop insurance payments while exhibiting such anomalous patterns as (1) having at least 2 consecutive years of crop insurance claims larger than those of similar farmers in the area and (2) frequently filing prevented planting claims when compared with similar farmers in the area.[15]
- A North Carolina farmer received about $720,000 in crop disaster payments that were based on suspicious crop insurance claims payments. RMA put this farmer's operation on its annual list because the farmer received crop insurance payments while exhibiting such anomalous patterns as (1) having unusually large yields on some land while experiencing severe losses on other land for the same crop during the same year and (2) filing insurance claims for 2 consecutive years that were significantly larger claims than those filed by similar farmers in the area.
- One farmer who operated farms in Kansas received over $635,000 in crop disaster payments that were based on suspicious crop insurance claims payments. RMA put this farmer's operation on its annual list because the farmer received crop insurance payments while exhibiting such anomalous patterns as (1) having a loss ratio 150 percent greater than other farmers within the area and (2) experiencing abnormally large crop insurance claims in comparison with similar farming operations in the county and repeating this behavior for multiple years.

Similarly, the FSA county officials we interviewed identified some farmers in their counties who received crop disaster payments that the FSA county officials believed were based on suspicious crop insurance claims payments. These FSA county officials told us that they were familiar with the farmers in their county and could identify those who may have received suspicious crop insurance payments, but because the county officials received the crop insurance claim information several years after the crop losses occurred, they could not verify the farmers' crop losses and relied on RMA data to issue the crop disaster payments. The FSA county officials provided the following as examples:

- One farmer in North Dakota received over $85,000 in disaster payments under the 2001 through 2007 crop disaster programs, claiming that disaster conditions caused losses to his crops. According to an FSA county official, the farmer's crop losses were likely due to poor farming practices because this farmer did not fertilize his crops.
- A farmer in North Carolina received almost $160,000 in disaster payments from 2001 through 2007, including about $60,000 for tobacco that he claimed was damaged or could not be harvested. According to an FSA county official, although this farmer received crop insurance payments, he did not have the required barn space to dry and cure the total amount of tobacco planted and had not obtained contracts necessary to sell the tobacco crop. The county official added that area farmers informed the FSA county office that this farmer experienced crop losses as a result of poor farming practices.

In commenting on crop disaster payments that they believed were based on suspicious crop insurance claims payments, some FSA county officials stated that they did not challenge or deny the applications for these crop disaster payments because they expected the applicants would appeal any challenge to USDA's National Appeals Division.[16] These officials added that in their past experience with appeals, USDA rarely upheld FSA county office decisions to deny payments. One official said that USDA generally approved appeals related to crop disaster applications unless the FSA county office produced evidence that the payment applicant did not meet program eligibility requirements. The official added that he did not collect such evidence because, at the time of the crop loss, he did not anticipate that a disaster program would provide assistance for those crop losses. However, according to our analysis of data from USDA's National Appeals Division, FSA was more likely to be favored in an appeal related to the 2001 through 2007 crop disaster programs than were the farmers. We found the National Appeals Division upheld FSA's denial of crop disaster payment applications for about 72 percent of the appeals, and the division overturned FSA's denial, deciding that the farmer should have received a crop disaster payment, for the remaining 28 percent.[17]

Although Weaknesses Exist in FSA's Data Systems, Hard Copy Files Show That Payments Complied with the Statutory Cap

Under the crop disaster programs from 2001 through 2007, a statutory payment cap allowed FSA to provide a farmer up to 95 percent of the expected value of the crop in the absence of a disaster. We found certain weaknesses in FSA's data systems, which precluded us from determining whether FSA's electronic data files are reliable for the purpose of assessing whether a crop disaster payment complied with this statutory cap. For example, FSA's data systems (1) could not be reliably merged using program year, tax identification number, tax identification number type, FSA state code, and FSA county code to determine whether payments complied with the statutory cap and (2) were not sufficiently documented. However, we assessed hard copy payment files for 75 selected farmers in the five states and found that the payments made to these farmers complied with the statutory payment cap.

We found that FSA could not provide documentation on how its systems captured and processed data in order to calculate disaster payments for crop losses from 2001 through 2007. Specifically, FSA officials could not provide us with business rules, system specifications, or processing algorithms associated with the payment calculations executed at FSA's Application Development Center in Kansas City, Missouri. Such documentation is important because it typically translates policies and procedures into specific, unambiguous rules that govern how data are entered, validated, stored, processed, and reported. As such, the documentation facilitates accurate and consistent implementation of policies and procedures. Although FSA officials provided copies of program guidance and described actions FSA has taken to ensure the quality of the data it generates, they could not provide sufficient documentation for us to verify the agency's stated actions. For example, FSA could not provide design specifications about the functional requirements of the data systems it used to capture information about disaster payments for crop losses from 2001 through 2007. Detailed design specifications are important because they are used for developing thorough test plans, maintaining the system, and ensuring that risks associated with building and operating the system are adequately controlled. Furthermore, FSA's documentation of the crop disaster program data systems does not meet Office of Management and Budget documentation guidelines.[18] These guidelines require federal agencies, among other things, to identify and document business rules; information relationships; and the functional requirements, capabilities, and interconnections of the computer systems. FSA officials could not provide documentation describing how its systems operated.

Table 3. Percentage of Expected Value Received by 75 Selected Farmers on Fields with Crop Losses, 2001 through 2007 Crop Disaster Programs

Percent of expected value	Number of fields
95	328
90-94	228
80-89	489
70-79	520
60-69	373
50-59	171
40-49	89
30-39	47
20-29	14
10-19	4
>0-9	0
Total	**2,263**

Source: GAO analysis of FSA data.

Also, for the purpose of assessing whether crop disaster payments complied with the statutory cap, we performed a detailed review of hard copy crop disaster payment files for 75 selected farmers who received payments under all three crop disaster programs from the five counties receiving the largest amount of crop disaster payments in each of five selected states. According to our analysis, these 75 selected farmers received payments that complied with the 95 percent statutory percentage cap on all of their 2,263 fields that sustained crop losses from 2001 through 2007. Overall, as shown in table 3, 328 of these fields qualified for a disaster payment that allowed the farmers to receive 95 percent of the expected value of their crops for these fields.

We also found that the total payment received by the 75 selected farmers for the three programs varied from $61,592 to $2,256,386. According to our analysis of the hard copy files, 24 percent of the fields we reviewed qualified for payments because disaster conditions prevented farmers from harvesting any crops from the fields; 69 percent because disaster conditions reduced the amount of crops produced on the fields; and 7 percent because disasters prevented farmers from planting crops on the fields.

Forty-nine of the 75 selected farmers received payments for at least one field they were unable to harvest. Furthermore, although not exceeding the 95 percent cap, the crop disaster programs provided 37 of these 49 farmers—who grew crops such as corn, cotton, soybeans, and wheat—90 percent or more of the expected value of the crops. However, these farmers did not incur harvesting costs for these fields. Based on our review of two academic studies,[19] about 15 percent of the cost of producing such crops can be associated with harvesting the crops. Thus, although these 37 farmers may have incurred about 85 percent of the cost of producing these crops, crop disaster program payments allowed these farmers to receive 90 percent or more of the expected value of the crops, even though FSA offices reduced farmers' crop disaster payments by a certain percentage—known as the "unharvested" payment factor—to reflect the fact that the farmers had not harvested these crops.

FSA Can Learn Lessons for the New Crop Disaster Program from Three Prior Programs

FSA's experience with ad hoc crop disaster programs provides lessons that could benefit the agency's implementation of the new program. First, under the past programs, FSA county officials could not verify the cause of a crop loss because of the lag—as much as 4 years—between the occurrence of a disaster-related crop loss and the application for a disaster payment for that loss. Under the new program, FSA officials will still face a lag time, and without more timely eligibility determinations, FSA county officials will be unable to verify that applicants experienced losses due to an eligible cause. Second, the lack of documentation in FSA's data systems for calculating and issuing payments under the ad hoc programs makes it difficult to validate the accuracy of those payments. A similar lack of documentation under the new program could hamper FSA officials' efforts to track payments and ensure the payments adhere to statutes, regulations, and FSA guidelines.

Lack of Timely Eligibility Determinations Provides Lessons for New Crop Disaster Program

Under the ad hoc crop disaster programs from 2001 through 2007, USDA regulations and program guidance specified disaster conditions—such as hail, drought, or excessive rainfall—that qualified as eligible causes of crop loss. As such, FSA county officials reviewed each payment application to determine whether the crop loss was eligible for payment. However, because the programs were enacted on an ad hoc basis after the disaster-related crop losses, these application reviews took place as many as 4 years after the losses occurred. With such a lag, we found that FSA county officials could not take actions, such as conducting field inspections, to validate whether the crops suffered damage as a result of a qualifying disaster condition. Instead, the FSA county officials relied on information farmers supplied on their disaster payment applications and information from RMA, such as crop insurance payment records, to determine if an eligible disaster condition caused a farmer's crop losses. Fourteen of the 27 FSA county officials we spoke with identified the absence of making timely cause of loss eligibility determinations as a concern under the 2001 through 2007 crop disaster programs, and many of these county officials said that having the opportunity to determine the eligibility of losses soon after the disaster would increase assurance that crop disaster program payments are proper. This opportunity could exist under the new Supplemental Revenue Assistance Payments Program.

Determining the cause of crop losses for each farmer will remain critically important under the Supplemental Revenue Assistance Payments Program because a farming operation must have lost at least 10 percent of production on at least one crop of economic significance as a result of an eligible disaster condition to qualify for a payment. Under the program, FSA county officials are to determine crop loss eligibility at least 1 year after crop losses occur because, under the new program guidelines, FSA officials are to make this determination using annual market prices for each crop to calculate payments, which are generally established at the end of the crop year. As a result, crop disaster payment applicants can submit their applications several months after their crop loss occurs, and FSA officials will continue to depend on information from farmers and RMA crop insurance data to determine whether applicants experienced crop losses due to an eligible disaster condition. For example, a farmer who planted corn in the spring of 2010 would not harvest that crop until fall. Therefore, if a disaster destroyed the corn during the summer, the farmer may wait until the fall of 2011—after the crop year for corn ended and when FSA could determine the market prices needed to calculate a payment and process a claim—before filing a loss claim. Without more timely eligibility determinations, FSA county officials will not have the opportunity to verify that payment applicants experienced crop losses due to an eligible disaster condition. Because farmers know that, under the new program, FSA cannot make determinations until the annual market prices for each crop are available to calculate payments, there is no incentive to file crop disaster claims when a crop loss occurs.

In contrast, under the federal crop insurance program, if farmers incur crop losses and file a claim with their insurance agent or company, the company assigns an adjuster who visits the farm at the time of the disaster-related loss and, using RMA guidance, determines the percentage of loss for the acres planted. The adjuster forwards the claim to the insurance company, which verifies and recalculates the claim. If all company and RMA requirements are met, the company pays the claim to the farmer.[20] According to RMA guidance, a farmer may destroy any of the damaged crops or replant a new crop after the insurance adjuster has inspected the farmer's crop loss and provided written consent that the farmer may take such actions. However, we have previously raised concerns of fraud and abuse of the crop insurance program's claims adjustment process. For example, in 2005,[21] we reported that crop insurance fraud cases, investigated by USDA's Office of Inspector General and resulting in criminal prosecutions between June 2003 and April 2005, show how farmers, sometimes in collusion with insurance agents and others, falsely claim prevented planting, weather damage, and low production. In addition, we found that several of these cases demonstrated the importance of having FSA and RMA work together to identify and share information on questionable farming practices and activities. Under the Supplemental Revenue Assistance Payments Program, as under the 2001 through 2007 crop disaster programs, FSA county officials receive information about crop losses at the time the farmer submits an application for payment. As a result, FSA officials may become aware of crop losses after the claims adjustment process and after farmers have planted a new crop on their fields that suffered disaster-related damage. Without notification of the crop losses closer to the time of the disaster, FSA county officials will not have the opportunity to verify the eligibility of crop losses.

Weaknesses in Data Systems Provide Lessons for New Crop Disaster Program

Under past crop disaster programs, FSA's automated payment system used information in multiple data systems to calculate and issue payments. However, we identified limitations in this payment system that prevented us from making a determination about the reliability of FSA's data files for the purpose of assessing the extent to which payments for the 2001 through 2007 crop disaster programs complied with the statutory payment cap that limited payments to no more than 95 percent of the expected value of the crop in the absence of a disaster. These limitations included a lack of sufficient documentation and our determination that FSA's data systems could not be reliably merged using program year, tax identification number, tax identification number type, FSA state code, and FSA county code for this purpose. For additional information, see appendix I.

We and others have previously reported on concerns with FSA's information technology systems. As we reported in 2008, FSA's information technology systems, which date to the 1980s, do not fully meet the agency's business needs or readily share data.[22] In August 2009, USDA's Office of Inspector General reported that integration of USDA's information management systems, including FSA and RMA systems, could improve the integrity of farm programs, such as the new crop disaster program.[23]

In the context of these information technology issues, in early 2010, FSA began issuing payments for the new crop disaster program using an interim payment system that has weaknesses. According to FSA documents, because of the significant amount of data required to calculate payments under the new crop disaster program, FSA does not expect to complete the development of a fully automated payment system that will allow the agency to issue timely payments to farmers who sustained crop losses in 2008. As a result, FSA developed an interim payment system that requires FSA county office staff to use a manual process to complete applications and calculate payments for 2008 crop losses, storing each application in a single spreadsheet maintained in FSA county offices. FSA staff at each county office manually enter applicant data into this spreadsheet to calculate applicants' payments, and an independent official verifies the accuracy of the data entry. According to program guidelines, once the payment calculations are complete, the FSA county office staff are to record the payment amounts in a Web-based system that automatically issues the payments. FSA officials said that once the agency fully develops the automated payment system, it plans to validate and make any necessary adjustments to the payments calculated and issued using the interim payment system. However, according to the FSA officials responsible for implementing the new crop disaster program, the agency did not develop a mechanism to link the final payment amounts in the Web-based system to the application data in the spreadsheets maintained in each FSA county office. Therefore, if USDA or an independent entity sought to audit the payments under the new crop disaster program to ensure they are proper, the auditor would have to manually review the files in each of about 2,300 FSA county offices. Also, the program and the auditors would not have the benefit of electronic edit checks to ensure the accuracy of payments.

Furthermore, according to FSA officials, the agency is still in early development stages of the final automated payment system and has not developed documentation of the data systems or written business rules that describe how the final automated system will calculate and issue payments. However, according to FSA officials responsible for developing the final payment system for the Supplemental Revenue Assistance Payments Program, FSA plans to issue the necessary documentation, including design specifications and functional requirements, and perform system testing. As of March 2010, FSA officials were uncertain when this documentation would be issued.

CONCLUSIONS

FSA helps the nation's farmers recover financially from natural disasters. For the three former ad hoc crop disaster programs, owing to the time between when a disaster occurred and applications for disaster payments were filed, FSA officials did not have the opportunity to verify whether an eligible disaster condition caused farmers' crop losses. Instead, FSA officials relied largely on information from farmers and RMA to determine the cause of crop losses. The Supplemental Revenue Assistance Payments Program provides an opportunity to eliminate this problem. Under this program, however, FSA county officials will not receive information about crop losses until the time the farmer submits an application for payment, which may occur after farmers have planted a new crop on their fields that suffered disaster-related damage. Without notification of the crop losses closer to the time of the disaster, FSA county officials will not have an opportunity to make timely loss eligibility determinations. Such determinations would reduce reliance on crop insurance information and the potential for disaster payments for suspicious crop losses.

Because of limitations in FSA's data systems, including insufficient systems documentation and the inability to reliably merge files from these systems using program year, tax identification number, tax identification number type, FSA state code, and FSA county code, the reliability of FSA's electronic data files for the purpose of assessing whether payments under the past crop disaster programs complied with relevant statutes and regulations is undetermined. Many of the limitations in FSA's data systems will most likely continue under the new crop disaster program because FSA county office staff are using a manual process to enter application data into spreadsheets and payment data into a Web-based system, and FSA does not plan to develop a mechanism to electronically link the final payments to the supporting spreadsheets. Without such a mechanism to link the Web-based system and the spreadsheets FSA uses to calculate and issue payments under the new crop disaster program in an integrated way, it will be difficult for USDA or audit organizations to evaluate the new program and to ensure that payments are properly made.

Recommendations for Executive Action

We are making the following three recommendations to the Secretary of Agriculture:

To better ensure that payments under the Supplemental Revenue Assistance Payments Program compensate farmers who experienced eligible crop losses, we recommend that the Secretary of Agriculture implement procedures so that FSA county officials are notified at the time of crop insurance claims for disaster-related losses so those officials have an opportunity to verify that crop disaster payment applicants experienced losses because of an eligible cause.

To ensure that crop disaster payments under the Supplemental Revenue Assistance Payments Program can be assessed as to whether they comply with relevant statutes and regulations, we recommend that the Secretary of Agriculture direct the Administrator of the Farm Service Agency to

- develop and maintain data system documentation, including written business rules, of the interim payment system and the final automated payment system that are used to calculate and issue crop disaster payments; and
- develop and implement a mechanism to link Web-based payments to the application data in the spreadsheets maintained in the FSA county offices that would result in an integrated interim payment system.

Appendix I. Objectives, Scope, and Methodology

Our objectives were to determine (1) how the U.S. Department of Agriculture's (USDA) Farm Service Agency (FSA) administered its crop disaster programs for losses from 2001 through 2007 and the results of payments under these programs and (2) what lessons FSA can learn from its experience with the previous crop disaster programs for managing its new crop disaster program.

Objective 1

To determine how FSA administered its crop disaster programs for crop losses from 2001 through 2007, we reviewed statutes, regulations, and guidance, such as the *FSA Handbook on the Crop Disaster Program, 5-DAP (Revision 2)*, as well as relevant studies prepared by the USDA's Office of Inspector General and the Congressional Research Service and our own past reports. In addition, we spoke with relevant USDA officials in headquarters and in FSA's Application Development Center in Kansas City, Missouri.

Because FSA bases its disaster assistance payments largely on USDA's Risk Management Agency (RMA) data, we also obtained information on suspicious crop insurance claims payments identified by RMA, which is responsible for administering the crop insurance program, and the Center for Agribusiness Excellence, which is an independent organization that conducts data mining on crop insurance and farm program data. Specifically, RMA uses data mining to identify patterns in crop insurance claims payments that are consistent with the potential for fraud and abuse. For example, these patterns include

- farmers, agents, and adjusters linked in irregular behavior that suggests collusion;
- farmers who for several consecutive years received most of their crop insurance payments from prevented planting claims;
- farmers who appear to have claimed the production amounts for multiple fields as only one field's yield, thereby creating an artificial loss on their other fields; and
- farmers who, in comparison with their peers, have excessive harvested losses over many years.

We compared RMA information with FSA records of crop disaster payments to identify payments to farmers that RMA identified as receiving suspicious crop insurance claims payments from 2001 through 2007.

Specifically, we identified crop disaster payments made to farmers who RMA identified as receiving suspicious crop insurance payments for at least 1 year of the crop disaster program under which the farmer received a disaster payment. We interviewed agency officials and reviewed relevant documentation to assess the reliability of the RMA data and determined the data to be sufficiently reliable for the purposes of our report.

We also obtained and analyzed data files from FSA to determine how FSA applied legal requirements and policy directives articulated in the statutes, regulations, and guidance in administering the programs. Specifically, we obtained the following data files:

- Producer Payment Reporting System file, which contains summary information on farm program payments made to individuals and entities;
- crop disaster program payment history file, which contains information on the dollar amount of crop disaster program payments;
- crop disaster program crop loss application file, which contains information from the applications that farmers submit when applying for crop disaster program payments;
- crop disaster program crop prices file, which contains the crop prices used to calculate payments under the crop disaster programs;

- USDA National Agricultural Statistics Service crop prices file, which contains crop prices used to calculate payments under multiple federal farm programs; and
- permitted entity file, which contains information on individuals and entities receiving farm program payments.

  We used these data to determine the distribution of crop disaster program payments to recipients. To assess the reliability of these data, we
- obtained and reviewed the available documentation about the data elements in the data files;
- performed electronic testing on the data elements that we used;
- reconciled the two sources of crop disaster program payment data—Producer Payment Reporting System and crop disaster program payment history records—by matching common data elements including FSA state code, FSA county code, and tax identification number;
- worked with FSA Application Development Center staff to determine how to merge all of the data files because FSA did not have written business rules or overall system documentation;
- discussed our results from merging these data files with officials in FSA's Production, Emergency, and Compliance Division and in FSA's Application Development Center, which administers and oversees the crop disaster program payments; and
- compared the results of merging all data files to FSA county office hard copy payment records that contain the calculations for the statutory payment cap.

We also attempted to use FSA's data files to determine if any payments exceeded the statutory payment cap of no more than 95 percent of the crop's expected value in the absence of a disaster. More specifically, the sum of the disaster payment, the value of the salvageable crops, and any crop insurance payments cannot exceed 95 percent of the crop's expected value. In attempting to determine whether payments exceeded the statutory cap of 95 percent of the crop's expected value in the absence of a disaster, we merged the crop disaster program crop loss records and crop disaster program payment history records. We found that the crop disaster payment crop loss application records could not be reliably merged with the crop disaster program payment history records using the following data elements—program year, tax identification number, tax identification number type, FSA state code, and FSA county code. We also found discrepancies between the data that resulted from merging the data files and the hard copy payment records that we obtained for selected farmers. Specifically, we found discrepancies in some of the data elements—insurance payments and expected values of production from the crop disaster program crop loss application records, as well as crop prices that FSA uses to calculate the statutory payment cap. A potential complex alternative method for using FSA's data systems to compare crop disaster payments to statutory payment caps might have permitted a comparison of estimated disaster payments with statutory payment caps. Even if this alternative method were viable, additional research would have been necessary to reach a different conclusion about the reliability of FSA's data systems for the purpose of determining the extent to which actual disaster payments met statutory payment caps. This additional research would have required data reliability assessments of additional specific data elements, an examination of the differences between estimated and actual disaster payments at the detail and summary levels, and validating calculated fields not saved or recorded by FSA. We did not fully pursue this alternative method owing to insufficient documentation of FSA's data systems and a consideration of the large amount of time and effort it would have required. Therefore, the reliability of FSA's electronic data files for the purpose of assessing whether a crop disaster payment complied with a statutory cap is undetermined.

In summary, (1) the payment data from the reconciled crop disaster program payment data—Producer Payment Reporting System and crop disaster program payment history records—were sufficiently reliable for determining the distribution of crop disaster payments by state, program, and type of recipient and (2) the reliability of FSA's electronic data files for the purpose of assessing whether payments under the past crop disaster programs complied with relevant statutes and regulations is undetermined.

In addition, we identified the four states with the highest dollar amount of total crop disaster program payments: Kansas, North Dakota, South Dakota, and Texas. We also selected North Carolina, another state with high payment levels, to expand geographic dispersion. We identified the 27 counties representing the top 20 percent of the crop disaster payments FSA administered in each of those five states. We interviewed FSA officials in each of these 27 counties about their experiences administering crop disaster programs. Within each of these 27 counties, we identified the farmers representing the top 10 percent of total crop disaster payments and randomly selected 15 of these farmers in each county that received disaster payments under all three programs, and we collected their payment records from the FSA county office that administered their payments. Although these farmers were selected randomly from the top 27 counties in these five states, because this selection does not constitute a probability sample of farmers receiving crop disaster payments, it is not generalizable to a larger population.

Because we could not reliably merge the data files to determine whether payments complied with the statutory payment cap, we reviewed the hard copy payment records for 75 farmers. To select these 75 farmers, we identified the county administering the largest dollar amount of disaster payments within each of our five selected states and analyzed the payment records we collected for 15 farmers in each of these five counties to determine the total payments each of the 75 farmers received through crop insurance payments, sales of salvageable crops, and crop disaster payments. We then compared this total with the farmer's expected value of production in the absence of a disaster to arrive at the total value as a percent of expected production. We analyzed field-level disaster payment data for these selected farmers. A field, in this report, refers to the lowest, detailed level at which a crop loss is defined and includes RMA- and FSA-defined crop characteristics such as the crop price, farming practices, insurance coverage, and planting period for units and subunits that describe contractual relationships or different crop yields associated with the acreage or producer share. For example, a field might be a farmer's 20 acres (not necessarily contiguous) devoted to a corn crop—but it would only be classified as a "field" if that farmer filed a claim and received a disaster payment for that specific corn crop.

Objective 2

To determine what lessons FSA can learn from its experience with past crop disaster programs for managing the new crop disaster program, we reviewed relevant statutes, regulations, and guidance, including the *FSA Handbook on the Supplemental Revenue Assistance Payments Program, SURE-1*. We also interviewed FSA officials from the agency's Production, Emergency, and Compliance Division; FSA's Application Development Center in Kansas City, Missouri; and the counties in the five states we examined. We asked these officials to identify challenges, if any, they faced in administering past programs and spoke with them about their plans for administering the new program. We analyzed this information to determine how FSA could use lessons learned to manage the new program.

We conducted this performance audit from November 2008 through June 2010, in accordance with generally accepted government auditing standards. Those standards require that we plan and perform the audit to obtain sufficient, appropriate evidence to provide a reasonable basis for our findings and conclusions based on our audit objectives. We believe that the evidence obtained provides a reasonable basis for our findings and conclusions based on our audit objectives.

APPENDIX II. SUPPLEMENTAL REVENUE ASSISTANCE PAYMENTS PROGRAM

The Food, Conservation, and Energy Act of 2008 (the 2008 farm bill) created the Supplemental Revenue Assistance Payments Program to assist farmers for crop losses incurred on or before September 30, 2011. Under the program, USDA provides crop disaster payments based on a farmer's revenue from all crops in all counties. That is, the program considers the impact of a disaster on a farmer's entire operation, including revenue losses from crops that sustained damage, as well as revenue gains from crops that were successfully grown and harvested. In general, if the farmer's revenue is less than a guaranteed level of revenue, which is based on the farmer's production history, the farmer receives a payment. In contrast, if the farmer's revenue is equal to or greater than the guaranteed level of revenue (i.e., revenue losses are offset by revenue gains) the farmer does not receive a payment.

Eligibility Requirements and Payment Limitations

To be eligible under the new program, a farming operation must be located in or contiguous to counties that received a USDA secretarial disaster designation (see figure 2 for the counties that met this requirement in 2008), and have lost at least 10 percent of production on at least one crop of economic significance.[24] Eligible disaster conditions include damaging weather, weather-related disease, and weather-related insect infestation. Alternatively, a farming operation must incur eligible total crop losses of greater than 50 percent of the normal production, including a loss of at least 10 percent of production on at least one crop of economic significance.

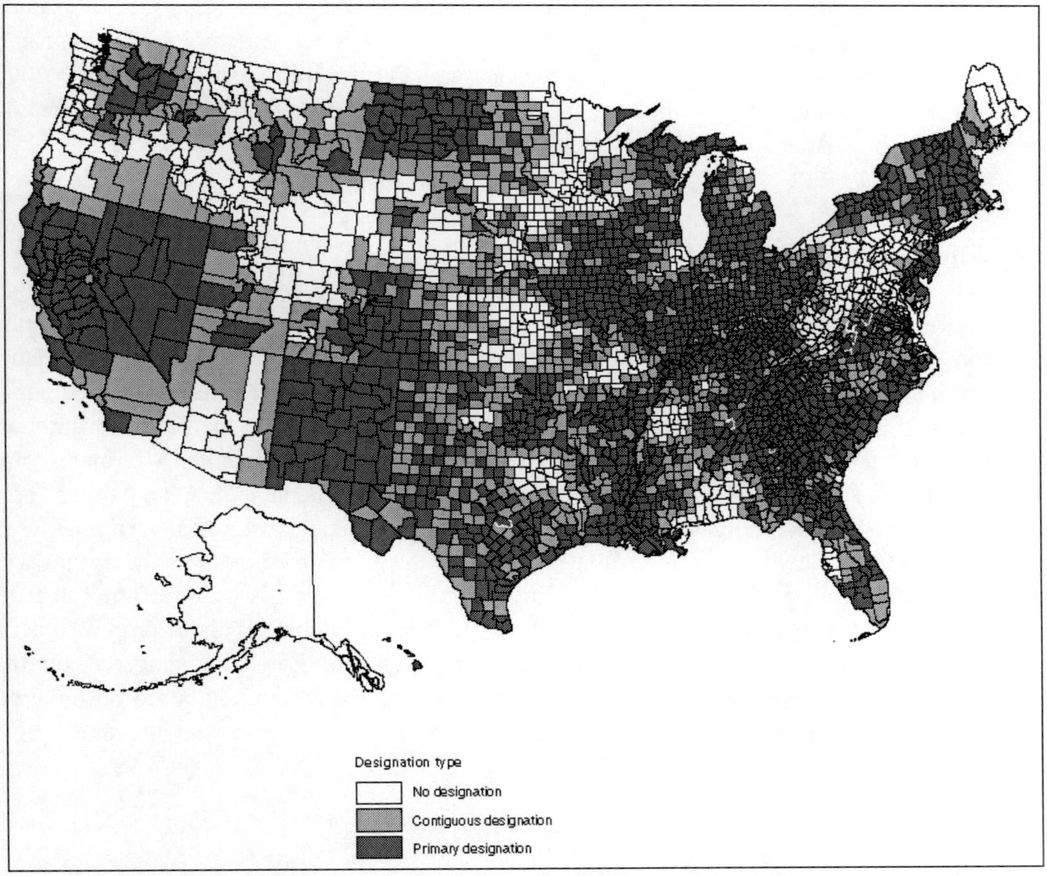

Sources: GAO analysis of USDA data; Map Information (map).

Figure 2. USDA Secretarial Disaster Designations for 2008, by County

Furthermore, farmers must have purchased either federal crop insurance coverage or be covered under the Noninsured Crop Disaster Assistance Program for all crops of economic significance on their farming operation in order to qualify for a disaster payment. The Supplemental Revenue Assistance Payments Program considers revenue losses or gains from crops that are eligible for coverage through crop insurance or the Noninsured Crop Disaster Assistance Program. However, an amendment to the 2008 farm bill extended the date by which the federal crop insurance program and the Noninsured Crop Disaster Assistance Program required farmers to purchase coverage for their 2009 crops to be eligible for payment. Also, the Supplemental Revenue Assistance Payments Program includes an income eligibility requirement that prohibits any individual or a farming operation with an average adjusted gross income that exceeds $2.5 million, over the previous 3 tax years immediately preceding the applicable crop year, from receiving program payments, unless 75 percent or more of their income is from farming. For 2009 and subsequent crop years, individuals and entities with an average adjusted gross income of $500,000 or more, excluding income from farming, are not eligible to receive payments.

In addition, there are two basic payment limitations under the Supplemental Revenue Assistance Payments Program. First, the 2008 farm bill prohibits any person from receiving more than $100,000 in combined payments from the Supplemental Revenue Assistance Payments Program; the Livestock Forage Program; the Livestock Indemnity Program; and Emergency Assistance for Livestock, Honeybees, and Farm-raised Fish. Second, the 2008 farm bill limits payments by prohibiting a farmer's guaranteed revenue level from exceeding 90 percent of the farmer's expected revenue in the absence of a disaster.

Payment Calculation

USDA calculates payments under the Supplemental Revenue Assistance Payments Program by comparing a farmer's total revenue with the farmer's guaranteed level of revenue. If the farmer's total revenue is less than the guaranteed level of revenue, the payment is equal to 60 percent of the difference between the two. In order to calculate the payment amount, USDA must determine the total revenue and the guaranteed level of revenue. A farmer's total revenue includes the actual value of all crops, crop insurance payments, and other farm program payments, including other disaster payments and some farm subsidy payments. A farmer's guaranteed level of revenue equals the sum of the guaranteed revenue the farmer will receive from each crop. For insured crops, the guaranteed revenue is based on the level of crop insurance coverage the farmer purchased for each crop. Higher levels of crop insurance coverage result in higher guaranteed revenue for that crop. For crops covered by the Noninsured Crop Disaster Assistance Program, the guaranteed revenue is based on the crop price, the number of acres the farmer planted or intended to plant, and the amount of harvested crops.

Special Provisions for 2008 Payments

The American Recovery and Reinvestment Act of 2009 expanded eligibility and increased the benefits farmers could receive for the 2008 crop year. The act created an extension of the date by which farmers must have purchased crop insurance coverage or coverage through the Noninsured Crop Disaster Assistance Program for their 2008 crops to be eligible for payment. Regarding increased benefits, the statute allowed farmers to receive potentially larger payments by altering the method for calculating a farmer's guaranteed revenue.

Appendix III. Selected Information on Distribution of 2001 through 2007 Crop Disaster Program Payments

FSA administered a total of $6.9 billion in payments for the three crop disaster programs from 2001 through 2007. The state receiving the largest dollar amount in payments under the three programs was Texas, which received a total of $867.5 million in crop disaster payments under the 2001 through 2007 programs. Table 4 shows the dollar amount of crop disaster payments that states received under each of the three programs and as a combined total for all three programs from 2001 through 2007.

Table 4. Crop Disaster Program Payments for 2001 through 2007, by State

State	2001-2002 program	2003-2005 program	2005-2007 program	Total
Texas	$310,405,053	$283,002,363	$274,141,304	**$867,548,720**
North Dakota	228,194,676	290,486,210	177,649,567	**696,330,453**
Kansas	225,650,813	195,782,810	169,357,163	**590,790,786**
South Dakota	215,822,272	156,250,855	176,213,853	**548,286,980**
Nebraska	169,204,178	104,174,004	53,824,443	**327,202,625**
Minnesota	83,927,610	142,593,584	99,530,035	**326,051,229**
Colorado	103,080,100	95,343,964	56,627,499	**255,051,563**
North Carolina	77,893,857	76,962,245	85,418,178	**240,274,280**
Georgia	80,977,637	75,417,739	74,927,314	**231,322,690**
California	60,454,530	79,464,918	61,254,939	**201,174,387**
Montana	90,622,087	68,775,072	40,260,580	**199,657,739**
Oklahoma	63,016,075	35,203,089	82,805,472	**181,024,636**
Iowa	47,060,748	82,526,995	32,257,278	**161,845,021**
Wisconsin	33,195,463	84,220,977	42,851,238	**160,267,678**
Missouri	45,996,079	58,345,102	44,416,459	**148,757,640**
Ohio	73,597,267	37,957,270	21,092,656	**132,647,193**
Michigan	61,666,602	44,377,925	25,487,765	**131,532,292**
Illinois	44,872,563	41,950,176	37,028,516	**123,851,255**
Florida	47,127,857	42,946,938	30,304,659	**120,379,454**
Indiana	41,137,104	38,528,136	20,007,651	**99,672,891**
Idaho	34,037,278	50,533,014	11,937,763	**96,508,055**
Washington	34,011,192	42,403,015	15,041,983	**91,456,190**
Mississippi	39,571,669	17,509,226	25,503,700	**82,584,595**
South Carolina	36,985,971	21,594,238	23,762,775	**82,342,984**
Alabama	27,338,196	20,684,316	33,214,332	**81,236,844**
Arkansas	27,072,564	20,965,310	24,564,548	**72,602,422**
Louisiana	36,530,697	22,604,777	11,793,312	**70,928,786**
Tennessee	11,800,552	17,929,741	39,560,820	**69,291,113**
New York	25,709,582	30,028,720	13,035,764	**68,774,066**
Kentucky	11,462,659	15,806,469	33,100,340	**60,369,468**
Pennsylvania	31,865,771	13,641,250	12,488,804	**57,995,825**
Virginia	21,079,878	14,716,189	22,153,092	**57,949,159**
Oregon	23,285,671	14,646,815	8,904,272	**46,836,758**
Wyoming	12,532,123	16,346,080	7,123,421	**36,001,624**
Maryland	14,450,410	7,573,288	13,469,150	**35,492,848**
New Mexico	11,301,600	16,561,748	5,595,315	**33,458,663**
Utah	13,367,311	9,784,309	3,516,302	**26,667,922**
New Jersey	7,046,761	5,822,770	4,600,040	**17,469,571**
Maine	2,142,602	11,564,866	1,883,451	**15,590,919**
Massachusetts	5,177,016	5,358,485	4,825,335	**15,360,836**
Puerto Rico	5,651,715	8,282,014	1,258,089	**15,191,818**
Vermont	8,178,614	6,346,072	611,637	**15,136,323**
Arizona	5,746,541	5,706,784	1,976,987	**13,430,312**
Delaware	3,950,004	2,564,679	6,146,483	**12,661,166**

Table 4. (Continued)

State	2001-2002 program	2003-2005 program	2005-2007 program	Total
Nevada	4,244,861	3,826,882	1,578,496	**9,650,239**
Connecticut	1,839,161	4,238,166	2,888,210	**8,965,537**
West Virginia	827,993	1,678,058	1,071,123	**3,577,174**
New Hampshire	1,214,449	615,909	451,162	**2,281,520**
Guam	725,399	636,152	82,771	**1,444,322**
Hawaii	209,323	697,300	356,092	**1,262,715**
Rhode Island	348,815	316,556	380,939	**1,046,310**
Alaska	174,585	387,808	19,177	**581,570**
Northern Mariana Islands	55,351	196,626	21,156	**273,133**
American Samoa	0	248,756	0	**248,756**
Virgin Islands	0	41,207	10,193	51,400
Total	**$2,563,838,885**	**$2,446,167,967**	**$1,938,383,603**	**$6,948,390,455**

Source: GAO analysis of FSA data.

Table 5. Number of Recipients and Total Payments for the 2001 through 2007 Crop Disaster Programs, by Payment Size

Payment size	Recipients		Total payments		
	Number	Percent	Total	Percent	Average
$1-500	74,496	12.8	$18,863,685	0.3	$253
501-1,000	60,031	10.3	44,256,980	0.6	737
1,001-2,000	80,129	13.8	116,915,493	1.7	1,459
2,001-3,000	52,125	9.0	128,797,558	1.9	2,471
3,001-4,000	37,687	6.5	130,953,339	1.9	3,475
4,001-5,000	28,886	5.0	129,459,526	1.9	4,482
5,001-7,500	50,853	8.8	313,033,620	4.5	6,156
7,501-10,000	33,665	5.8	292,018,904	4.2	8,674
10,001-15,000	42,857	7.4	526,351,065	7.6	12,282
15,001-20,000	26,678	4.6	462,330,171	6.7	17,330
20,001-25,000	18,493	3.2	413,913,203	6.0	22,382
25,001-50,000	43,079	7.4	1,507,598,878	21.7	34,996
50,001-100,000	22,927	4.0	1,584,613,935	22.8	69,116
100,001-500,000	8,362	1.4	1,235,599,099	17.8	147,764
500,001-1,000,000	50	0.0	32,893,115	0.5	657,862
1,000,001-5,000,000	8	0.0	10,791,884	0.2	1,348,986
Total/average	**580,326**	**100.0**	**$6,948,390,455**	**100.0**	**$11,973**

Source: GAO analysis of FSA data.

More recipients of 2001 through 2007 crop disaster program payments (80,129 recipients) received a total of $1,001 to $2,000 under the three programs combined than any other payment level. In addition, the recipients of total crop disaster payments from 2001 through 2007 that were larger than $1 million received an average payment of $1.3 million. Table 5 shows the number of recipients and their total payments under the 2001 through 2007 crop disaster programs, distributed by total payment size.

Table 6. Payments and Number of Recipients of 2001 through 2007 Crop Disaster Program Payments, by Type of Recipient

Crop disaster program	Individuals		Entities		Total	
	Number of recipients	Payments	Number of recipients	Payments	Number of recipients	Payments
2001-2002 program	324,169	$1,835,356,576	56,860	$728,482,309	381,029	$2,563,838,885
2003-2005 program	276,189	1,712,160,806	53,808	$734,007,161	329,997	2,446,167,967
2005-2007 program	247,995	1,327,490,815	52,346	$610,892,788	300,341	1,938,383,603
Total	[a]	**$4,875,008,197**	[a]	**$2,073,382,258**	[a]	**$6,948,390,455**

Source: GAO analysis of FSA data.

[a]The number of recipients is not additive since some individuals and entities may have received payments under multiple programs.

Finally, when reviewing the farming structure of the 2001 through 2007 crop disaster program payment recipients, we found that the majority of recipients were individuals. Individuals received a total of about $4.9 billion in payments, while entities received about $2 billion under the crop disaster programs from 2001 through 2007. Table 6 shows the number of recipients and the payments they received under each crop disaster program and for all three programs combined, distributed by type of recipient.

APPENDIX IV. COMMENTS FROM THE U.S. DEPARTMENT OF AGRICULTURE

Note: GAO comments supplementing those in the report text appear at the end of this appendix. Page numbers in draft report may differ from those in this report.

See comment 1.
See comment 2.
See comment 2.

USDA

United States Department of Agriculture

Farm and Foreign Agricultural Services

Farm Service Agency

Operations Review and Analysis Staff

1400 Independence Ave. SW
Stop 0540
Washington, DC
20250-0501

TO: Lisa Shames
Director
Natural Resources and Environment
Government Accountability Office

MAY 1 8 2010

FROM: James W. Miller
Under Secretary
Farm and Foreign Agricultural Services

SUBJECT: Government Accountability Office (GAO) Draft Report Entitled, "USDA CROP DISASTER PROGRAMS: Lessons Learned Can Improve Implementation of New Crop Assistance Program", GA0-10-548

GAO conducted an audit to assess the effectiveness of Farm Service Agency's (FSA) program delivery of three multiyear crop disaster programs operated from 2001 through 2007, and to identify lessons learned that could improve the implementation of the new Supplemental Revenue Assistance Payments (SURE) Program, authorized under the 2008 Farm Bill. FSA is providing the following comments that specifically address where FSA does not agree with GAO's finding as identified below.

The "Highlights" page of the draft report incorrectly states that FSA officials did not provide systems documentation such as specifications and business rules on how FSA used data in its systems to calculate crop disaster payments. FSA made available and provided to GAO for review, all requirements specifications, handbook documentation, and other system documentation utilized in the delivery of the crop disaster programs contained in the draft report.

Page 7 of the draft report references that eligible causes of loss under the disaster programs were eligible for crop disaster payments if the losses resulted from any of the following: (1) damaging weather, such as drought, excessive moisture, hail, freeze, tornado, or hurricane; (2) and adverse natural occurrence, such as earthquake; or (3) a condition related to damaging weather or an adverse natural occurrence, such as excessive wind, excessive heat, saltwater intrusion, rationing of irrigation water, disease, or insect infestation. FSA considers excessive wind and excessive heat as an adverse weather condition and not as a related weather condition.

Page 8 of the draft report incorrectly references Risk Management Agency (RMA) as the agency who uses the term "uninsured crops". This reference should be removed. The wording of sentence should reflect that crops, crop types, intended uses, and practices for which Federal crop insurance or Noninsured Crop Disaster Assistance Program (NAP)

See comment 3.
See comment 4.
See comment 5.
See comment 6.
See comment 5.
See comment 6.

was not purchased, were not eligible for payment under the crop disaster program implemented for crop losses in 2005, 2006, or 2007.

FSA does not agree with GAO's conclusion on pages 12 and 13 of the draft report that FSA made questionable crop disaster payments to farmers identified by RMA as having received suspicious crop insurance payments. Specifically, GAO's conclusion questions $395 million that FSA paid to farmers under the 2001 through 2007 crop disaster programs because RMA identified the crop insurance payments to those farmers as possibly suspicious. On pages 5 and 6 of the draft report, it is pointed out that RMA has identified 45 patterns of crop insurance payments that RMA defines as anomalous, such as receiving crop insurance payments while experiencing high frequency of losses in comparison with surrounding farming operations; using poor farming practices; or exhibiting irregular behavior with insurance agents or adjusters that suggest collusion. RMA's data mining does not identify specific instances of fraud or abuse of the crop insurance program; rather it identifies anomalous patterns of crop insurance claim payments that are consistent with the potential for fraud and abuse and considers these payments as "suspicious". RMA places farmers who exhibit such patterns on an annual list, after the year in which crop insurance claims payments are made, to monitor their current or future farming practices. RMA provides its annual list to FSA, and FSA notifies the selected farmers that crop inspections will be conducted. The draft report does not provide information on FSA's use of the suspicious payment report and that FSA conducts a minimum of 2 documented field inspections with representative digital photographs that have an embedded date and time with GPS points, and that the inspections are required within 30 calendar days after the final planting date and before harvest becomes general in the area. If producers listed on the report have not filed an acreage report with FSA, the producers are requested to identify the location of the planted crops being reviewed to ensure that inspections can begin to document such items as tillage methods, weed control, application of fertilizer, and how the crop compares with similar crops in the general area. In addition, the draft report does not address that FSA was not authorized to disapprove crop disaster program applications solely because a farmer was identified on RMA's suspicious payment report. The draft report does not provide information on the number of incorrect payments or the dollar amount of incorrect payments because the producer was determined to have acted fraudulently. The draft report does not include the process utilized by FSA for review and approval of crop disaster program applications, or the process for collection of payments that were determined to be in error. Further, during previous discussions with GAO on the three examples provided on pages 14 and 15 of the draft report, FSA recommended that GAO determine whether or not any of the three producers listed received crop insurance payments that were incorrect or based on fraudulent claims. The draft report does not provide additional information on any action by RMA to obtain refunds of indemnities.

Page 17 of the draft report discussed the lack of documentation on how FSA's automated systems captured and processed data to calculate disaster payments for crop losses. FSA

See comment 1.
See comment 7.
See comment 7.
See comment 7.

made available and provided to GAO for review, all requirements specifications, handbook documentation, and other system documentation utilized in the delivery of the crop disaster programs contained in the draft report. This collaboration was intended to assist GAO in its understanding of the business rules and the computations required for determination of program benefits. In addition, FSA staff participated in teleconferences and exchanged emails to assist GAO, and FSA is willing to again make these documents available to GAO.

Also on page 17 of the draft report, GAO states that FSA's data systems could not be reliably merged. FSA worked with GAO to explain the automated processes and the tracking of data in the automated systems. During a meeting held in Kansas City, GAO was focused on how to recalculate the "Estimated Calculated Payment Report" according to the 5-DAP (Rev. 2) handbook and compare that amount to the Producer Payment Reporting System (PPRS). FSA provided supporting documentation and verified the production files needed to support this effort. Prior to the meeting held in Kansas City, GAO visited the Wharton County, Texas office and had the Estimated Calculated Payment reports that GAO wanted to recreate by using the live data provided by FSA. GAO raised a concern that the payment history data could be different than what was in the PPRS. The primary focus for GAO was to tie the PPRS payment back to the Crop Disaster files (field, unit, crop, acres indemnity payment, harvested amount and the expected yield). Payment history records are rolled up to the producer level when sent to the National Payment Service (NPS) and subsequently PPRS. Many units and crops may be tied to the actual payment amount. The actual payment amount is calculated based on the payment grouping which includes: unit, state/county location, crop, crop type, planting period, practice and insured type. There can be multiple groupings calculated and included in a payment to a producer.

Further confusion was encountered by GAO when trying to interpret the internal indicators and values in the files to determine if the calculation was for single or multiple market crops; yield based crops; value loss crops; quality adjustments, or whether the 95% Cap reductions applied to the pay crop. FSA agrees the internal coding of the data files used to determine these conditions was difficult to understand.

GAO created a SAS data set of the payment history to try and reconcile the Calculated Estimated Payment amount to PPRS. There was confusion around how eligibility conditions that can occur prior to sending the record to NPS can change the payment amounts recorded in PPRS. Eligibility conditions include reductions for permitted entity share, AGI share, ineligibility, payment limitations, and combined producers. Data files used to support this evaluation could have changed between the time of issuing a payment and when the files were sent to GAO for their review.

Page 19 of the draft report identifies concerns surrounding a farmer's inability to harvest crops and the fact that 37 farmers received 90 percent or more of the expected value of

See comment 8.
See comment 9.
See comment 10.
See comment 2.

the crops however they only incurred 85 percent of the cost of producing these crops due to not incurring harvest expenses, and implies that FSA paid for costs not incurred by the farmer. As required by statute, FSA did apply an unharvested payment factor for the specific crop acreage that was either prevented from planting or that was not harvested, and this factor did reduce the disaster benefit to the farmer.

Page 24 of the draft report references that FSA will validate 2008 Supplemental Revenue Assistance Payments (SURE) Program payments after FSA fully develops an automated payment system. For 2008, FSA does not have the resources to develop an automated payment system for SURE. FSA does plan to use an interim process developed using RMA data and a workbook application to validate 2008 SURE payments.

In addressing the first GAO recommendations on pages 25 and 26, the FSA Administrator does not exercise administrative control over filing crop insurance claims so that notification could be provided to FSA county officials. The RMA Administrator would be the responsible party to alert FSA when crop insurance claims are filed. In addition, RMA is responsible for verifying the validity of crop insurance claims.

On page 37 of Appendix II of the draft report, FSA would like to clarify that the guarantee for the Noninsured Crop Disaster Assistance Program is similar to the crop insurance calculation. Similar to the crop insurance calculation, the NAP calculation for guaranteed revenue is based on the acres planted or intended to be planted, the adjusted NAP approved yield, the catastrophic level of coverage offered under NAP with an increase in price coverage from 55 percent to 100 percent, and the crop price.

Thank you for the opportunity to provide comments on the subject draft report.

The following are GAO's comments on the U.S. Department of Agriculture's letter, dated May 18, 2010.

GAO's Comments

1. We appreciate FSA officials' cooperation in discussing the agency's data systems with us. In April 2009, we visited USDA's Application Development Center in Kansas City, Missouri; interviewed officials responsible for each program file; and requested documentation for all files used in determining payments under each of the crop disaster programs. Specifically, in order to understand how FSA's data systems operate, we requested 10 items: (1) descriptions of all data elements, (2) code values for each variable, (3) key required to join the files, (4) system documentation required to use the data field both within and between files, (5) business rules, (6) tables showing the relationships between the various files, (7) data descriptions, (8) state and county codes, (9) information on how each file is related to the other files, and (10) process flow charts that should provide system details. FSA provided the first three items requested but not the remaining seven. Instead, FSA referred us to handbooks for each of the crop disaster programs, but these handbooks are standard operating procedures for county office staff to implement each program and do not take the place of systems documentation. As late as March 5, 2010, we asked FSA officials about systems specifications and user requirements for the ad hoc crop

disaster programs and the Supplemental Revenue Assistance Payments Program. These officials stated that they may not have provided these documents, but even if they had, the documents for the ad hoc disaster assistance programs would not be usable for our purposes since they were not official, and the documents for Supplemental Revenue Assistance Payments Program are in the initial phases of development. Under these circumstances, we stand by our statement that FSA officials could not provide systems documentation, such as specifications and business rules on how FSA used data in its systems to calculate crop disaster payments.

2. We made these technical changes as appropriate.
3. We recognize that FSA received claims for disaster-related crop losses, and the funds to pay for these losses, years after these crop losses occurred. We modified the text to be consistent with our characterization of FSA payments in the rest of the report.
4. We revised this report to note that FSA inspects fields for practices in addition to those we discussed in a draft of this report.
5. We do not question FSA's approval of crop disaster payments. Instead, we recommend that FSA county officials be notified at the time of crop insurance claims for these losses so these officials have an opportunity to verify that crop disaster payment applicants experienced losses because of an eligible cause. In general, we did not seek to validate individual applications for crop disaster payments.
6. In this report, we focused on FSA's crop disaster payments and not on RMA's crop insurance claims payments. FSA bases its crop disaster payments primarily on RMA's crop insurance data. As we noted in this report, we found that about 6 percent of FSA's crop disaster payments went to farmers who were identified by RMA's data mining as having received suspicious crop insurance claims payments during that same period. We did not follow up on whether farmers had acted fraudulently or whether RMA took any actions to obtain refunds of crop insurance claims payments because these issues were not the focus of this report.
7. We acknowledge that the data systems for the ad hoc crop disaster programs are complex and include numerous data files. Nonetheless, reconciling the information in farmers' disaster applications and their payments was important in addressing part of our first objective: how FSA administered its three ad hoc crop disaster programs for crop losses from 2001 through 2007. To this end, in February 2009, we met with FSA Wharton County, Texas, officials to understand how, within a county office, the estimated disaster payments were calculated. In April 2009, we visited USDA's Application Development Center to discuss the files we needed, and how the files should be linked to determine how the actual payments were calculated. At that time, center officials explained that the system—files and their linkages—was not well documented. On several occasions, we requested information on the formulas and variables used to recreate the actual payments, but center officials did not respond to our requests. Because center officials could not provide us with documentation for business rules and file specifications (see response to comment 1), we asked these officials if we could use specific variables—tax identification number, tax identification type, FSA state code, and FSA county code—maintained in the history file to determine whether payments complied with the statutory cap that payments not exceed 95 percent of the crop's expected value in the absence of the disaster.

These officials noted that this approach should provide the information we needed. From July 2009 through December 2009, we found discrepancies in this approach and contacted center officials to gain additional clarification on this approach. In each case, center officials continued to confirm that this approach seemed reasonable. In October 2009, we provided center officials with a list of farmers whose payments appeared to exceed the statutory cap, resulting in overpayments, but FSA did not provide comments. In December 2009, we provided FSA headquarters officials with a more refined list of farmers who appeared to have been paid in excess of the statutory cap. FSA headquarters officials responded that they would investigate the farmers on this list. In December 2009, these officials examined the apparent overpayments, found that the payments were made correctly, and informed us that the originally agreed upon approach would not provide us with accurate calculations. Because we had already invested significant time and resources on the approach FSA had told us represented a reasonable approach, and because we still lacked adequate documentation of the system, we used hard copy payment files for 75 selected farmers in five states to determine if these farmers' payments complied with the statutory payment cap. For these 75 farmers, we found that the payments complied with the cap.

As USDA observes, the system, and its internal coding, used to calculate payments (and determine compliance with the payment cap) is very difficult to understand. Although these systems are difficult to understand, delays in and lack of responses to our questions further complicated our analyses. We also agree with USDA that eligibility conditions that are not well documented are very difficult to discern. Finally, although we requested that all files cover the same time periods, FSA did not provide us with consistent files.

8. We revised this report to reflect the use of the unharvested payment factor. As we note, however, even with the use of this factor, farmers may still have received payments that exceeded their costs of producing these crops.
9. In response to USDA's comment that FSA has limited resources for developing the automated payment system for 2008, we revised this report to more clearly acknowledge that FSA verifies the data entries. Furthermore, as we state in this report, FSA officials said that once the agency fully develops the automated payment system, it plans to validate and make any necessary adjustments to the payments it calculates and issues using the interim payment system.
10. We revised this report to recommend that the Secretary of Agriculture implement procedures so that FSA county officials have timely notice of crop insurance claims for disaster-related losses.

Related GAO Products

Crop Insurance: Opportunities Exist to Reduce the Costs of Administering the Program. GAO-09-445. Washington, D.C.: April 29, 2009.

Information Technology: Agriculture Needs to Strengthen Management Practices for Stabilizing and Modernizing Its Farm Program Delivery Systems. GAO-08-657. Washington, D.C.: May 16, 2008.

Supplemental Appropriations: Opportunities Exist to Increase Transparency and Provide Additional Controls. GAO-08-314. Washington, D.C.: January 31, 2008.

Agricultural Conservation: Farm Program Payments Are an Important Factor in Landowners' Decisions to Convert Grassland to Cropland. GAO-07-1054. Washington, D.C.: September 10, 2007.

Suggested Areas for Oversight for the 110th Congress. GAO-07-235R. Washington, D.C.: November 17, 2006.

Crop Insurance: Actions Needed to Reduce Program's Vulnerability to Fraud, Waste, and Abuse. GAO-05-528. Washington, D.C.: September 30, 2005.

Crop Insurance: USDA Needs to Improve Oversight of Insurance Companies and Develop a Policy to Address Any Future Insolvencies. GAO-04-517. Washington, D.C.: June 1, 2004.

Agricultural Conservation: USDA Needs to Better Ensure Protection of Highly Erodible Cropland and Wetlands. GAO-03-418. Washington, D.C.: April 21, 2003.

End Notes

[1] The Agricultural Assistance Act of 2003, Pub. L. No. 108-7, tit. II, 117 Stat. 538; the Military Construction Appropriations and Emergency Hurricane Supplemental Appropriations Act, 2005, Pub. L. No. 108-324, div. II, § 101, 118 Stat. 1220, 1232 (2004); and the U.S. Troop Readiness, Veterans' Care, Katrina Recovery, and Iraq Accountability Appropriations Act, 2007, Pub. L. No. 110-28, tit. IX, 121 Stat. 112, 211.

[2] We have also reported on the lack of transparency in funding conducted under emergency-designated supplemental appropriations. See GAO, *Supplemental Appropriations: Opportunities Exist to Increase Transparency and Provide Additional Controls,* GAO-08-314 (Washington, D.C.: Jan. 31, 2008).

[3] A crop year is measured from the time the crop is planted through the time it is harvested and may not correspond with the calendar year.

[4] The Consolidated Appropriations Resolution, 2003 and the Military Construction Appropriations and Emergency Hurricane Supplemental Appropriations Act, 2005, allowed farmers who had failed to purchase insurance to receive payments for crop losses incurred in 2001 or 2002 and 2003, 2004, or 2005, respectively, if the farmers signed a statement agreeing to purchase insurance in each of the next 2 years.

[5] RMA uses noninsurable crops to mean crops that are agricultural commodities for which the catastrophic risk protection level of crop insurance is not available, including crops grown for food; crops planted and grown for livestock consumption; and crops grown for fiber, such as cotton and flax.

[6] In addition, the American Recovery and Reinvestment Act of 2009 expanded eligibility and increased the benefits farmers could receive for the 2008 crop year.

[7] A field, in this report, refers to the lowest, detailed level at which a crop loss is defined and includes RMA- and FSA-defined crop characteristics such as the crop price, farming practices, insurance coverage, and planting period for units and subunits that describe contractual relationships or different crop yields associated with the acreage or producer share.

[8] FSA defines an economically significant crop as one that has contributed or would have contributed or is expected to contribute 5 percent or more of the total expected revenue from all crops to the farming operation.

[9] U.S. Department of Agriculture, Office of Inspector General, *Disaster Assistance Payments for Crop Years 2001 and 2002* (Feb. 8, 2006).

[10] GAO, *Crop Insurance: Actions Needed to Reduce Program's Vulnerability to Fraud, Waste, and Abuse*, GAO-05-528 (Washington, D.C.: Sept. 30, 2005). In addition, we reported on the federal crop insurance

program in *Crop Insurance: Opportunities Exist to Reduce the Costs of Administering the Program*, GAO-09-445 (Washington, D.C.: Apr. 29, 2009) and *Crop Insurance: USDA Needs to Improve Oversight of Insurance Companies and Develop a Policy to Address Any Future Insolvencies*, GAO-04-517 (Washington, D.C.: June 1, 2004). See also, GAO, *Suggested Areas for Oversight for the 110th Congress*, GAO-07-235R (Washington, D.C.: Nov. 17, 2006).

[11] Major cost-saving opportunities are those that can limit costs and reduce waste across agencies and programs. This information is accessible through GAO's *High Risk and Other Major Government Management Challenges* page at www.gao.gov/highrisk.

[12] U.S. Department of Agriculture, Office of Inspector General, *Major USDA Management Challenges* (Aug. 11, 2009).

[13] GAO-05-528.

[14] These officials told us that crop insurance fraud cases are highly complex and involve a significant number of documents that must be reviewed and presented in court and that the dollar value of crop insurance cases frequently is not as large as in other cases, such as drug trafficking or some white-collar crime.

[15] Insurance companies pay farmers who were unable to plant the insured crop because of an insured cause of loss that is general in their surrounding area, such as weather conditions causing wet fields, and that prevents other farmers from planting acreages with similar characteristics.

[16] In a prior report, FSA officials identified having their decisions overturned by the National Appeals Division as a hindrance to their enforcement of certain agricultural conservation provisions. GAO, *Agricultural Conservation: USDA Needs to Better Ensure Protection of Highly Erodible Cropland and Wetlands*, GAO-03-418 (Washington, D.C.: Apr. 21, 2003).

[17] According to an FSA official, the 72 percent of appeals that favored FSA includes appeals that may have been decided on technical and procedural issues, as well as appeals that were decided based on the merit of the farmer's crop disaster payment application.

[18] Office of Management and Budget, Circular No. A-130, Revised, transmittal Memorandum No. 4 (Nov. 28, 2000).

[19] See, Iowa State University Extension, *Estimated Costs of Crop Production in Iowa—2010*, FM 1712 (Ames, Iowa, December 2009) and University of Illinois Extension, *Cost to Produce Corn and Soybeans in Illinois—2007*, FEFO 08-05 (Urbana, Ill., March 2008).

[20] All paid claims are subject to review by the insurance companies and various government agencies, including RMA and USDA's Office of Inspector General.

[21] GAO-05-528.

[22] GAO, *Information Technology: Agriculture Needs to Strengthen Management Practices for Stabilizing and Modernizing Its Farm Program Delivery Systems*, GAO-08-657 (Washington, D.C.: May 16, 2008).

[23] U.S. Department of Agriculture, Office of Inspector General, *Major USDA Management Challenges*.

[24] FSA defines an economically significant crop as one that has contributed or would have contributed or is expected to contribute 5 percent or more of the total expected revenue from all crops to the farming operation.

Chapter 7

CROP INSURANCE: OPPORTUNITIES EXIST TO REDUCE THE COSTS OF ADMINISTERING THE PROGRAM

United States Government Accountability Office

WHY GAO DID THIS STUDY

The U.S. Department of Agriculture (USDA) administers the federal crop insurance program with private insurance companies, which, in turn, work with insurance agencies that sell crop insurance. In 2008, according to USDA, the program cost $6.5 billion, including about $2.0 billion in allowances to insurance companies to cover their administrative and operating (A&O) expenses, such as salaries and sales commissions to agencies. GAO was asked to examine (1) the reasons for recent substantial increases in A&O allowances, and the purposes for which insurance companies use these allowances, and (2) insurance agencies' expenses for selling federal crop insurance policies, and questionable practices, if any, that agencies use to compete for business among farmers. GAO analyzed USDA and private insurers' data, among other things.

WHAT GAO RECOMMENDS

GAO recommends that USDA implement a methodology so that the A&O allowance more closely aligns with expenses, as it did before crop prices rose in 2006; require companies to annually report commissions to insurance agencies, by policy; and study costs of delivering crop insurance policies to establish a standard method for assessing agencies' reasonable costs. RMA agreed with two of our three recommendations, arguing that collecting commission data by policy may not be valuable. GAO believes that such data would better enable RMA to negotiate the A&O allowance it pays companies.

WHAT GAO FOUND

Between 2000 and 2009, companies' A&O allowances nearly tripled, primarily because USDA's calculation method for A&O allowances considers the value of the crop, rather than the crop insurance industry's actual expenses for selling and servicing policies, which generally remained stable. This increase in the A&O allowances occurred without a proportional increase in the number of policies, acres, or amount of insurance coverage purchased. The higher A&O allowances occurred because of higher crop prices since 2006. Per policy, the allowance rose from a national average of $836 in 2006 to an expected $1,417 in 2009. Companies have used most of the higher allowances to raise commissions, in an effort to compete for insurance agencies' portfolios of crop insurance policies. USDA data show that commissions increased more sharply in states with historically larger insurance underwriting gains, which add to company profits. For example, the average commission paid per policy in 5 Corn Belt states increased by 86 percent from 2006 to 2007, and by 43 percent in the other 45 states. Companies reported to USDA that their expenses to administer the program in 2007 exceeded their allowances. However, GAO determined that these expenses exceeded allowances largely because of the higher commissions paid to insurance agencies.

According to GAO's analysis, crop insurance agencies' sales commissions have outpaced their expenses for selling policies. Commissions per policy increased by an average of about 16 percent per year from 2000 to 2009, compared with an increase of about 3 percent per year for insurance agents' wages, which are the largest factor in agencies' expenses. For 2007 through 2009, commissions will exceed wage-adjusted commissions by $2.87 billion. According to USDA officials, higher commissions can create more incentive for rebating, which is the practice of offering something of monetary value to farmers to attract their business. USDA prohibits this practice, as do most states. USDA and state insurance regulators are working to reduce the potential for this practice.

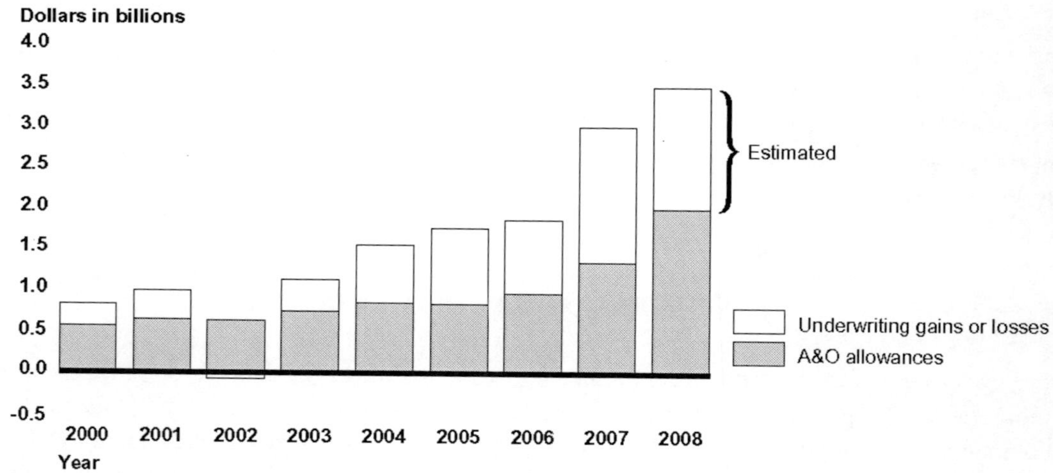

Source: USDA.

A&O Allowances and Underwriting Gains or Losses Paid to Companies, 2000 through 2008

ABBREVIATIONS

A&O	administrative and operating
NAIC	National Association of Insurance Commissioners
RMA	Risk Management Agency
SRA	standard reinsurance agreement
USDA	U.S. Department of Agriculture

April 29, 2009

The Honorable Henry A. Waxman
Chairman
Committee on Energy and Commerce
House of Representatives

The Honorable Edolphus Towns
Chairman
The Honorable Darrell Issa
Ranking Member
Committee on Oversight and Government Reform
House of Representatives

The Honorable Jim Cooper
House of Representatives

Federal crop insurance protects participating farmers against the financial losses caused by natural disasters, such as droughts, floods, and hurricanes, as well as declines in crop prices. In 2008, the crop insurance program provided about $90 billion in insurance coverage for 272 million acres of farmland at a cost of $6.5 billion to the federal government. To implement the federal crop insurance program, the U.S. Department of Agriculture's (USDA) Risk Management Agency (RMA) partners with 16 private insurance companies, which sell and service the insurance policies and share a percentage of the risk of loss and opportunity for gain associated with the policies. RMA pays insurance companies a percentage of the premiums on policies sold to cover the administrative and operating (A&O) expenses of selling and servicing these policies. These expenses are generally described in RMA guidance and can include company overhead, such as employee salaries, fees paid to insurance adjusters to verify claims, and sales commissions paid to the insurance agencies and their agents who sell crop insurance to farmers. These agencies and agents generally operate independently of the 16 insurance companies and can change companies from year to year.

We have reported for many years on the costs of the crop insurance program associated with A&O allowances. In May and June, 2007, we testified that RMA should ensure that expenses for delivering the crop insurance program are reasonable.[1] Specifically, we noted that the federal government spent more than $6.8 billion from 2002 through 2006 to administer the program—with A&O allowances accounting for over half of these expenditures—and recommended that Congress authorize RMA to renegotiate its agreement with the companies that sell and service crop insurance policies. Subsequently, Congress, through the Food, Conservation, and Energy Act of 2008 (the 2008 Farm Bill), reduced the A&O allowance payment rate for most crop insurance policies by 2.3 percentage points, effective in 2009. This reduction is expected to result in financial savings of almost $1 billion through 2013. The 2008 Farm Bill also directed RMA to consider alternative methods for determining A&O payment rates as well as other methods, taking into account current financial conditions, to ensure the continued availability of the program. In 2006, we identified the need for better oversight of the federal crop insurance program to ensure that its funds are spent as economically, efficiently, and effectively as possible.[2] Furthermore, in 1997, we reported that A&O allowances exceeded the companies' expenses that can be reasonably associated with selling and servicing crop insurance policies.[3] We noted that alternative arrangements for determining A&O allowances offered potential for savings. These alternative arrangements included paying companies a flat fee per policy, plus a lower percentage of the premium on the policy. Furthermore, we noted that USDA's Farm Service Agency had administered a type of crop insurance—catastrophic insurance—at a lower cost to the government than did private insurance companies.

While the 2008 Farm Bill reduced the A&O allowance rate, other factors also affect A&O allowances to insurance companies. Because allowances are a percentage of insurance premiums, they increase when the value of policies that companies sell increases, such as when crop prices rise. According to USDA, since 2007, the prices for major crops—such as corn, soybeans, and wheat—have been among the highest on record, and prices in 2009 and beyond are expected to remain relatively high.[4] In response to these rising crop prices, A&O allowances increased from about $960 million in 2006 to about $2 billion in 2008.

In this context, you asked that we examine (1) the reasons for the substantial increases in A&O allowances in recent years, and the purposes for which insurance companies use these allowances, and (2) insurance agencies' expenses for selling federal crop insurance policies, and questionable practices, if any, that agencies use to compete for business among farmers.

To examine the reasons for the substantial increases in A&O allowances in recent years and the purposes for which insurance companies use these allowances, we interviewed RMA officials and officials from each of the 16 companies that participate in the federal crop insurance program. In addition, we reviewed and analyzed RMA and company data concerning companies' uses of the allowances from 2000 through 2007. The sources of these data included expense reports that the companies submitted to RMA listing the amounts that they charge to various expense categories. We also reviewed RMA's reporting guidelines for companies and discussed these guidelines with company officials. In addition, we reviewed examples of companies' contracts with insurance agencies. We selected these contracts on the basis of the volume of business between the insurance company and the agency and, when possible, regional diversity. For the purpose of this report, commissions include profit-sharing bonuses that an insurance company pays to an insurance agency on the basis of profits for a given year and transfer bonuses that a company pays to an agency that transfers its portfolio of crop insurance policies that it sells (book of business) to the company. To examine insurance agencies' expenses for selling federal crop insurance policies, and questionable practices, if any, that agencies use to compete for business from farmers, we interviewed officials of eight insurance agencies and reviewed documents that some of these officials provided. We also interviewed officials from trade associations representing insurance agents. In addition, we interviewed officials from RMA and the National Association of Insurance

Commissioners (NAIC), an association of state insurance regulators, and discussed with RMA its investigations of questionable competitive practices.

We conducted this performance audit from January 2008 through April 2009 in accordance with generally accepted government auditing standards. Those standards require that we plan and perform the audit to obtain sufficient, appropriate evidence to provide a reasonable basis for our findings and conclusions based on our audit objectives. We believe that the evidence obtained provides a reasonable basis for our findings and conclusions based on our audit objectives. Appendix I contains more detailed information on our scope and methodology.

BACKGROUND

Farming is an inherently risky enterprise. In conducting their operations, farmers are exposed to financial losses because of production risks—droughts, floods, hurricanes, and other natural disasters—as well as price risks. For decades, the federal government has played an active role in helping to mitigate the effects of these risks on farm income by promoting the use of crop insurance.

Through the federal crop insurance program, farmers insure against losses on more than 100 crops. The federal government encourages farmers' participation by subsidizing their insurance premiums and acting as the primary reinsurer for the private insurance companies that take on the risk of covering, or "underwriting," losses to insured farmers. These companies achieve underwriting gains when insurance premiums exceed the claims they must pay farmers for crop losses, and they incur underwriting losses if claims paid on the policies exceed the premiums. To cover the expenses of selling and servicing crop insurance policies, the federal government pays companies an A&O allowance. In turn, insurance companies use this money to cover their overhead expenses, such as payroll and rent, and to pay commissions to insurance agencies and agents. Companies also incur expenses associated with verifying—adjusting—the amount of loss claimed. These loss adjustment expenses include, for example, travel expenses to farmers' fields. The relationships among the federal government, private insurance companies, agencies, agents, and farmers are illustrated in figure 1.

To encourage widespread participation in the crop insurance program, the federal government pays the costs of selling and servicing crop insurance policies through the A&O allowance. As designed, this allowance increases when companies sell policies to more farmers, insure additional acreage, or sell a higher level of insurance coverage on acres that are already insured. However, A&O allowances can also increase as a result of higher crop prices without corresponding changes in the number of policies sold to farmers, insured acreage, or levels of coverage. Such increases in A&O allowances—when decoupled from the federal crop insurance program's interest in promoting more insured acreage and higher levels of coverage—can create additional incentives for insurance companies to expand their market share by raising commission rates.

In 2008, RMA provided about $2.0 billion in A&O allowances and an estimated $1.5 billion in underwriting gains to crop insurance companies. Figure 2 shows the A&O allowances and underwriting gains or losses paid to companies for 2000 through 2008.

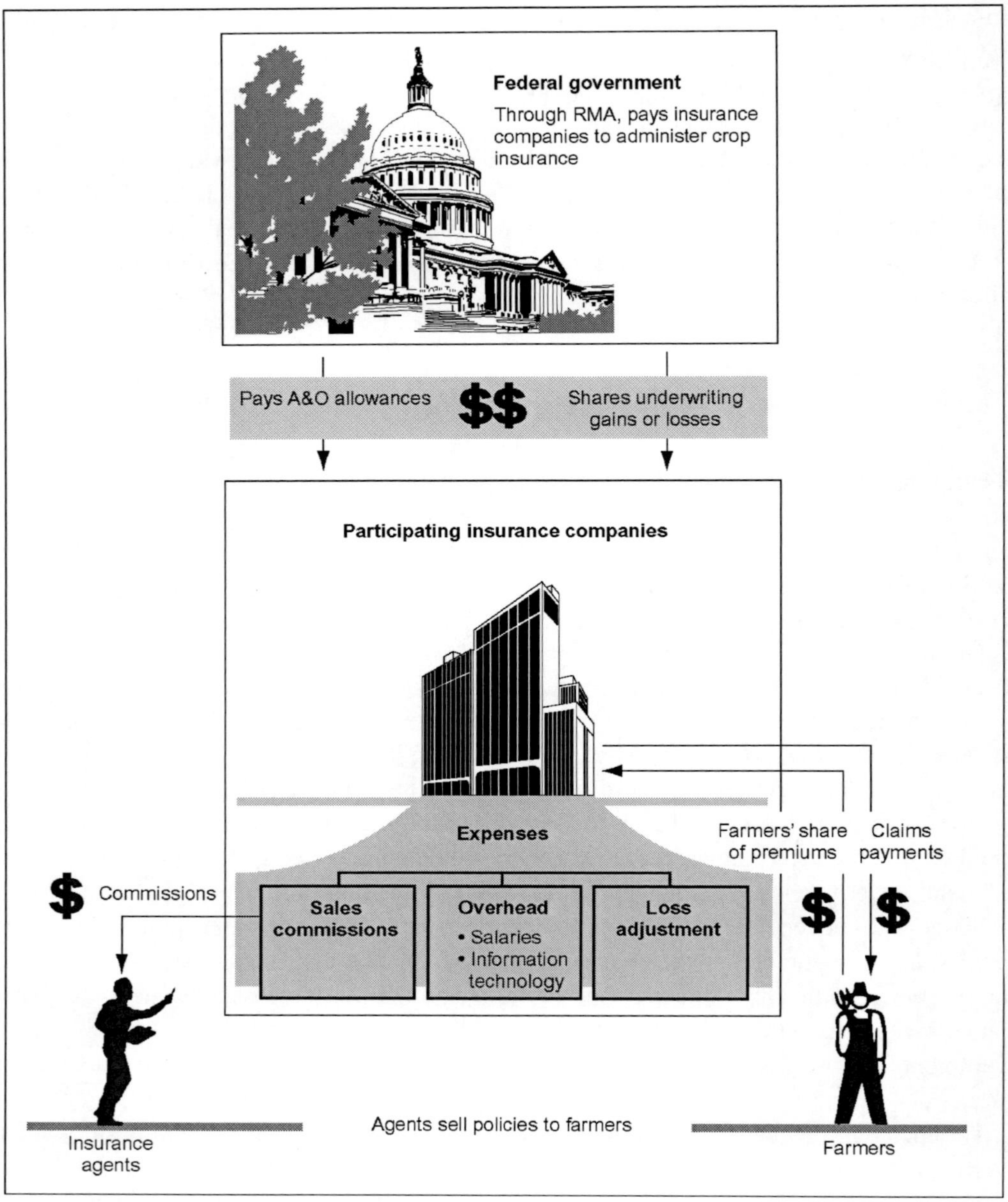

Sources: GAO; Art Explosion.

Figure 1. How Money Flows through the Federal Crop Insurance Program

Taking into account all payments, the crop insurance program cost taxpayers about $31 billion for 2000 through 2008, according to the most recent available estimate from the Center for Agricultural and Rural Development at Iowa State University.[5] According to our analysis, RMA paid about $1.93 for every $1.00 in payments to farmers, with the other $0.93 going to insurance companies over the period. Since 2006, when crop prices began to rise sharply, RMA has paid about $2.29 for every $1.00 that reached the farmer, with the balance going to insurance companies.

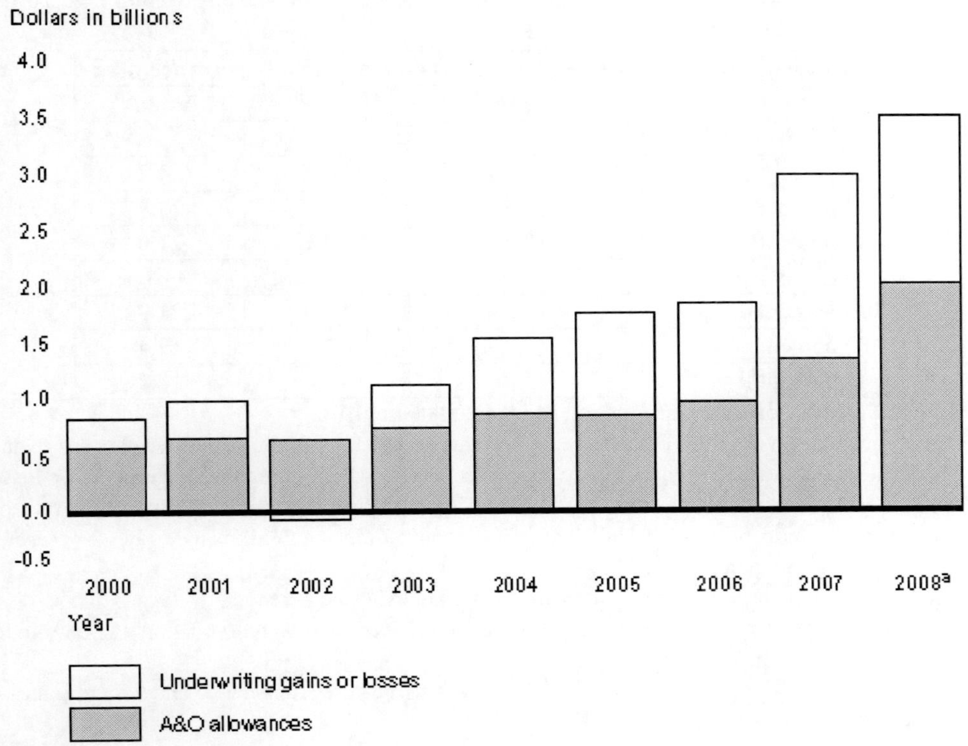

Source: RMA.

[a] Underwriting gains for 2008 are estimated, as of April 15, 2009.

Figure 2. Crop Insurance A&O Allowances and Underwriting Gains or Losses Paid to Companies, 2000 through 2008

The policies that insurance companies underwrite and service are sold by more than 12,000 insurance agents. Some insurance agencies sell only crop insurance, while others also sell other lines of property and casualty insurance, such as automobile insurance and homeowner's insurance. These agencies, which are generally independent contractors and receive sales commissions for selling the policies, can sell policies on behalf of multiple crop insurance companies. Farmers must purchase policies by certain "sales closing" dates. These dates correspond to a time before planting season for a given crop in a certain region of the nation.

RMA is responsible for administering the federal crop insurance program through a cooperative financial agreement called the standard reinsurance agreement (SRA), which can be renegotiated once during a 5-year period, or as directed by Congress. The SRA incorporates the terms and conditions by which the private insurance companies that sell and service crop insurance policies are to abide. Under the 2008 Farm Bill, RMA may renegotiate the financial terms and conditions of the SRA, effective for the 2011 reinsurance year, beginning July 1, 2010. According to RMA officials, this effort will begin in the spring of 2009. For 2008 and 2009, RMA approved 16 insurance companies to provide federal crop insurance.

Table 1. A&O Allowance Rates, by Coverage Level, 2006 through 2008 and 2009

Coverage level, by year	A&O allowance rate, by type of insurance plan		
	Revenue[a]	Area[b]	Yield[c]
2006 through 2008			
75 percent or less	20.8	22.4	24.2
80 percent	18.7	20.1	21.7
85 percent	18.1	19.4	21.0
2009			
75 percent or less	18.5	12.0	21.9
80 percent	16.4	12.0	19.4
85 percent	15.8	12.0	18.7

Source: GAO analysis of RMA information and the 2008 Farm Bill.

Note: The coverage level is the percentage of revenue or production that a farmer chooses to insure. This table does not show catastrophic insurance plans, which compensate farmers for losses in production exceeding 50 percent of their average historic production at a payment rate of 55 percent of the crop price. The 2008 Farm Bill reduced the A&O allowance rate for these plans from 8 percent to 6 percent.

[a] Revenue insurance plans protect farmers against losses in expected revenue.

[b] Area insurance plans protect farmers against losses in revenue or production, using a county index as the basis for determining a loss.

[c] Yield plans also include other insurance plans—such as pasture, rangeland, and forage plans—and protect farmers against losses in production.

Premiums for the policies are set by RMA and depend, in part, on the price of the insured crop, although premiums also vary according to the type of insurance plan and the coverage levels that farmers select. A&O allowances are calculated as a fixed percentage of the premium, and they vary depending upon the plan and coverage levels, as shown in table 1.

For most policies, the 2008 Farm Bill reduced the A&O allowance rate by 2.3 percentage points beginning in 2009. However, the bill provides an exception to cover higher loss adjustment expenses when needed. Specifically, if a state's losses are 20 percent higher than the total premiums for that state, only one-half of the 2.3 percentage-point reduction would apply. In addition, the reduction in the A&O allowance rate was larger for area insurance plans than for other plans.

The 2008 Farm Bill also repeals a provision of the Federal Crop Insurance Reform and Department of Agriculture Reorganization Act of 1994 that allowed providers to implement "premium reduction plans" with RMA approval. Through these plans, companies could offer a premium discount to farmers that is equal to the amount that the companies' A&O expenses fell below their A&O allowances for a given year. Thus, these plans offered an incentive for companies to reduce A&O expenses, because they allowed companies to compete for more business by, in effect, reducing the premiums they charged farmers for crop insurance. RMA established guidelines for the submission of the plans in a final interim rule in the *Federal Register* on July 20, 2005. In commenting on this rule, state insurance regulators expressed concerns that the plans would result in industry consolidation, reducing competition in the long run, and that the plans could create pressure for insurance companies to reduce essential operating expenses, thereby disadvantaging newer companies compared with larger, established companies.operating expenses, thereby disadvantaging newer companies compared with larger, established companies.

State insurance regulators also expressed concerns that the plans constituted a legal form of rebating, the practice of offering something of monetary value to farmers to attract their business. Rebating is generally prohibited by the SRA and by most states, and the 2008 Farm Bill limits the compensation an individual can receive for selling or servicing a crop insurance policy in which he or she has a substantial beneficial interest.

Higher Crop Prices Sharply Raised A&O Allowances, and Insurance Companies Used a Large Share of These Increases to Compete for More Business

Companies' A&O allowances nearly tripled from 2000 to 2009, primarily because the method that RMA uses to calculate A&O allowances considers the value of the crop and not the crop insurance industry's actual expenses for selling and servicing policies. Companies spent a large share of their higher A&O allowances on commission payments, in part in an effort to compete for business from insurance agencies. They also reported expenses that are not clearly related to selling and servicing policies, such as legal fees.

Substantially Higher A&O Allowances Have Occurred Primarily because of Sharp Increases in Crop Prices

A&O allowances nearly tripled—from \$552 million in 2000 to an estimated \$1.6 billion in 2009, according to our analysis of RMA data. The change from 2006 to 2009 was particularly large, rising from an average of \$836 per policy to an expected \$1,417 per policy. These increases occurred primarily because RMA calculates the allowance as a percentage of the premiums on crop insurance policies, rather than the crop insurance industry's actual expenses to sell and service policies. Crop insurance premiums change when crop prices change. Thus, the allowance increased sharply from 2006 through 2009, when the prices of major crops increased.

Figure 3 shows the prices for these crops—corn, soybeans, and wheat—that RMA used in calculating A&O allowances for 2000 through 2009.

These three crops represented about 71 percent of the crop insurance premiums in 2008.

According to RMA, A&O allowances will decrease in 2009 because crop prices are expected to decrease and because of the reduction in the A&O allowance rate for most crop insurance policies, as mandated in the 2008 Farm Bill. However, the prices for corn, soybeans, and wheat—the top three crops in the crop insurance program, by premium—are expected to remain relatively high. Thus, using RMA's estimate of premiums and the current allowance rate, we estimated that allowances in 2009 will be \$1,417 per policy, 69 percent higher than in 2006, although down from \$1,751 per policy in 2008.

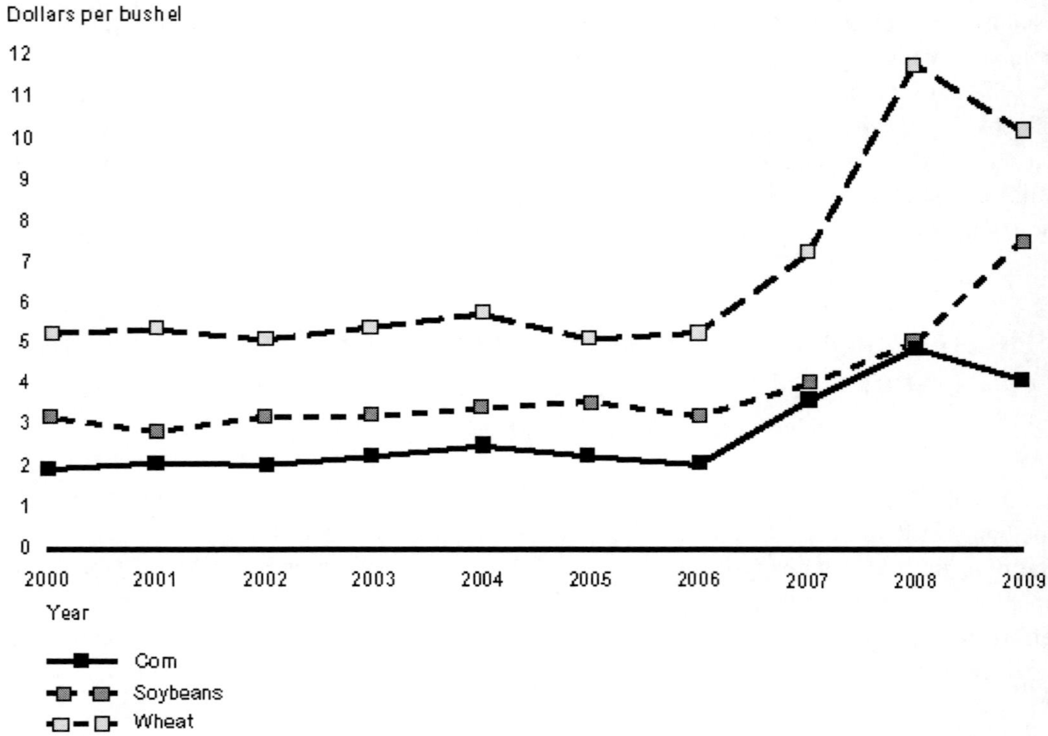

Source: RMA.

Note: Crop prices in this figure are for yield insurance plans, which were the plans most widely available for this period.

Figure 3. Corn, Soybean, and Wheat Prices That RMA Used in Calculating A&O Allowances, 2000 through 2009

The current method for calculating A&O allowances has caused allowance payments to increase along with crop prices, but without a proportional increase in the number of policies, acres, or coverage levels. For 2000 through 2008, A&O allowances increased sharply despite a 13 percent decrease in the number of crop insurance policies—the principal factor affecting companies' workloads and costs.[6] This increase in A&O allowances has also been substantially greater than the increase in the number of acres covered by the program. Since 2000, the number of acres insured has increased slightly—by 7 percent—excluding insurance for pasture and rangeland. These types of insurance tend to cover large acreages in a single policy and, therefore, add many acres to the program without a proportional increase in the number of policies or in companies' workloads. With the addition of pasture and rangeland insurance, the number of acres insured has increased by 32 percent since 2000, but these policies represent only about 1 percent of all crop insurance policies. Nor are coverage levels—which have increased from an average of about 61 percent of crop value in 2000 to an average of 67 percent of crop value in 2008—a major factor in the rapid increase in A&O allowances.

Because crop prices are a principal factor in the method for calculating A&O allowances, the allowance fluctuates as crop prices rise and fall. Fluctuations make it more difficult for insurance companies to budget and operate effectively over the long term. Although USDA expects that crop prices will remain relatively high for the next several years, prices are also expected to be volatile because of energy markets, among other things. Crop prices are increasingly tied to these markets because of the growing production of ethanol. When oil prices increase, ethanol prices generally increase, which raises demand for corn, the primary ethanol feedstock.

Companies Have Used a Large Share of Higher A&O Allowances to Compete for More Business

Companies generally base insurance agencies' commissions on a percentage of the premiums that agencies bring to the companies. Thus, as crop prices have increased, so have commissions. Figure 4 shows the change in premiums, A&O allowances, and commissions from 2000 through 2009.

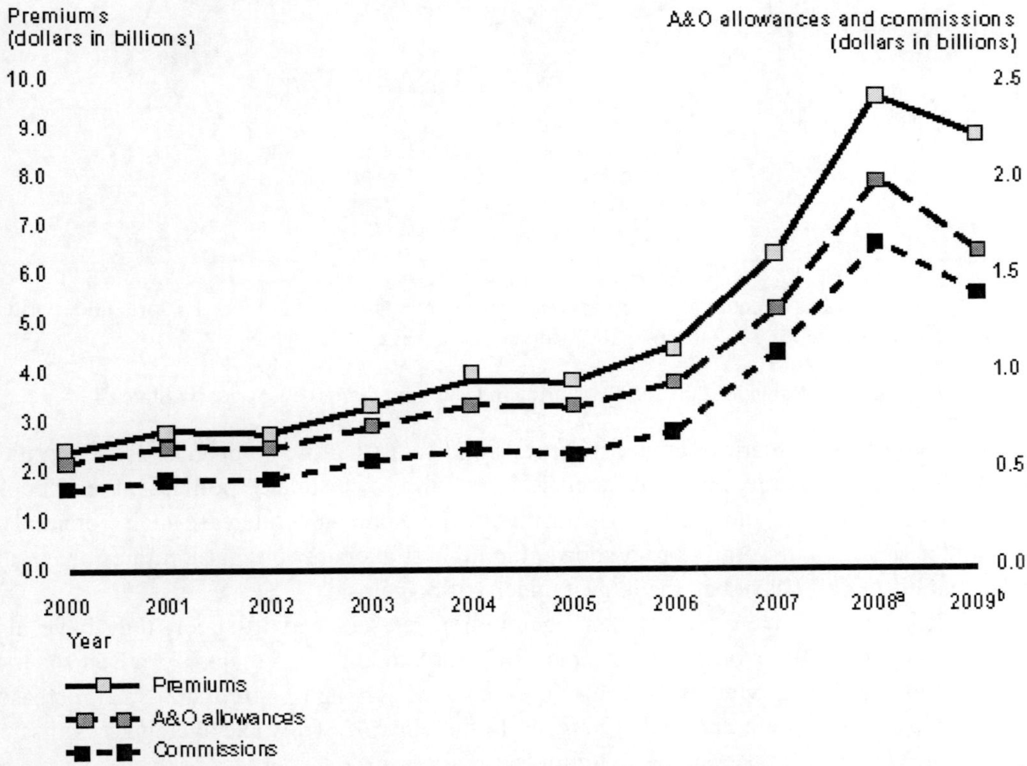

Source: GAO analysis of data that the insurance companies provided to RMA.

[a] For 2008, commissions are estimated on the basis of 2008 premiums and the assumption that commission rates remained the same as they were in 2007.

[b] For 2009, A&O allowances and commissions are estimated.

Figure 4. Crop Insurance Premiums, A&O Allowances, and Commissions, 2000 through 2009

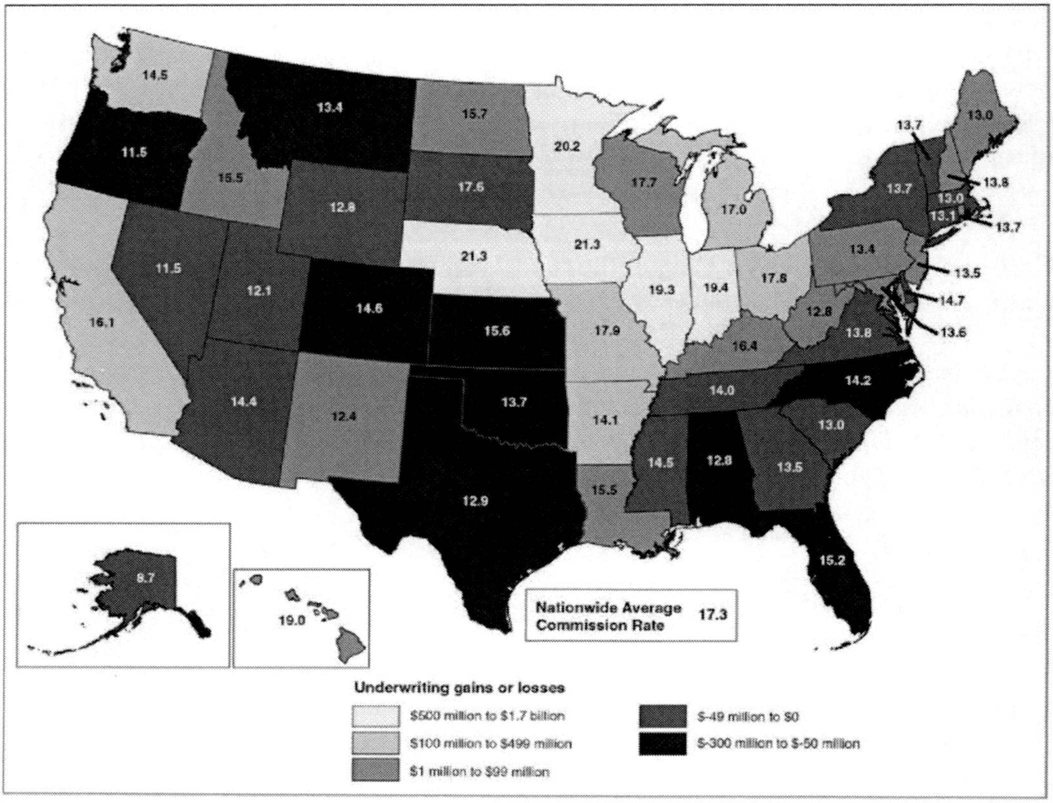

Sources: GAO analysis of RMA data and data that the insurance companies provided to RMA; Map Resources (map).

Note: Commission rates are commissions expressed as a percentage of premiums. Historic underwriting gains or losses are for 2000 through 2007, the latest data available.

Figure 5. Commission Rates for 2007 and Historic Underwriting Gains or Losses, by State

The geographic pattern in commission rates indicates that the companies are using their A&O allowances to attract insurance agencies' portfolios of insurance policies—their "books of business." Obtaining more books of business helps companies increase their potential to earn underwriting gains. As figure 5 shows, the highest average commission rates are in the states that historically have had the largest underwriting gains.

While companies have paid higher commission rates in certain states, they have also increased the rates nationwide. For example, from 2006 to 2007 in 5 major Corn Belt states—Illinois, Indiana, Iowa, Minnesota, and Nebraska—the average commission rate increased from 17.6 percent of premium to 20.3 percent. In the other 45 states, the average commission rate increased from 13.0 percent of premium to 14.2 percent.

In terms of commission dollars, the average commission paid per policy from 2006 to 2007 increased more in the 5 major Corn Belt states overall than in the other states, rising by a total of 86 percent in these 5 states compared with 43 percent in the other 45 states. For 2007, in the 5 Corn Belt states, crop insurance companies paid a total of $506 million in commissions—which is about $9 million more than the total A&O allowance that the companies received from RMA for these states. According to crop insurance company officials, having used their A&O allowance for commissions, they rely on underwriting gains in such states to pay their overhead expenses and fees to insurance adjusters, who verify claims that are filed. Appendix II contains additional information on commissions paid in 2006 and 2007.

Company officials confirmed that they increased commission rates to compete for the insurance agencies' books of business. Obtaining more books of business helps companies increase their potential to earn underwriting gains.

Because RMA sets the premiums for crop insurance policies, companies cannot compete by reducing premiums. Nor do they often have the opportunity to insure new crop acres or sell more policies overall. Thus, one of the key ways for companies to increase their market share is to draw insurance agencies (and their books of business) away from competing companies by raising the agencies' commission rates. In addition, company officials told us that some insurance agencies have considerable leverage in negotiating with companies for sales commissions because these insurance agencies have long-standing relationships with farmers whose crop insurance policies have historically produced high underwriting gains. Thus, companies compete against one another, offering higher and higher commissions until the increase in A&O allowances is exhausted. Insurance agencies have benefited from the increases in A&O allowances without selling more policies.

In addition to increasing commission rates in certain states, some insurance companies seek to attract agencies' books of business by offering commission rates on the basis of the agency's size. That is, many of the commission contracts we reviewed provided higher commission rates to agencies that sell insurance in larger quantities.

Even as they compete for insurance agencies' books of business on commissions, companies can also try to retain their current agencies' business by providing in-kind services, such as policy processing services and mailings to inform farmers about policies. These services usually entail an investment in information technology, such as quoting software that calculates farmer-specific premiums that agencies can use to market the various policies.

RMA does not know how much an individual company spends on commissions to each of the agencies with which it does business. RMA guidelines for reporting under the SRA direct insurance companies to report only their total commissions for each state in which they operate, not commission amounts paid to individual agencies. Information by state does not provide sufficient detail on commission expenses because such data do not allow RMA to assess whether the compensation paid to agencies is appropriate in relationship to the cost of selling and servicing crop insurance. RMA would be better able to set the A&O allowance rate when it renegotiates the SRA with insurance companies if it had more detailed information on commissions provided to individual agencies, such as commission data at the policy level. With such information on agencies' commissions, as well as their costs, RMA could assess whether the A&O allowances are reasonable for program delivery but not excessive, and adjust allowances as needed. Data by policy would enable RMA to better understand how compensation to agencies varies with agency size and the characteristics of policies sold, such as the type of insurance plan and expected underwriting gains. This understanding would enable RMA to better anticipate the effects of adjustments in A&O allowances on agencies. For example, this analysis may show that agencies that do business primarily in a part of the state with historically high underwriting gains received higher commission rates than agencies that do business in a part of the state with lower underwriting gains.

Companies' Reported Expenses Exceeded A&O Allowances, but High Commissions and Expenses That Were Inconsistent with RMA Guidance Explain This Difference

Despite the increases in A&O allowances, insurance companies reported to RMA that their expenses for delivering federal crop insurance for 2007 exceeded their A&O allowances by about $244 million. Company officials told us that new RMA regulations and recent changes have added a significant administrative burden. For example, they noted, when RMA introduces an insurance product, companies must update their information systems, train staff, and take on additional work, and RMA provides what companies view as insufficient time for them to do so. Furthermore, although RMA guidelines have long directed companies to perform additional review of all claims of more than $100,000, these reviews became more frequent when crop values started to increase significantly in 2007 and claim amounts rose accordingly. These activities made company operations more costly, according to company officials. Furthermore, insurance company officials told us that certain expenses vary by region of the country. For example, companies that operate in regions that tend to have crop losses more frequently incur higher overall A&O expenses because of higher loss adjustment expenses. Nevertheless, RMA officials noted that recent changes should have only marginally affected the cost of doing business.

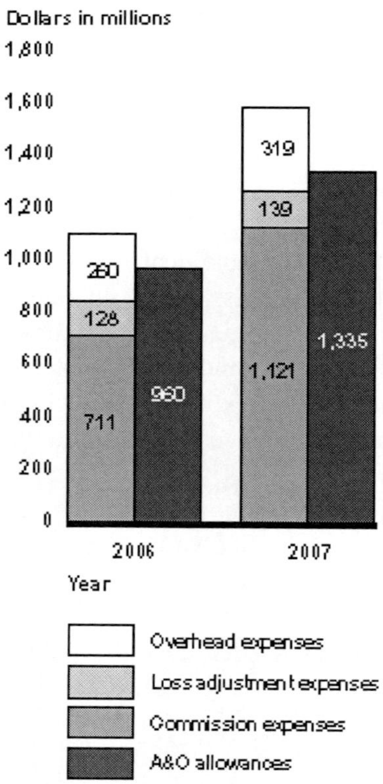

Source: GAO analysis of data that the insurance companies provided to RMA.

Figure 6. A&O Expenses and A&O Allowances That Crop Insurance Companies Reported to RMA, 2006 and 2007

We found that the amount by which companies' reported A&O expenses exceeded allowances was largely due to the increased spending on commissions, as well as to the reporting of expenses that was inconsistent with RMA guidance, rather than to greater administrative burdens. Although A&O allowances increased by 39 percent—from $960 million in 2006 to about $1.3 billion in 2007—companies increased the commissions they paid to agencies by 58 percent—from $711 million to about $1.1 billion. Figure 6 shows A&O expenses for 2006 and 2007 and the A&O allowances reported.

For individual agencies, commissions can be large, both in terms of actual dollars and in relationship to A&O allowance rates. For example, in 2007, companies paid 60 insurance agencies commissions that were at least $1.0 million and at least 20.0 percent of the premium value, which is about equal to the average A&O allowance rate of 20.4 percent paid to companies nationwide.

We also found that some insurance companies' reporting of program delivery expenses was inconsistent with RMA reporting guidance. For 2007, some companies reported profit-sharing bonuses, legal fees, and other expenses that were not directly related to the selling and servicing of crop insurance policies. RMA guidance states that these payments should not be included in the expense report, and, according to RMA officials, these payments are not program delivery expenses. For example, 10 of the 16 companies listed profit-sharing bonuses to insurance agencies as an expense to deliver the program. Similarly, 6 of the 16 insurance companies included reinsurance expenses that relate to business expansion, rather than to program delivery. Specifically, insurance companies pay premiums for commercial reinsurance to (1) reduce their risk of underwriting losses and (2) increase their capacity to sell more insurance. According to RMA guidance, reinsurance expenses should not be reported as A&O expenses. RMA officials told us that these types of expenses should be paid from underwriting gains because they are not associated with the direct sale and service of federal crop insurance to farmers. Finally, we found one company had included in its A&O expenses about $1 million in legal fees to defend itself against a lawsuit from another crop insurance company. However, the guidance notes that legal fees associated with delivering the program should pertain to defending lawsuits related to servicing policies. RMA officials agreed that such legal fees should not be included as an A&O expense. RMA and company officials stated that RMA's guidance on allowable expenses should be clarified.

Insurance Agencies' Commissions Have Outpaced Expenses, and Higher Commissions Can Create More Incentive for Rebating

The modest increase from 2000 through 2009 in insurance agencies' expenses for selling policies has not been commensurate with the dramatic increase in their commissions. Consequently, many agencies have apparently seen substantial increases in their profits from their crop insurance books of business; this is particularly true for states that have had high underwriting gains, such as the Corn Belt states. The growth in commissions can create more incentives for agents to engage in rebating, although RMA has taken steps to reduce the potential for this practice.

Insurance Agencies' Commissions Have Outpaced the Insurance Industry's Expenses, as Measured by Growth in Wages

Insurance agents' responsibilities can include (1) adequately informing farmers about applicable crop insurance policy provisions and (2) accurately preparing and completing the farmer's insurance application, certification of production history, acreage reports, and other sales-related documents. Agents also must properly maintain the crop insurance contract files. While acknowledging that their commissions have increased, insurance agency officials stated that selling crop insurance policies generally entails more work for agents and thus higher expenses than for other lines of property and casualty insurance, and that those expenses have increased in recent years. Table 2 provides examples of the expenses that agencies incur in selling crop insurance.

Much of the insurance agencies' work, according to the agency officials with whom we spoke, is related to the time required to help farmers choose the appropriate policy. These officials said agents generally (1) meet individually with farmers at various times during the year to update them on policies and compliance requirements, (2) mail farmers information on deadlines for reporting to the insurance agent on the number of acres planted and the amount of crop produced, and (3) provide seminars and annual meetings to help farmers understand the crop insurance options available to them. According to one insurance agency official, to service a crop insurance policy, an agent interacts with a farmer a minimum of six times a year. Another agency official told us that agents need to meet with the farmers at least four times a year.

In addition, some of agencies' crop insurance expenses are for services to farmers that are not described in RMA guidance but that help insurance agencies compete for farmers' business. Crop insurance agency officials told us that they compete on the basis of reputation, personal relationships, and additional services. These officials also noted that they advise farmers on how to best market their crops and increasingly provide advanced mapping services to farmers, such as creating and printing poster-size maps that display farmers' crop areas to help farmers manage their land. One insurance agency official said that the information technology needed for such services constituted the agency's biggest expense outside of payroll.

Table 2. Examples of Insurance Agencies' Crop Insurance Expenses

Type of expense	Example
Pay and benefits	Salaries, health insurance, and retirement
Education/Training	Training on software and changes in RMA regulations and requirements
Rent and equipment	Office space and vehicles
Information technology	Quoting software to help farmers select a crop insurance plan and coverage level that best meet their needs
Legal and professional	Liability insurance (errors and omissions insurance)

Source: GAO.

Although insurance agency officials told us that their crop insurance expenses are high, the documents they provided did not show that their sales expenses have increased at the same pace as their commissions. Because comprehensive information is not available on the expenses of the thousands of agencies that sell crop insurance, we examined the extent to which the growth in crop insurance commissions tracked trends in insurance industry expenses. We used 2000 as the base year in which crop insurance commissions are presumed to have been more closely aligned with expenses, before the increase in the A&O allowance. We then calculated what the commission per policy would have been for 2001 through 2009 if it had increased at the rate of change in insurance agents' wages. We used the rate of change in insurance agents' wages because, according to industry officials, wages account for agencies' largest expense. For this analysis, we used commission data from RMA and insurance agents' wage data for all lines of insurance from the Department of Labor's Bureau of Labor Statistics. In view of the 2008 Farm Bill's 2.3 percentage point reduction in A&O allowance rates for most insurance plans, we assumed that 2009 commission rates would decline by half of this amount—1.15 percentage points—relative to 2007, the most recent year for which RMA data on actual commission rates were available.[7]

On the basis of these assumptions, we found that the rate of increase in commission per policy to crop insurance agencies has significantly outpaced the rate of increase in insurance agents' wages. That is, the actual commissions increased by an average of about 16 percent per year from 2000 through 2009, compared with an increase of about 3 percent per year for commissions assumed to increase at the same rate as insurance agents' wages. Figure 7 shows these comparisons.

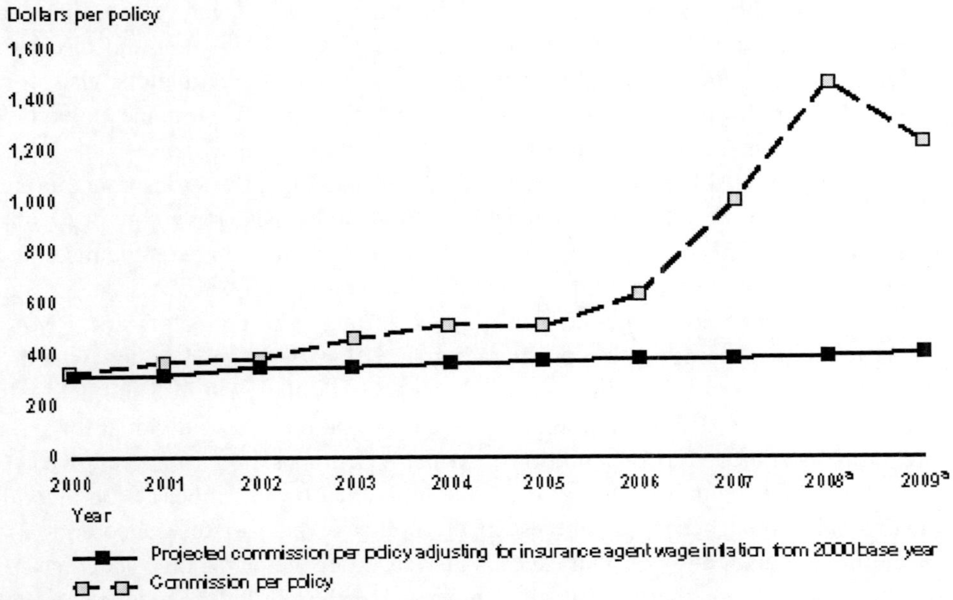

Source: GAO analysis of Bureau of Labor Statistics data and data that the insurance companies provided to RMA.

[a] Commission per policy is estimated for 2008 and 2009.

Figure 7. Actual Commission per Policy Compared with Projected Commission per Policy Adjusted for Insurance Agent Wage Inflation, 2000 through 2009

As figure 7 shows, with 2000 as a base year, if commissions had increased at the rate of increase in insurance agents' wages, the commission per policy in 2007 would have been $382, but the actual commission per policy that insurance companies paid to agencies in 2007 was $985—a difference of $603 per policy. According to our analysis, in 2007, with about 1.14 million crop insurance policies, actual commission payments exceeded the adjusted commissions by about $687 million. For 2007 through 2009, estimated commission payments exceed the adjusted commissions by about $2.87 billion.

Crop insurance industry officials with whom we spoke generally acknowledged that insurance agencies received higher profits as a result of increased commissions in 2007 and 2008. While some officials said agencies' more profitable financial years are balanced by less profitable years, others said that the method for calculating A&O allowances needs to be modified to bring it more in-line with reasonable expenses for delivering the crop insurance program. Finally, a number of insurance company officials supported limiting commissions, although they had differing views on the best way to implement such limits.

Higher Commission Payments for Insurance Agencies Can Create More Incentive to Use Rebating to Compete for Farmers' Business

According to RMA and NAIC officials, higher commissions have increased the incentives for rebating. The RMA officials indicated that as commissions have increased, the number of anecdotal reports of rebating has also increased. They also observed that rebating is more prevalent in states with higher commission rates. A number of insurance agency officials told us that they lost business to competitors that they believed engaged in rebating. According to RMA officials, rebating disrupts the crop insurance market and discriminates against farmers who purchase smaller policies. State insurance regulators also consider rebating unfair to policyholders because it results in pricing based on the policyholder's relationship to an agent, rather than on risk.

RMA has determined that the incidence of illegal rebating of crop insurance premiums has grown in recent years. To combat rebating, RMA and NAIC have sought to improve communication and coordination between RMA and states on complaints, ongoing investigations, data analyses, and enforcement. In December 2007, RMA issued a bulletin directing crop insurance companies to notify agencies that state regulators and RMA were aware that rebating schemes were proliferating and that RMA and states would work cooperatively to discover and eliminate such schemes. In addition, in July 2008, RMA issued guidance on a 2008 Farm Bill provision that bars compensation to an individual for selling or servicing crop insurance if two conditions are met. Compensation is not allowed, either directly, or indirectly through an entity, if (1) the individual or a member of the individual's family has a substantial beneficial interest in the policy or plan of insurance and (2) total compensation from that policy or plan exceeds 30 percent or the percentage specified in state law, whichever is less, of the total of all compensation the individual receives directly or indirectly for selling or servicing crop insurance. RMA and NAIC officials told us that enforcing antirebating laws is difficult because rebating is only uncovered when complaints are made, but these officials believe that their recent actions will reduce the potential use of this practice.

CONCLUSIONS

Federal crop insurance plays an important role in protecting farmers from losses due to natural disasters, and the private insurance companies that participate in the program are integral to its success. Nevertheless, in view of increasing pressure to reduce federal budget deficits, A&O allowances present an opportunity to reduce government spending without compromising the crop insurance program's safety net for farmers.

Because A&O allowances are linked to crop prices, the A&O calculation method and higher crop prices have significantly increased A&O allowances, and companies—competing for underwriting gains—have passed a larger proportion of this allowance to insurance agencies, especially in the Corn Belt. As a result, many insurance agencies have experienced a kind of windfall. Although the 2008 Farm Bill reduces A&O allowance rates, these allowances, as well as commissions for 2009, are still likely to be well above the levels that occurred before crop prices increased in recent years. In addition, because crop prices have become increasingly volatile, the allowances are subject to large declines, which could make it more difficult for insurance companies and agencies to budget and operate effectively.

A&O allowances can better reflect reasonable business expenses, adjusted for costs in different regions of the country. Linking A&O allowances to reasonable expenses would also help stabilize the allowances that insurance companies receive. Furthermore, the 2008 Farm Bill directs RMA to consider alternative methods to determine the A&O allowance rate that would also provide savings for taxpayers. This effort could be more effective if RMA were to collect information on the commissions that companies have paid to individual agencies, as well as the individual agencies' expenses. This information would enable RMA to appropriately modify the A&O calculation method and monitor whether this revised method produces sufficient allowances to cover reasonable expenses.

Finally, many companies reported expenses to RMA that were not clearly related to selling and servicing crop insurance policies. Such reporting is due, at least in part, to inadequate guidance. Improved guidance would enable RMA to accurately track the insurance companies' crop insurance delivery expenses.

RECOMMENDATIONS FOR EXECUTIVE ACTION

To better ensure that the A&O allowances provided to the crop insurance industry are sufficient for program delivery, but not excessive, we recommend that the Secretary of Agriculture direct the Administrator of the Risk Management Agency to develop a new methodology for calculating the A&O allowance so that it is more closely aligned with expenses, in terms of dollars per policy, as was the allowance in place before 2006, when crop prices increased sharply. SRA renegotiations should achieve this goal. Once this alignment is completed, the Administrator should minimize annual fluctuations in A&O allowances that are unrelated to business expenses, while recognizing variations in delivery expenses across regions of the country.

To assist in maintaining the relationship between A&O allowances and reasonable business expenses, we further recommend that the Secretary of Agriculture direct the Administrator of the Risk Management Agency to require that companies annually report the commissions they paid to insurance agencies, by policy, to the Risk Management Agency. The agency should also conduct a study of the costs associated with selling and servicing crop insurance policies to establish a standard method for assessing agencies' reasonable costs in selling and servicing policies.

Finally, to accurately track the insurance companies' expenses for delivering crop insurance, we recommend that the Secretary of Agriculture direct the Administrator of the Risk Management Agency to clarify the current guidance on reporting these expenses and specify what expenses are permitted.

APPENDIX I. OBJECTIVES, SCOPE, AND METHODOLOGY

We were asked to examine (1) the reasons for the substantial increases in administrative and operating (A&O) allowances in recent years, and the purposes for which insurance companies use these allowances, and (2) insurance agencies' expenses for selling federal crop insurance policies, and questionable practices, if any, that agencies use to compete for business among farmers.

To examine the reasons for the substantial increases in A&O allowances in recent years, and the purposes for which insurance companies use these allowances, we interviewed U.S. Department of Agriculture (USDA) officials from the Risk Management Agency (RMA) and officials from each of the 16 insurance companies that participate in the federal crop insurance program. In addition, we reviewed and analyzed RMA and company data concerning companies' uses of the allowances from 2000 through 2007. The sources of these data included expense reports that the 16 companies submitted to RMA listing the amounts that they charge to various expense categories. We also reviewed reports that the companies submitted to RMA listing the amount of commission and the commission rate paid to insurance agencies by state during 2006 and 2007. For the purpose of this report, commissions include profit-sharing bonuses that an insurance company pays to an insurance agency on the basis of profits for a given year and transfer bonuses that a company pays to an agency that transfers its business to the company. In addition, we analyzed data from RMA's *Summary of Business* and reviewed RMA's analysis of companies' financial data.

For our analysis of company data, we used both data reported directly to RMA as well as data from company expense reports. RMA data on premiums were complete for all years. Company expense report data on both premiums and commissions were complete for 2006 and 2007, but were only partially complete for the other years (85 percent complete for 2000, 89 percent complete for 2001, 70 percent complete for 2002, 71 percent complete for 2003, 85 percent complete for 2004, and 89 percent complete for 2005). Data were missing largely because of changes in company structure, such as mergers, acquisitions, and companies' going out of business. We took the following steps to correct for the missing data to avoid overstating any change over time (since data were more often missing in earlier years). We assumed the data on commissions, as reported in company expense reports, were missing to the same extent as the data on premiums reported in the same place. We therefore adjusted the data on total commissions paid, by year, by the same fraction necessary to adjust the premiums reported on the company expense reports to bring it up to the amount of premiums reported to RMA, which we knew to be the more reliable number.

We also reviewed examples of companies' contracts with insurance agencies. We selected these contracts on the basis of the volume of business between the insurance company and the agency and, when possible, regional diversity. Furthermore, we reviewed RMA's reporting guidelines for crop insurance companies and discussed these guidelines with company officials. In addition, we interviewed National Association of Insurance Commissioners (NAIC) officials to better understand allowable expenses.

To examine insurance agencies' expenses for selling federal crop insurance policies and questionable practices, if any, that agencies use to compete for business from farmers, we interviewed officials of eight insurance agencies and reviewed documents that some of these officials provided, including their income statements. We based our selection of insurance agencies on premium volume, regional location, crop type, and proximity to crop insurance companies. We examined the extent to which the growth in crop insurance commissions tracked trends in insurance industry expenses. We used 2000 as the base year in which crop insurance commissions are presumed to have been more closely aligned with expenses, before the increase in the A&O allowance. We then calculated what the commission per policy would have been for 2001 through 2009 if it had increased at the rate of change in insurance agents' wages. We used the rate of change in insurance agents' wages because, according to industry officials, wages account for agencies' largest expense. For this analysis, we used commission data from RMA and insurance agents' wage data for all lines of insurance from the Department of Labor's Bureau of Labor Statistics. In view of the Food, Conservation, and Energy Act of 2008's 2.3 percentage point reduction in A&O allowance rates for most insurance policies, we assumed that 2009 commission rates would decline by half of this amount—1.15 percentage points—relative to 2007, the most recent year for which RMA data on actual commission rates were available. We then calculated what the commission per policy would have been for 2001 through 2009 if it had increased at the rate of change in insurance agents' wages. We also interviewed officials from trade associations representing insurance agents. In addition, we interviewed officials from RMA and NAIC and discussed with RMA its investigations of questionable competitive practices.

In addressing the objectives, we also reviewed prior GAO work and additional relevant academic studies assessing the federal crop insurance program. Furthermore, we reviewed analyses of premium reduction plans as well as the *Federal Register* listing and associated comments regarding these plans. We did not independently verify the Bureau of Labor Statistics, RMA, and company data, but we discussed with agency and company officials, as appropriate, the measures they take to ensure the accuracy of these data. For the purposes for which these data were used in this report, these measures seemed reasonable. We conducted this performance audit from January 2008 through April 2009 in accordance with generally accepted government auditing standards. Those standards require that we plan and perform the audit to obtain sufficient, appropriate evidence to provide a reasonable basis for our findings and conclusions based on our audit objectives. We believe that the evidence obtained provides a reasonable basis for our findings and conclusions based on our audit objectives.

APPENDIX II. COMMISSIONS, PERCENTAGE CHANGE IN COMMISSION PER POLICY, AND UNDERWRITING GAINS OR LOSSES

State	Commissions[a]				
	Year		Change	Percentage change per policy	Underwriting gains or losses 2000 through 2007
	2006	2007			
Illinois	$78,412,807	$119,829,350	$41,416,542	61.2%	$1,440,877,198
Iowa	63,736,297	127,604,411	63,868,114	106.6	1,680,044,379
Minnesota	55,246,417	105,270,295	50,023,877	92.9	982,031,875
North Dakota	54,469,829	83,846,615	29,376,786	56.5	11,015,469
Nebraska	51,187,444	95,367,265	44,179,821	93.6	757,012,039
Texas	49,519,189	60,393,008	10,873,819	9.8	(216,112,758)
South Dakota	42,668,604	74,586,111	31,917,506	76.7	(36,492,553)
Kansas	39,891,250	68,827,161	28,935,911	76.6	(289,751,007)
Indiana	33,780,007	58,304,916	24,524,908	76.2	659,564,954
California	26,778,219	30,044,334	3,266,116	13.5	498,321,632
Florida	21,385,507	19,295,620	(2,089,887)	(1.7)	(212,135,483)
Ohio	21,121,885	34,418,894	13,297,008	63.5	262,618,216
Missouri	20,461,507	33,626,430	13,164,923	63.1	400,298,610
Wisconsin	16,912,717	27,967,272	11,054,555	69.3	51,497,302
Colorado	13,261,396	20,134,952	6,873,555	47.7	(163,381,278)
Montana	12,269,982	16,088,903	3,818,921	34.9	(163,126,743)
Georgia	12,184,145	12,398,701	214,556	(4.0)	(38,377,197)
Michigan	12,049,758	19,751,624	7,701,866	67.7	140,498,209
North Carolina	11,588,482	15,484,827	3,896,345	31.6	(146,898,874)
Oklahoma	8,053,897	12,154,386	4,100,489	47.7	(144,451,805)
Washington	6,917,606	8,309,144	1,391,538	24.1	104,710,814
Arkansas	6,693,417	8,660,735	1,967,318	16.3	131,815,766
Mississippi	6,238,658	8,675,622	2,436,964	20.3	(42,324,473)
Kentucky	5,937,255	9,887,195	3,949,941	61.5	29,311,314
Idaho	5,840,670	6,668,574	827,904	9.4	97,428,583
Louisiana	5,421,460	7,982,734	2,561,274	39.8	37,685,157
Alabama	4,624,019	5,054,420	430,402	5.9	(66,285,056)
Tennessee	4,605,565	6,541,555	1,935,991	33.4	(3,110,142)
Pennsylvania	4,054,763	5,984,085	1,929,322	57.5	25,969,560
South Carolina	4,008,829	5,017,032	1,008,203	23.2	(42,446,340)
Virginia	3,370,504	5,139,069	1,768,565	50.8	(22,158,038)
Oregon	2,428,333	2,804,002	375,668	16.7	(85,129,309)
New York	2,315,523	2,990,658	675,135	34.4	(2,260,430)
Maryland	2,205,660	3,253,648	1,047,988	51.1	21,445,930
New Mexico	1,391,397	1,755,658	364,261	28.0	16,163,333
Arizona	1,221,424	1,055,695	(165,729)	(5.0)	(6,313,709)

(Continued)

State	Commissions[a]				
	Year		Change	Percentage change per policy	Underwriting gains or losses 2000 through 2007
	2006	2007			
Wyoming	903,310	1,675,054	771,744	90.2	(39,087,279)
Delaware	771,875	1,282,352	510,478	63.9	(876,791)
Maine	649,107	700,797	51,690	13.8	3,304,735
Connecticut	427,090	549,218	122,127	32.9	(9,580,108)
New Jersey	331,242	571,616	240,374	76.7	13,121,040
Massachusetts	280,498	378,626	98,128	41.5	(12,479,868)
Utah	234,411	257,585	23,174	26.9	(4,473,986)
Hawaii	183,442	340,909	157,467	42.4	4,451,873
West Virginia	164,075	236,474	72,399	52.2	727,834
Vermont	115,109	198,056	82,947	83.6	(1,309,708)
Nevada	109,527	92,555	(16,972)	(4.4)	(5,231,273)
New Hampshire	41,727	52,269	10,541	35.8	287,382
Rhode Island	7,797	11,562	3,765	71.5	211,129
Alaska	2,803	3,080	276	19.0	(44,194)
Total	**$716,476,439**	**$1,131,525,055**	**$415,048,616**	**59.3%**	**$5,616,575,931**

Source: GAO analysis of the data that the insurance companies provided to RMA.

Note: Companies report commissions each year by state. Companies also submit to RMA an expense report, in which total commissions represent one of several itemized expenses. The total commissions in the two reports are not equal because RMA guidance stipulates that companies include commissions based on profit-sharing in the state commission report but not in the expense report. Therefore, the total commissions in this table, which are based on the state commission report, are not equal to the total commissions noted elsewhere in this report.

[a] Commissions are rounded to the nearest dollar.

APPENDIX III. COMMENTS FROM THE U.S. DEPARTMENT OF AGRICULTURE

Note: GAO comments supplementing those in the report text appear at the end of this appendix.

USDA

US GAO

2009 APR -8 AM 11:06

APR 3 2009

United States
Department of
Agriculture

Risk
Management
Agency

1400 Independence
Avenue, SW
Stop 0801
Washington, DC
20250-0806

Ms. Lisa Shames
Director, Natural Resources and Environment
Government Accountability Office
441 G Street, NW
Washington, DC 20548

Dear Ms. Shames:

Thank you for the opportunity to review and provide comments on the Government Accountability Office's (GAO) draft report on *Crop Insurance: Opportunities Exist to Reduce the Costs of Administering the Program* (GAO-09-445).

The Risk Management Agency (RMA) provides the following response and comments to the recommendations contained in the draft report:

> GAO Recommendation 1: Develop a new methodology for calculating Administrative and Operating (A&O) subsidy so that it is more closely aligned with actual delivery expenses in terms of dollars per policy. Once this alignment is completed, RMA should minimize annual fluctuations in A&O allowances that are unrelated to business expenses while recognizing variations in delivery expenses across regions of the country.
>
> RMA Response: RMA has considered the GAO recommendations regarding the alignment of A&O subsidy with actual delivery expenses, and considers the recommendations generally consistent with the direction and guidance provided within the 2008 Farm Bill. As part of the next renegotiation with the private insurance companies, RMA will be evaluating potential alternative A&O calculation methodologies for establishing an appropriate reimbursement for services performed.
>
> GAO Recommendation 2: Require that companies annually report to RMA the commissions they paid to insurance agencies, by policy.
>
> RMA Response: RMA has two major concerns with the recommendation that the companies annually report commissions they pay to insurance agencies by policy. First, companies often pay insurance agencies' commissions or other compensation on a basis other than by policy. Compensation is sometimes paid when an agency transfers a book of business to the company, reaches aggregate premium volume thresholds, achieves overall success in meeting reporting deadlines, or meets policy retention goals, as just a few

See comment 1.
See comment 2.
See comments 3 and 4.

examples. Meeting the recommendation for reporting by policy would require the companies or RMA to devise an allocation system for commissions that are not usually paid on a per policy basis. Consequently, gathering and reporting this data by policy would represent a significant administrative burden both for the companies and RMA.

Second, it is not clear that such detailed data would be valuable in attempting to identify true program delivery costs or in devising a better A&O reimbursement structure. Since 2005, RMA has collected information on the amount each company spends for agent compensation in each state. This information, along with informed estimates of true delivery costs, or the results of the study recommended by GAO, can form the basis for aligning the A&O reimbursement structure more closely to actual delivery costs. It is unclear how access to policy-level data on company compensation payments would add significantly to this effort.

During the exit conference, RMA raised this issue. Neither in the conference nor in the draft report does GAO explain or provide examples of how such detailed information would contribute significantly to the objective of aligning the A&O reimbursement with true delivery costs. Consequently, until more explanation and rationale are given, RMA is not inclined to agree to this recommendation.

GAO Recommendation 3: Conduct a study of the costs associated with selling and servicing crop insurance policies to establish a standard method for assessing agencies' reasonable costs in selling and servicing policies.

RMA Response: RMA agrees that a study of the costs associated with selling and servicing crop insurance policies can be useful in evaluating commission expenses paid by insurance companies and in establishing an appropriate rate of reimbursement. RMA will pursue initiating a study contingent on the availability of funds.

GAO Recommendation 4: Clarify the current guidance on expense reporting and specify what expenses are permitted.

RMA Response: RMA agrees to clarify the expense reporting guidance for the 2011 reinsurance year.

RMA appreciates the opportunity to work with your staff during the course of this audit. Should you have any questions regarding this response, please contact Michael Hand, RMA Deputy Administrator for Compliance/Audit Liaison Officer at 202-720-0642.

Sincerely,

William J. Murphy
Acting Administrator

Following are GAO's comments on the Risk Management Agency's letter dated April 3, 2009.

GAO Comments

1. We do not agree that gathering and reporting data on commissions paid to insurance agencies by policy would significantly increase the "administrative burden" on RMA and insurance companies. First, RMA, which currently collects commission data aggregated at the state level, could require that companies report two additional data fields in the policy records they currently submit to RMA—commissions and other compensation. These records can already contain over 300 such data fields. Once these changes are implemented, the recurring costs should be minimal. In conjunction with these changes, RMA could develop and provide allocation guidance to prorate compensation that is not provided on a per-policy basis so that this compensation could be apportioned to individual policies. Second, providing policy-level data would eliminate the need for companies to provide data aggregated at the state level, which could offset the additional burden that RMA believes would result. Furthermore, given the magnitude of commission payments—an estimated $1.7 billion in 2008—additional reporting would result in analyses that would strengthen transparency and accountability in the use of taxpayer funds.
2. We disagree with RMA's statement that more detailed commission data may not be valuable. With data on commissions paid to insurance agencies by policy, RMA would be better able to establish whether the compensation paid to agencies is appropriate in relationship to the agencies' costs of selling and servicing crop insurance. Tracking commissions by state, as RMA does currently, does not provide RMA with sufficient detail to take into account differences among agencies, such as location and size.
3. We disagree with RMA's assertion that we did not adequately justify this recommendation in the draft provided to RMA. We noted the following in the draft:

- RMA does not know how much an individual company spends on commissions to each of the agencies with which it does business.
- Information by state does not provide sufficient detail on commission expenses. RMA would be better able to set the A&O allowance rate when it negotiates the standard reinsurance agreement (SRA) with insurance companies if it had more detailed information on commissions provided to individual agencies.
- With information on agencies' commissions, as well their costs, RMA could assess whether the A&O allowances are reasonable for program delivery but not excessive, and adjust allowances as needed.

  Nonetheless, we have provided additional examples in the report to make our explanation more explicit.

4. During the exit conference with RMA officials, we explained, as we had in the draft report, that information at the policy level would inform RMA of the amounts that companies pay agencies for selling and servicing policies and thus would improve RMA's position in renegotiating the SRA. An RMA official told us that RMA knew from commission data currently collected at the state level that agencies in a given state earn commissions that are higher on average than those in other states. We responded, however, that RMA cannot determine, solely on the basis of state-level data, whether commissions vary across agencies within a state.

Related GAO Products

Crop Insurance: Continuing Efforts Are Needed to Improve Program Integrity and Ensure Program Costs Are Reasonable. GAO-07-944T. Washington, D.C.: June 7, 2007.

Crop Insurance: Continuing Efforts Are Needed to Improve Program Integrity and Ensure Program Costs Are Reasonable. GAO-07-819T. Washington, D.C.: May 3, 2007.

Crop Insurance: More Needs To Be Done to Reduce Program's Vulnerability to Fraud, Waste, and Abuse. GAO-06-878T. Washington, D.C.: June 15, 2006.

Crop Insurance: Actions Needed to Reduce Program's Vulnerability to Fraud, Waste, and Abuse. GAO-05-528. Washington, D.C.: September 30, 2005.

Crop Insurance: USDA Needs to Improve Oversight of Insurance Companies and Develop a Policy to Address Any Future Insolvencies. GAO-04-517. Washington, D.C.: June 1, 2004.

Department of Agriculture: Status of Efforts to Address Major Financial Management Challenges. GAO-03-871T. Washington, D.C.: June 10, 2003.

Crop Insurance: USDA Needs a Better Estimate of Improper Payments to Strengthen Controls Over Claims. GAO/RCED-99-266. Washington, D.C.: September 22, 1999.

Crop Insurance: Increases in Insured Crop Prices and Premium Rates Raise the Administrative Expense Reimbursement Paid to Companies. GAO/RCED-98-115R. Washington, D.C.: March 20, 1998.

Crop Insurance: Opportunities Exist to Reduce Government Costs for Private-Sector Delivery. GAO/RCED-97-70. Washington, D.C.: April 17, 1997.

End Notes

[1] GAO, *Crop Insurance: Continuing Efforts Are Needed to Improve Program Integrity and Ensure Program Costs Are Reasonable*, GAO-07-944T (Washington, D.C.: June 7, 2007); and *Crop Insurance: Continuing Efforts Are Needed to Improve Program Integrity and Ensure Program Costs Are Reasonable*, GAO-07-819T (Washington, D.C.: May 3, 2007).

[2] GAO, *Suggested Areas for Oversight for the 110th Congress*, GAO-07-235R (Washington, D.C.: Nov. 17, 2006).

[3] GAO, *Crop Insurance: Opportunities Exist to Reduce Government Costs for Private-Sector Delivery*, GAO/RCED-97-70 (Washington, D.C.: Apr. 17, 1997).

[4] USDA, Office of the Chief Economist and World Agricultural Outlook Board, *USDA Agricultural Long-Term Projections to 2018* (Washington, D.C.: February 2009).

[5] The cost of crop insurance to taxpayers is equal to A&O allowances, plus underwriting gains paid to companies, plus claims paid to farmers, minus the premiums that farmers pay.

[6] Specifically, crop insurance "units"—the individual farms that may be covered under a single policy—drive the companies' workload. The number of units covered has remained relatively stable since 2000.

[7] Company officials told us that although they could not predict the commission rate for 2009, they did not expect that it would decline by the full 2.3 percentage points.

CHAPTER SOURCES

The following chapters have been previously published:

Chapter 1 – This is an edited, reformatted and augmented version of Congressional Research Service publication, Report RS21212, dated April 28, 2010.

Chapter 2 – This is an edited, reformatted and augmented version of Congressional Research Service publication, Report R40452, dated May 20, 2010.

Chapter 3 – This is an edited, reformatted and augmented version of Congressional Research Service publication, Report RL34207, dated January 28, 2009.

Chapter 4 – This is an edited, reformatted and augmented version of Congressional Research Service publication, Report R40532, dated May 28, 2010.

Chapter 5 – This is an edited, reformatted and augmented version of Congressional Research Service publication, Report R40966, dated June 10, 2010.

Chapter 6 – This is an edited, reformatted and augmented version of United States Government Accountability Office publication GAO-10-548, dated June 2010

Chapter 7 – This is an edited, reformatted and augmented version of United States Government Accountability Office publication GAO-09-445, dated April 2009

INDEX

D

E

F

G

H

I

L

M

N

O

P

Q

R